NORMANDY
gastronomique

NORMANDY
gastronomique

JANE SIGAL

FOREWORD BY ANNE WILLAN

PHOTOGRAPHY BY DEBBIE PATTERSON

SERIES EDITOR MARIE-PIERRE MOINE

ABBEVILLE PRESS
NEW YORK LONDON PARIS

First published in the
United States of America
in 1993 by
Abbeville Press
488 Madison Avenue
New York, NY 10022

First published in Great Britain in 1993 by
Conran Octopus Limited
37 Shelton Street
London WC2H 9HN

ISBN 1-55859-496-5

Senior Editor **SARAH PEARCE**
Art Editor **KAREN BOWEN**
Copy Editor **NORMA MACMILLAN**
Editorial Assistant **JANE CHAPMAN**
Additional Picture Research **NADINE BAZAR**
Production **JILL MACEY**

NOTE ON RECIPES. Many recipes specify crème fraîche as
an ingredient. Where this is unavailable, the same
amount of whipping cream can be substituted, but
care must be taken not to allow a sauce to boil after
the cream has been added.

CONTENTS

FOREWORD

For ten happy years of my life, Normandy was home ground. On weekends, holidays, and the long days of northern summer we escaped the pressures of Paris for a red brick villa outside Dieppe, the nearest point of coast. It was here I took the children to build sand castles and watch the fishermen bring in their catch – pop-eyed cod, spotted plaice, the occasional turbot, and Dover sole with their tails still flapping in protest. First thing in the morning we would dispatch the children to the farm for the morning's milk, warm from the cow, with a stop at the *boulangerie* for croissants en route.

Normandy Gastronomique, and the meticulously drafted text by Jane Sigal, brings it all back. She revels, as we did, in the small details of rural life – the design of fishing boats, the backchat of street markets, and the ornamental brickwork of pigeonhouses – as well as the grander scene to be found in cities like Rouen and Caen. And the scene *is* grand, for Normandy is a large province, bounded by the sea to the north, and reaching south past the busy Seine waterway to the sunlit basin of the Loire. Between Monet's Impressionist garden at Giverny on the eastern boundary and the shifting sands of Mont-Saint-Michel in the west lies some of the richest farming country in the world. This is the home of Camembert and Pont-L'Evêque cheese, of *andouille* sausages, Calvados, and crème fraîche. Not for nothing were Rouennais merchants able to endow a whole tower of their cathedral in return for a dispensation allowing butter to stay on the table during the Lenten fast.

Jane Sigal graduated with the *grand diplôme* from La Varenne, then joined us there in the editorial office. She has acted as research assistant for Patricia Wells, whose food guides on France are classics. When Jane describes a dish and then gives the recipe, you can be sure she has not only tasted it on the spot, but also tried it out exhaustively at home. She offers old favorites such as *moules à la crème* and *poulet Vallée d'Auge* with Calvados, cream, and apples, as well as new ideas such as Warm Scallop Salad with Cress, and a Green Apple Sorbet, which I cannot wait to try. Between the covers of one book, the Normans have never had it so good!

TOP *Normandy, at heart: a characteristic piece of painted decoration on a* maison à colombage, *or half-timbered house, near Dieppe.*

ABOVE *With his old* moque *raised in a toast, a Norman farmer advertises naturally fermented apple cider drawn from a keg, on a painted sign in Honfleur.*

RIGHT *A new harvest for the Dieppe market: cherries from the Seine Valley, the first leeks, and* choux nouveaux, *spring cabbage.*

INTRODUCTION

Overheard one Saturday morning at the Lisieux farmers' market: "How do you like your Camembert?" enquires the cheese merchant to find out whether the preference is for a fresh or more fragrant taste. "*J'aime un coeur tendre*," quips the customer, "I like a soft heart."

In Normandy, cheese merits a dialogue: There is more than one morally correct way to eat Camembert, and it can be discussed with wit and humanity.

This chitchat also reveals that this cheese merchant has an array of Camemberts, of varying ages, to offer. He must have a cheese cellar, or perhaps several, for ripening his cheeses. And he must have trained for years to become an *affineur*. Furthermore, someone made the cheese for him to age. Maybe this someone also milked the cow to make the cheese. In addition, the climate here is just clammy enough, the soil just dank enough, to make good pastureland for the cows to graze.

In Normandy, I was constantly reminded that for an ordinary exchange like this to take place, an entire culture was built and battles fought to protect its very commonness.

A NORMAN ODYSSEY

In my quest for "Normandy Gastronomique," I concentrated on what actually exists in Normandy today, both the new-fangled and the classic. When I sought the one-time, it was to make sense of modern times.

For my research, I traveled to the source. I went to the fishing port in Granville and spent time at the Café des Marins with the fishermen. I quizzed Victor Letouzé, carrot farmer in Créances: Where do you get a good meal around here? I visited Union Isigny-Sainte-Mère, an industrial dairy, and Bernadette Auvré, who makes Neufchâtel cheese on her farm to help make ends meet.

I wandered in all seasons. I froze my feet in the market in Dieppe in January, ate in empty restaurants in February, and was run off the road near Honfleur on the first sunny weekend in May. I found that this cheese, cream, apple, and fish corner of France holds its own against the buttery pastries of Brittany next door, the sprawl of Parisian taste, the fashion storms of squash flowers blown in from Provence.

What I did uncover often turned my own prejudices upside down. While I thought I didn't like tripe and the sausage called *andouille*, I found them delicious once I met the people who made them and tasted the best examples.

ABOVE Omaha Beach, whose wide expanses witnessed the Normandy landings in 1944; everywhere in this stretch of Manche one sees reminders of those world-changing events. Today, farmers raise mussels here by twirling strings of the shellfish around giant poles planted at the water's edge.
LEFT Storybook Normandy. A Norman cow, with her tell-tale brown "spectacles," grazes in a farmer's orchard beneath trees in blossom.

Cap de la Hague

Barfleur

CHERBOURG

Cotentin

MANCHE

Bessin

Isigny-
sur-Mer

Créances

Pirou

La Chapelle-
en-Juger

Coutances

Blainville
-sur-Mer

Villedieu-
les-Poêles

Granville

Bocage

Vire

Le Mont-St-Michel

Domfront

La Ferté-Macé

CALVADOS

CAEN

Courseulles-
sur-Mer

Honfleur

Trouville
Deauville

Pont l'Évêque

*Pays
d'Auge*

Lisieux

Livarot

Camembert

Argentan

ORNE

Alabaster Coast

SEINE

Fécamp

Étretat

Pays de Caux

Yvetot

St-Romain-
de-Colbosc

Le Havre

Val

Pont-Audemer

Roumois

Cormeilles

Lieuvin

Le Neubourg

Bernay

Pays d'Ouche

L'Aigle

Mortagne-
au-Perche

ALENÇON

Perche

I learned that far from being hardened types inured to death, the people who raise animals for slaughter are the most conscious of the value of life.

Specialties I had somehow missed before in my journeys to Normandy came into view. I was convinced *pain brié* had vanished. Then I began to find this bread in every nook and cranny.

To put contemporary Normandy in context, I went to any museum of rural life I could. And when one was closed (some open only on weekends or in July and August), I went regardless. Jacques Monthulé, the mayor of Mesnilbus, a small village in the Manche, opened the Musée des Marais for me. Then he gave me a private lesson on how people lived here until the 1950s.

After visiting the Musée de la Ferme du Cotentin, I became fascinated by farm machinery. I saw how little farming had changed over the centuries: a flat roller that used to be fashioned of wood or stone and pulled by a horse is now metal and tractor-drawn. I spent hours with my nose in dictionaries of farm implements and machinery to learn the names for the tools I saw.

Everywhere I went there was new vocabulary to learn: for sheep farming, fattening oysters, cidermaking, cheesemaking, bread-baking.

Much of what I encountered belongs on a list of endangered traditions. Members of the Confrérie Gastronomique Normande de la Tripière Fertoise, in nostalgic memory of medieval guilds, still dress in robes trimmed in yellow and green to judge the best *tripes en brochette*, the celebrated tripe of La Ferté-Macé.

And when I want to smile, I think about my interview with Roger Lemorton. From October to November, during *les vendanges normandes*, Monsieur Lemorton and his son, Didier, still pick their apple and pear trees by hand to make Domfrontais cider, *poiré* (pear cider), *pommeau* (an apple apéritif), and Calvados. "I much prefer *poiré* to that bitter-tasting stuff," says Roger Lemorton, pulling a face. "What is it? Ah yes, Coke."

But I found plenty to be discouraged about. Many of the artisans I met will be the last to ply their trade. When Jacques Leterrier, the sole baker in Le Vast who still makes regional breads in a wood-fired oven, retires in five years, there will be no one to take over. "We are the last generation," says Annick Collette, winner of the *tripière d'or*, the sought-after trophy, for her *tripe à la mode de Caen*. "Our children don't want to stick with the business."

And native taste seems to be drifting from the local and flavorful to the general and bland. Most people buy beer today, not cider. I ate with farmers who cooked their poor chickens until they were done and then cooked them an extra hour. I shared their purchased cardboard-like apple tarts.

"We are losing our heritage," says Robert Jollit, retired cheese merchant in Pont-Audemer. "Normandy is too rich. The old ways hold out only in poor regions where people don't have the money for progress."

Proximity to Paris and ready-made clients there have long guaranteed a market for this booming agricultural and fishing province. Normans rarely emigrated for economic reasons the way Savoyards and Basques did. On the contrary, Paris spills over into Normandy on weekends and in summer.

Surprisingly, it is the out-of-towners who often help shore up wobbly traditions. Locals don't want to face in restaurants the identical dishes they eat at home. But Parisians come looking for the very regional specialties that Normans spurn. They are willing to pay more for hand-crafted blood sausage, Pont-l'Evêque cheese, smoked ham – products that require long hours, expertise, and the finest ingredients.

Still, just because a cheese, sausage, or cider is farm-made doesn't mean it is better than the factory variety. I have tasted dairy cheeses made with much more care than the farm version.

And novel isn't necessarily bad. I found farmers who raised English venison and Asian quails, who fattened special breeds of duck for *foie gras,* and grazed goats – all immigrants to Normandy. These men and women take on their work with all the passion of creation.

I was just as impressed by people who had dug up old specialties and fiddled with them to please a modern palate. Cidermakers replant native varieties of apples but make an industrial cider. Farmers prepare *confiture de lait,* a half-forgotten preserve, and flavor it with hazelnut, coconut, or vanilla. Bakers sell an enriched version of *brasillé,* once "the poor man's cake." Chefs team up a farm cheese from the Pays de Bray with a North African import, *brik* dough. Or they handle *andouille* – Norman soul food – with culinary manners befitting caviar.

"People should be free to change to earn a living," says Patrick Ramelet, chef-owner of the Auberge du Beau Lieu in Forges-les-Eaux. "It's an evolution."

THE LAY OF THE LAND

Outside Normandy, most people in France couldn't name the five administrative *départements* that make up this ancient province. But in the land between the Epte and Avre rivers – land given by Charles the Simple to Rollo, the Viking ruler – the locals talk about Seine-Maritime, Eure, Calvados, Orne, and Manche.

They also mention Upper and Lower Normandy. Upper Normandy is the high chalk and limestone plateau in eastern Normandy, including Seine-Maritime and Eure. Most of Lower Normandy, taking in Calvados, Orne, and Manche, is a sandstone and granite mass, which slouches toward the West.

Even more than *départements* or other divisions, though, it is in terms of their own *pays* – the geographical and geological parcel of land they call home – that they think. Thus, for instance, the Orne *département* in Lower Normandy contains (portions of) the Pays d'Auge, Pays d'Ouche, Perche, and Bocage. To further complicate local geography, the Bocage divides into even smaller plots: the pear cider-producing region around Domfront is known as the Domfrontais, while the ribbon of land bordering the Orne river as it loops its way through the rocky escarpments of the northern Bocage is called the Suisse Normande.

And these *pays* do not respect administrative boundaries, so you can find yourself traveling from Calvados into the Orne and then into Manche and all the time remain in the Bocage.

The line-up of different *pays* in Normandy gives an idea of the diversity within this one patch of France bordering the English Channel. Although certain food themes – fish, poultry, dairy products, and apples, distilled or not – cross Normandy, each *pays* has its own specialties and local preferences. In the Pays de Bray, people favor Neufchâtel, the regional cheese. But in *pays* west of here, native taste finds Neufchâtel too salty.

Just how Normans feel about their *pays* was illustrated by a middle-aged couple I met in a café in Neufchâtel-en-Bray. She was from the Pays de Caux and he from the Pays de Bray, both in Seine-Maritime. "I never had anything to do with the Pays de Bray before I met him," she said nodding at her partner. Smiling to herself she added: "I thought people there were different from us."

ABOVE *An ancient Citroen on a bread run in La Bouille. Christian Artu bakes pastries, baguettes,* and *pain brié, a regional bread, for this village in the Seine Valley.*
LEFT *A half-timbered barn in the orchard at Père Jules, Léon Desfrièches' cider and Calvados farm near Lisieux. In Calvados, you will find the most rural of rural scenes.*

ABOVE Lunch break at a sidewalk café:
moules à la marinière *(mussels in white wine),*
frites, *and* baguette. *And for dessert?*
ABOVE RIGHT Old-world style in a pâtisserie
in Cherbourg.
RIGHT In Le Vast, Jacques Leterrier makes his
coarse-textured brioche with creamery butter and
farm eggs. I tasted local breads and baked
products wherever I could find them throughout
Normandy, but found unquestionably the best
examples – and most thriving traditions –
in Manche.

TASTING NORMANDY

Ironclad recipes do not exist, except in cook books. Recipes are ephemeral, lasting only the length of a meal. Next time the apples in the tart will be a different variety, the lamb's lettuce, or mâche, in today's salad out of season.

Also, each cook has his own way with the same recipe. The Demanneville bakery in Dieppe makes a rustic variation of Douillon, the Norman apple dumpling. My favorite version happens to come from the Auberge du Vieux Puits (see page 61).

The recipes here are those of the chefs and farmwives, bistrotiers and cidermakers I met who were generous enough to share them. They are recipes from cooks who prepare them to pamper their families or make their customers sit up and pay attention.

Of course, all the recipes have passed through my hands. In addition to filling in the blanks when certain crucial information was missing or correcting obvious errors, I did modify an occasional recipe. This happened when I felt the original was really quite good but off-putting in some way – too difficult, a garish sauce, overcooked. But often I let recipes stand, noting what the reader could expect to find when preparing it and how to change it if desired. In all cases I establish in the introduction just what my interventions, if any, have been.

Also, I did the picking and choosing. Some recipes are quick and easy, others simple but long-simmered. A few require special ingredients, while many can be made with supermarket staples. There is celebratory fare and everyday dishes. The cordon bleu cook will find something here as will the dabbler. The selection reflects both the individual *cuisinière* and the spirit of Normandy, a unique invention of the moment and the classic repertoire of Norman cooking.

ABOVE Apples and apple tart, the essence of Normandy.
LEFT Along with cider and Calvados, milk and cream, a farmwife at the market in Pirou Plage sells homemade piquette, the fresh curd cheese of the Manche.

TOP Trawlers in Dieppe.
*ABOVE This way to the beach: a weathered sign
on an antiques shop.*
*RIGHT The long oysters, or creuses, of Normandy
on sale. Fish merchants present the lemon as a
gift to good customers.*

SEINE-MARITIME

Stretching along the English Channel coast, bordered on the west by the Seine river, Seine-Maritime offers a bit of everything Normandy is noted for gastronomically.

There is abundant seafood that has traveled only a short distance from where it was caught; sprawling apple orchards; cheese still made by hand; and half-timbered farms with flocks of waddling ducks. Still, Seine-Maritime boasts a culinary repertoire all its own.

Off the coast, dubbed the Côte d'Albâtre because of its white cliffs, fishermen pull in the best gray sole and the fattest scallops in Normandy. Behind the shore, on the Caux plateau, a cidermaker has replanted local varieties of apple and produces vintage ciders. The regional cheese is not Camembert, but Neufchâtel, and it comes only from a sunken, clayey strip of land called the Pays de Bray. And in the protected Seine Valley, one committed poultry farmer raises a near-extinct breed of duck from Duclair.

THE ALABASTER COAST

Every day, weather permitting, a few fishermen cast off from Saint-Aubin-sur-Mer in aluminum *doris*, the local fishing boats. They head out from this small seaside village on the Alabaster Coast in search of *la petite pêche* – lobsters, crabs, striped bass, sole – which hides in the rocks just offshore.

Seen from these vessels bobbing in the water, the chalk cliffs of the Côte d'Albatre soar over the beaches. Here you can study the Pays de Caux's geological history depicted in the stone. Layers of gray flint and yellow marl, clay and alluvial mud stand out, all topped by grassy banks.

From Le Tréport to Etretat, the cliffs have provided a dramatic backdrop for centuries of fishing and mollusk gathering. In some places, the pounding surf has carved *valleuses*, as the deep caverns in the rock are called, forming hanging cliffs.

Weather and tides also shaped the famous needle rocks at the quiet resort of Etretat. On the beach near these sculptured rocks, thatched fishermen's huts have been restored, and today you can see them as Courbet and Monet painted them in the 19th century.

In the protected gaps between the cliffs, people have come together and established villages and, later, watering places. Every coastal town has its esplanade and pebble beach, where a few independent fishermen moor their dories even today.

ABOVE The pebble beaches and tall cliffs of the Alabaster Coast, one characteristic face of Seine-Maritime and the setting for the region's bountiful fishing.
LEFT Bags of cider apples shortly after picking.

LOBSTERING

Bundled in sweaters and rubber overalls against the wet January morning, two fishermen cruise in their dory toward the lobster pots off the Alabaster Coast. One steers the aluminum boat, the other, in the bow, scans the water for the colorful flags that signal the traps.

They have no hydraulic lines for hauling up the 44-pound pots; it is all done with manpower. Two legs brace against the side of the boat while four arms pull hand over hand. One after the other the traps are retrieved, lobsters and crabs are tossed into plastic bins, and then the traps are lowered back into the water.

Why are some lobsters a tasteless disappointment? According to fishermen in Saint-Valéry-en-Caux, Normandy's lobster capital, the answer may be the lobster's habitat. Off the coast of Normandy, they claim, where lobsters live in iodine-rich waters, the lobsters caught are especially good to eat.

Fishermen from Quiberville, near Dieppe, often scout for striped bass below the Ailly lighthouse, below the Varengeville cemetery. This perched site contains the graves of mariners and artists, including Georges Braque (a native of Normandy), who came to stay in this patch of the Alabaster Coast. It is the perfect resting place for a sailor, with unobstructed seascape as far as the eye can see.

With one foray completed, the fishermen head back to the beaches of Pourville, Varengeville, Quiberville, Sainte-Marguerite, Veules-les-Roses, Veulettes, and Saint-Aubin-sur-Mer. There they offload their catch, to be sold by wives and girlfriends at the water's edge.

Other fishermen dock their trawlers in Dieppe. From April to October, they bring to market Dover sole, skate, brill, turbot, and mackerel and, in the fall, whiting, cod, scallops, and herring. The largest fishing port on the Alabaster Coast, Dieppe has given its name to several fish recipes.

Marmite dieppoise may have started out as a chunky fisherman's stew prepared with the day's catch. Today, however, it usually appears as a more refined affair with filleted or shelled seafood because customers do not like bones. Generally it includes an expensive array of ingredients – scallops, sole, monkfish, turbot, *langoustines*, and shrimp – all poached in a spicy court-bouillon. Restaurants often present the murky poaching liquid first on its own, as a soup. Little toasts, grated Gruyère, and pungent *rouille* sauce are served alongside, much like Mediterranean *bouillabaisse*. Several restaurants in Dieppe specialize in this dish; one, the Marmite Dieppoise, has even taken its name from it.

Sole Dieppoise (see page 38), with a flour-thickened sauce enriched with cream and butter, remains a fixture in Dieppe's traditional restaurants. Cooks faithfully prepare it the old-fashioned way, ignoring culinary and health trends.

It is impossible to talk about sole without mentioning the *sole normande* debate. Is it Norman or the invention of a Parisian cook? Composed of poached sole fillets, with a garnish of mussels, shrimp, smelts, and mushrooms (plus oysters and crayfish, depending on the cook), the dish is probably a city creation. But if *sole normande* is technically Parisian, its spiritual roots are definitely Norman, and the dish is alive and well in its adoptive home.

The Seine Bay contains the largest scallop bed in the English Channel, and Dieppe celebrates this with an annual fair in mid-November. The *foire aux harengs et à la coquille Saint-Jacques*, or herring and scallop fair, arrives at the same time as the scallop season and the advent of herring off the Normandy coast.

The fair takes place in old Dieppe, on the Quai Henri-IV where the passenger port is located. By afternoon, tourists and locals, *frites*-vendors, and fairground rides crowd the narrow quay. On one side, you are hemmed in by cafés and seafood shacks and, on the other, by Dieppe–Newhaven ships, at least five stories tall. Cooks charbroil fish in sawed-off oil drums, and the odors of grilled herring settle in your clothing. Fish merchants sell fresh herring and scallops. While Beaujolais Nouveau, another November event, may seem out of place here, it easily outsells local cider. Drinking, eating, and browsing continue until nightfall, when a fireworks display lights the sky.

Besides Dieppe, Fécamp counts as the other important fishing port on the Alabaster Coast. France's primary port for cod, Fécamp is also home to several industries associated with fishing, including cod-drying plants and herring-curing factories. There is a museum here devoted to the history of cod fishing (see the Visitor's Guide), with exhibits that tell the stories of the far-ranging seamen who sailed to Newfoundland on six-month ventures.

LEFT A tractor with a doris, *the local fishing boat, in tow. Originally, the* doris *was a frail, wooden craft in which Norman fishermen shuttled to their catch in the freezing waters off Newfoundland. The modern version is larger and built of sturdy aluminum. Today's* doris *fishermen never stray far from the Alabaster Coast.*
BELOW A quiet morning at the Dieppe fish market, after the early rush.

SUPERIOR SCALLOPS

For Gilles Tournadre, who is uncompromising about his ingredients, only Dieppe rates as a source for his scallops. "The biggest and most beautiful scallops come from Dieppe," states Monsieur Tournadre, chef-owner of the two-star restaurant Gill in Rouen. "The coquilles Saint-Jacques further along the coast in Brittany are smaller and just not as good."
With their ivory color, firm texture, and sweet taste, scallops may be the most revered mollusk in France. Supplies would dwindle overnight if regulations did not protect the population: Fishermen could drag their metal nets along the sea bottom for scallops year round as this mollusk does not migrate.
Official scallop season varies from place to place; in some areas even the hours of harvesting are restricted, with helicopters policing the waters. In the Baie de Seine, the fount of Monsieur Tournadre's scallops, rules limit scallop harvesting to seven-and-a-half months during the year, October through mid-May.

TOP Giving good weight at the farmers' market in Dieppe. This farmer's modest offerings include herbs and hen's eggs.
RIGHT The source of Normandy's fine cooking: fresh produce from the open-air market.
FAR RIGHT A butcher advertises "Special today Guinea Fowl" and "Eat French mutton."

Apart from fish, Fécamp's gastronomic offerings include Benedictine. Not far from the port, in the opulent Palais Bénédictine, 27 herbs, roots, and spices are infused in pure alcohol and distilled, then aged in oak before surfacing as the liqueur with tenuous links to the Benedictine Abbey of Fécamp.

After a visit to the Benedictine museum (see the Visitor's Guide) – really a journey into fine-tuned salesmanship – come back down to earth at the Dieppe market. Here farmers and fishwives peddle their goods in the traditional way.

The fishing community from the Alabaster Coast mingles with the farmers from the Pays de Caux and Pays de Bray. A half-dozen fish carts face the arcades around the harbor near the Quai Henri-IV. Stallholders, wearing stained white aprons over their coats, hawk skate wings, sole, sanddab, plaice, and turbot as well as mussels and cockles.

The farmers set up around the Café des Tribunaux and the Eglise Saint-Jacques, a quarter that looks very much as it did when Walter Richard Sickert painted it at the turn of the century. On one folding table, a farmwife has arranged her offerings: two varieties of cultivated mushrooms. Nearby, a watercress grower declaims and points to his merchandise, grown in spring water. Norman snails are on sale at another stand. Everywhere there are pitchers of crème fraîche, baskets of eggs, and chickens in plastic bags.

Amid all this commerce, a Salvation Army officer proffers books and pamphlets describing the Army's soulful mission. The familiar marching music plays softly.

CIDRES DE CRU

All the signals suggest a dull cider: The Duché de Longueville's 12,000 tons of cider apples await processing on a concrete slab the size of a suburban parking lot; stainless steel tanks of 1,500 gallons hold the apple juice, regulating its fermentation by pressure; the resulting cider is filtered and pasteurized. And the finished cider tastes, well, surprisingly good.

This is not traditional cider. It lacks the body and bitter edge of the authentic drink, but it has plenty of apple flavor.

The Duché de Longueville factory began replanting local cider apples in the 1960s. From 40 varieties, they selected five to make vintage, rather than blended, ciders. (Each contains 90 to 95 percent of a single apple variety.) They are named after the apple from which they are made: Antoinette, Gros Oeillet, Bedan, Argile Rouge Bruyère, and Muscadet de Dieppe. All the ciders — dry, semisweet, and sweet varieties — have the distinct taste of a particular apple.

*ABOVE May in a valley of the Pays de Caux.
Wisteria at its peak frames a window.
RIGHT Apple trees in bloom on a Norman
farmstead: a spring scene from the countryside
behind Dieppe.
FAR RIGHT Endless fields of grain in the
Pays de Caux.*

THE PAYS DE CAUX

Fog descends quickly in the Pays de Caux, with nightfall. It slows even madcap drivers, and you move ahead at the pace of a cow. It provides fuel for chitchat, and neighbors exchange stories of circling for hours to find a friend's door.

This damp weather, along with fertile top soil, nurtures most growing things and keeps the countryside an exuberant green. Grass carpets even the ruins at Lillebonne, giving a Norman stamp to this Gallo-Roman amphitheater.

The Caux plateau, named for its chalky mass, is covered with fields: corn, wheat, flax, and *betterave*, which includes sugar beet and forage beet as well as table beet. To see this cultivated land at its best, set out early on a clear morning, when the slanting sunlight tints the landscape with a pink glow. In June, when the flax blossoms, the countryside is flooded with blue flowers.

Farmers here have long sought to tame the bitter winds that sweep the plateau. Their solution is easy to spot along any country lane: double rows of thick oak trees, beeches, or elms planted on high banks. Behind this naturally growing barrier, you see the traditional Cauchois property – farmhouse, outbuildings, and apple orchard. The whole farm demarked by its windbreak of trees is known as a *clos masure.*

The orchard has done double duty for centuries, supplying cider for farm workers and grass for dairy cows. This combination has created the eternal Norman scene of spotted cows sleeping under pink-blossomed apple trees.

Not very long ago, in addition to their work as windscreen, the grand trees supplied the material for furniture in the Norman home. It was traditional for a landowner to fell a tree for his daughter's

wedding. The tree was cut and the wood carted to a local cabinetmaker, who decorated the wedding chest according to the girl's wishes. A nest of lovebirds always adorned a wedding chest. But a bride-to-be then chose further embellishments, such as sheaves of wheat or musical instruments, according to her taste and background. An excellent place to study the rural furniture of Normandy is the Château de Martainville.

Another château not to miss is the 17th-century Château de Miromesnil, the birthplace of Guy de Maupassant and now home of the Comtesse Bertrand de Vogüé. The *potager*, or kitchen garden, here will dazzle you if you have ever planted a seed and watched it grow. Under the countess's watchful eye, the lowly vegetable patch has been upgraded to decorative art.

Fruits and vegetables flourish in plots bordered by a colorful display of daffodils, roses, clematis, delphiniums, and dahlias, depending on the season. Fruit trees, espaliered to maximize their exposure to the sun, hug the pale-rose walls. Late summer and fall, when the ripening vegetables are at their peak, is prime viewing time.

Along with ornamental gardens, dovecotes, or *pigeonniers*, once distinguished the estate of an aristocratic proprietor from a rustic one. The Pays de Caux has centuries-old dovecotes, often intricately designed, which stand as testaments to former customs. There's even a *route des pigeonniers* here, which guides you to superb examples.

Before the Revolution, the *pigeonnier* symbolized a lord's power and standing; only a seigneur could keep as many pigeons as he wanted, for fertilizer as well as for food. The greedy birds regularly polished off the newly planted grain in nearby fields, leaving disgruntled farmers. In 1789, this archaic privilege was abolished.

In some places in the Pays de Caux, you can find culinary specialties that haven't traveled even to the next town. In Saint-Romain-de-Colbosc, for instance, the *charcuteries* on the square all offer a stubby blood sausage, laced with Calvados and cream. In contrast to the *boudin* from Mortagne-au-Perche (see page 99), *boudin* capital of the Orne *département*, the fat in the Saint-Romain sausage is not chopped and blended with the pig's blood. Instead, it is cut in a long bar and arranged lengthwise in the sausage. When a slice is cut, you see a square of fat.

The high chalk plateau of the Pays de Caux is cut by several valleys. Formerly, saw mills, flour mills, and cider factories dotted the valleys. They once harnessed the rivers' energy in water-power, though few remain. Today, fish farmers profit from the rushing streams, mainly raising trout. Most offer a secluded spot for weekend fishing.

The Durdent, Sâane, Scie, and Varenne river valleys all make good routes for exploring Cauchois village life. One of the nicest areas to wander is the cider region between the towns of Auffay and Le Bois-Robert. Here, you can spend a day on the *route de la pomme et du cidre*. In May, the landscape offers a breathtaking vista – pink and white apple blossoms cradled in tones of green.

At any time of year, you can shop at the Auffay or Longueville-sur-Scie market, filling a hamper with Neufchâtel cheese, duck pâté, and country bread. Then you can sample single-variety ciders at a *cidrerie* and, from mid-June to mid-July, pick your own raspberries, strawberries, and black and red currants.

Between visits to cider factories and berry farms, there are ruins, châteaux, and bread ovens to investigate. (The Tudor-style *four à pain* outside Le Catelier is coiffed with a thatched roof.) And for a pause, the country *café-épiceries* provide coffee, cider, and company.

TOP AND ABOVE Snapshots from the ornamental kitchen garden at the Château de Miromesnil near Dieppe.
RIGHT Miromesnil's classic façade.

ABOVE *Forges-les-Eaux faïence by Grigore Fusle.
The last faïence workshop here was abandoned
around 1925, but Fusle, a Romanian ceramic artist,
later re-created this hand-painted, glazed pottery.
He duplicated 19th-century colors, designs, and
the signature* cul noir, *or black back.*
FAR LEFT *Churns in the Pays de Bray once used for
curdling milk to make Neufchâtel.
These belong to Bernadette Auvré, cheesemaker
in Mesnil-Mauger.*
LEFT *Neufchâtel cheese molds. Unlike most cheeses,
which drain in molds and take their
shape from them, Neufchâtel is stamped with
molds resembling cookie cutters.*

THE PAYS DE BRAY

Entering the Pays de Bray from the Caux plateau, you immediately notice a difference. The intensively farmed Pays de Caux gives way to rolling hills spotted with apple trees and grazing cows. There is not a wheat field in sight.

This low-lying, bucolic region, or *boutonnière* (buttonhole) as it is called, extends some 44 miles (70 kilometers), from about Londinières behind Dieppe southeast to Beauvais. The clay soil here retains water, making excellent pasturage. As a result, the whole area is practically one enormous dairy farm.

The Pays de Bray is the source of many cheeses and cheese products, including Neufchâtel, Petit-Suisse, and *fromage blanc*. Neufchâtel possesses an *appellation d'origine contrôlée* guaranteeing its area of production and other characteristics. This soft, salty cheese with a downy rind contains 45 percent butterfat by law and is the oldest Norman cheese; documents refer to Neufchâtel cheese as early as 1050.

Perhaps because Neufchâtel is relatively simple to make, farmwives produce it to supplement their income. About 40 farms in the region manufacture and age Neufchâtel (see right) in varying shapes and sizes, each with its own descriptive name: *bonde, briquette, carré, coeur, double-bonde,* and *gros-coeur* (bung, brick, square, heart, double bung, big-heart).

Many cheesemakers along the *route du fromage de Neufchâtel* welcome visitors. They post a sign advertising the cheese: a white heart on a red ground with two golden lions, the symbol of Normandy. You also find farm Neufchâtel at local markets and in grocery stores. It's always marked *fermier*. Saturday is market day in the small town of Neufchâtel-en-Bray, and farmers spread out around the Eglise Notre-Dame. To see the cheesemaking equipment, visit La Ferme de Bray near Sommery, a living museum.

Gervais-Danone, which produces most of the Petit-Suisse eaten by schoolchildren in France, has two factories in the Pays de Bray, where much of the local milk goes. According to local tradition, the beloved Petit-Suisse was invented around 1890 by a Bray dairymaid and a Swiss cheesemaker who added cream to drained curds.

But the Pays de Bray features more than homespun attractions. The spa town of Forges-les-Eaux draws a well-bred crowd with its casino, iron-rich waters, and other entertainments. Here you can also enjoy the beautiful faïence (on display at the town hall) created after the Revolution by an Englishman named Wood.

THE VAL DE SEINE

From the four-lane *autoroute de Normandie*, a road zigzags down to the village of La Bouille in the Seine Valley. The abrupt descent spotlights the contrast between the protected valley and the exposed surrounding countryside.

Driving from La Bouille toward Duclair, one orchard follows another and stone farmhouses with billowy thatched roofs line the road. In the village of Bardouville, an old bread oven stands by the side of the road, identifiable by the beehive bulge at the back. It is a beautiful example of the type

FARM NEUFCHATEL

Bernadette Auvré's cheesemaking room is as warm and damp as a greenhouse. Here, this farmwife makes Neufchâtel every morning, the old-fashioned way. She sets buckets of warm milk from the family's 25 cows to curdle, slowly, with rennet. The next day she pours the wet curds into plastic laundry baskets lined with cheesecloth. When the whey has trickled out, she wraps the cloth around the curds and sets a board over it. Then she hoists a water-filled bucket on top to force out any remaining whey. Twelve hours later, she works a crumbled Neufchâtel, covered with bloomy rind, into the curds. Once "seeded," the curds are ready for molding – stamping, really – then salting. The cheeses finish drying for 24 hours in a room with a sweet lactic aroma. Finally she moves them to a cool, moist cellar where she turns and tends them for two weeks until they are ripe enough to wear the Neufchâtel fermier label.

found in Normandy (see page 50). Once used for storing such utensils as bread paddles and rakes, the cabin attached to the oven now serves as a workshop.

In Anneville-sur-Seine, you come across the Ferme du Canardier. Here, a *maître canardier éleveur* raises the famed Duclair breed of duck, named for the market town just across the river.

The best place to see the effects of the microclimate in the Seine valley is along the *route des fruits*. First you roll onto the ferry (*bac*) to Duclair, along with other cars, trucks, and foot passengers. Cars with "76" license plates (indicating cars registered in Seine-Maritime) go free, while others pay a small fee. Skimming across the Seine, you spot the names "Henri" and "Denise" etched on the two towers of the Hôtel de la Poste. Monsieur Henri Denise is believed to be the inventor of the celebrated *canard à la rouennaise* (see opposite), prepared throughout the Seine valley even today.

The *route des fruits* begins after Duclair and continues along the meandering river to Jumièges. Fruit trees pack the ribbon of land between white cliffs and beacons. At day's end the beacons flash red signals to guide boats and barges on the Seine.

The river carries warm, damp air to this inland valley, and the cliffs guard the orchards against the wind that rustles in the oaks, beeches, and elms on the enclosing plateau. As a result, apple trees here burst into bloom in late April – weeks before those on the frosty Caux plateau. Delicate fruits such as pears, cherries, and plums all thrive in this coddled setting.

In warm weather, *arboriculteurs*, or fruit-tree growers, set up roadside stands, and you can buy their harvest direct from the farm. Also, at the *base de plein air* (local recreation area) outside Mesnil-sous-Jumièges, growers sell cherries, red currants, pears, and apples, according to the season.

Further along the river to the west, past sober abbey ruins, flamboyant mansions, and mighty castles, is Caudebec-en-Caux. While Caudebec has no culinary specialties of its own, it can brag about its *fête du cidre*, or cider festival, held in even-numbered years in late September, when the whole town joins in traditional cidermaking.

Rouen, straddling the Seine, is a showcase for Normandy's gastronomic offerings, with excellent restaurants and markets that feature fruit grown in the Seine valley and seafood plucked from the waters off the Alabaster Coast. Butchers in this capital of Seine-Maritime regularly garner prizes for *boudin* and other *charcuterie*. Poultrymen sell Rouennais ducks as well as ducks from Duclair.

In the town's pedestrian streets, lined with wood-ribbed houses, candy stores advertise *sucre de pomme de Rouen*, an old-fashioned candy stick made from sugar and apple extract. The *mirliton de Rouen* is often mentioned in books as a regional specialty, but it is hard to find. Gilles Tournadre, at the restaurant Gill in Rouen, makes one. His recipe, with almond cream wrapped in puff pastry, is based on early cook books from the region.

Tableware shops display hand-painted reproductions of Rouen dishes – now made in northern France. After you roam the cobbled lanes of Rouen and admire the Gothic Notre-Dame Cathedral portrayed in different lights by Monet, have a look at genuine Rouen faïence at the Musée de la Céramique, which presents a history of the famous pottery.

Today, a special connection exists between this heirloom faïence and regional cuisine. The Rouennais restaurateur who sets out this pottery for you to discover will also track down Duclair duck for his *canard à la rouennaise*. This is a cook who will take the time to prepare sample dishes for his suppliers. In turn, these men and women will strive to grow, raise, or catch produce with as much flavor as in the old days.

VERITABLE CANARD DE DUCLAIR

Robert Maugard raises chickens, guinea fowl, and several breeds of duck at the Ferme du Canardier in Anneville-sur Seine. But his passion is the canard de Duclair. "Look at my duck," says Monsieur Maugard, pointing with his knife at the bird he is deboning. "In an ordinary duck the liver would be half that size."

Outside, his ducks peck at corn and wheat in the fresh air, but they flee, quacking, as we approach. "The Duclairs are the black ones with the white 'bib'," he explains as they turn their backs on us. But their favorite food is grass. "In March," he says, "when the grass starts to grow again, their skin turns yellow with the change in diet."

The breed is said to be a mix, originally the offspring of domestic, local mothers and wild fathers. When the ducks are killed, their weight averages 5 pounds, with most of that concentrated in breast meat. (By comparison, the canard rouennais weighs in at 3 pounds, with a considerable amount of fat.)

These are canards au sang – ducks strangled and not bled – destined for such gastronomic dishes as canard à la rouennaise. This manner of dispatching birds has been outlawed in France except where these recent regulations would interfere with tradition, such as around Duclair.

Mindful of critics in this matter, farmers such as Robert Maugard first stun the ducks with an electric shock. Still, Monsieur Maugard clucks at electrocution, which he feels induces more stress than the time-tested method.

According to legend, the first canards au sang appeared spontaneously, the result of overcrowding on the boats that used to ferry market gardeners and livestock across the Seine to Duclair. One plucky farmer, the tale goes, turned the smothered ducks to profit by selling them to restaurateurs.

Henri Denise, formerly chef-owner of the Hôtel de la Poste in Duclair, is credited with inventing canard à la rouennaise. For this recipe, a Duclair duck is first roasted in a hot oven for 17 minutes. The legs and breast meat are carved, then seasoned with sea salt, pepper from the mill, a grating of nutmeg, a pinch of ground cloves, and a little Dijon mustard. To make the sauce, red Bordeaux wine, laced with Cognac and port, is simmered with shallots and a purée of the duck liver and heart. The roasted carcass is crushed in a silver press that expels every bit of bloodied juice, which is added to thicken and flavor the sauce. Some recipes include a stuffing prepared with onion, fatty bacon, duck livers, parsley, and spices. Without doubt, canard à la rouennaise is the Duclair duck's supreme moment.

Though restaurants throughout the Val de Seine offer this specialty, the frumpy Hôtel de la Poste in Duclair remains the local institution for sampling the famous duck, here called "canard à la Denise." Surrounded by the birds in his work, perhaps Monsieur Maugard is less enthusiastic about seeing them on his dinner table? "Oh no!" he says. "I love duck."

LEFT Iris grows on the roof of a thatched cottage in the Seine Valley. Functional as well as ornamental, the iris holds the thatch in place and keeps it moist.

AUBERGE DU BEAU LIEU

LE FOSSÉ, FORGES-LES-EAUX, TEL 35 90 50 36

When Patrick Ramelet first took over the Auberge du Beau Lieu, he had to do his shopping in Paris. Local farmers did not produce the quality ingredients he wanted. However, slowly he developed relationships with the farmers, prodding and coaxing them, so that now most of his provisions come from the Pays de Bray.

Monsieur Ramelet is himself from Burgundy. But he has become more Norman than the locals. "The moment you live in a new place," he says, "your cooking evolves. You draw on fresh traditions and new ingredients." He's also lost the neighborhood clientele who expect steak and fries. Instead, people come from Rouen, Paris, and farther afield to sample his cooking, expertly tuned to the seasons and the surrounding Normandy countryside.

After ten years of hard work to establish their restaurant, Monsieur Ramelet and his wife, Marie-France, have no regrets. "You cannot put a price on the hours you work," he says. "We have realized a dream."

CROQUANT DE NEUFCHATEL A LA CREME D'HERBES FINES

Neufchâtel in Crispy Pastry with Herb Cream

An old cheese, Neufchâtel is still made largely on farms in the simplest way, with milk warm from the cow. Patrick Ramelet wraps this salty farm cheese in a North African import, brik dough, and fries the pastry in duck fat!

French supermarkets commonly sell packages of paper-thin round brik sheets. While brik, similar to filo and strudel dough, is normally used for this recipe, filo works just as well. Neufchâtel takes well to this melting-pot treatment. The mixture of melted cheese, herbed cream, buttery spinach, and crisp pastry is an inspired alternative to the copycat grilled cheese toasts on salad. Serve it as a first course or a light luncheon dish with salad. Or alternatively make it the cheese course in a formal dinner menu.

SERVES 4
½ **cup whipping cream**
2tbsp mixed chopped fresh herbs such as
tarragon, chives, and chervil
2tbsp unsalted butter
⅓**lb fresh spinach, stems removed**
1 clove garlic
8 sheets of *brik* dough or 4 sheets of filo
dough
1 egg, beaten to mix with a pinch of salt
1 Neufchâtel (7oz), rind removed and cut
into thin slices
3tbsp duck fat or vegetable oil
salt and freshly ground black pepper

Whip half the cream until it holds soft peaks. Stir in half the herbs and chill until ready to use.

Melt the butter in a saucepan. Add the spinach with a little salt and pepper and cook it over moderately high heat, stirring it with a fork stuck with the peeled garlic clove, just until the spinach wilts. Discard the garlic.

If using filo dough, cut each sheet into two 9½-inch rounds. Generously brush four of the dough sheets, either filo or *brik*, with the beaten egg mixture. Cover each sheet with a second sheet of dough. Put one-quarter of the spinach in the center of each, cover with slices of Neufchâtel, and top with a tablespoon of whipped cream.

For each pastry, fold one flap of the dough over the filling and brush the top with beaten egg. Continue folding the flaps of dough over the filling and brushing them with egg until the filling is completely enclosed in a square of dough.

Heat the fat or oil in a large frying pan over moderate heat. Put the pastries in the pan flap-side up, without crowding the pan. Fry them on both sides until browned, about 1 minute on each side, and drain on paper towels.

Stir the remaining herbs into the rest of the cream. Put the pastries on warmed plates and spoon the herb cream around them.

PAIN PERDU
DU BEAU LIEU

French Toast with Gingerbread Ice Cream and Sesame Wafers

Patrick Ramelet's recipe combines, on the same plate, something warm and something icy, a crispy texture and soft ones. This stream-lined version keeps the essence while skipping a few finishing touches. But if you like, add egg custard sauce and sautéed apples to the plate.

For Monsieur Ramelet, cooking is much more than just a creative exercise. "I try to please my clients," he says. "If they don't like a new dish, I take it off the menu."

SERVES 4
3 egg yolks
½ **cup crème fraîche**
1tbsp sugar
4 slices brioche loaf, cut ¾in thick
3tbsp unsalted butter
4 scoops Gingerbread Ice Cream (see page
32) or another flavor

FOR THE WAFERS
1 stick unsalted butter
2tbsp honey
¾ **cup sugar**
3tbsp flour
2tbsp sesame seeds

For the wafers, preheat the oven to 325°F.

Melt the butter with the honey, stirring until smooth, then let cool. Mix together the sugar, flour, and sesame seeds, then stir in the honey butter. The batter will be pasty.

Put tablespoons of the batter on a baking sheet, spacing them about 2 inches apart. With the back of a spoon, spread each lump of batter into a thin round 2½ inches in diameter.

Bake until the sesame wafers are lacy and deep golden, about 12–15 minutes.

It is tricky getting the wafers off the baking sheet. Let them stand about 1 minute or they will fall to soft pieces when you try to lift them off with a metal spatula. Do not wait too long or the wafers will harden and crumble. When the wafers are just cooled enough to be slightly firm, work quickly to remove them using a metal spatula and carefully drape each one over an upturned tumbler. Let them cool on the tumblers. The soft wafer will fall into a tulip shape on its own; if you try to mold it with a ramekin pressed over each wafer, the fragile wafer will tear.

Beat together the egg yolks, crème fraîche, and sugar. Soak the brioche slices in this egg mixture until the mixture is well absorbed but the brioche is still firm enough to keep its shape. Melt the butter in a large frying pan over moderate heat. Fry the brioche slices in the butter, without crowding the pan, until they are golden on both sides, 1–2 minutes in all.

Set a slice of brioche on each plate. Put a scoop of gingerbread ice cream in four of the nicest tulip-shaped wafers, place a wafer alongside the brioche, and serve immediately.

GLACE PAIN D'EPICES

Gingerbread Ice Cream

There is a cerebral element to Patrick Ramelet's cooking as well as a sensual one. So the food at the Auberge du Beau Lieu does not merely taste good, it also gives you something to think about, gastronomically.

This ice cream recipe uses French gingerbread, pain d'épices, but where this is not available, other dry-textured gingerbread can be substituted with equally good results.

MAKES ABOUT 1QT
2 cups milk
¾ cup sugar
8 egg yolks
5oz French *pain d'épices*, crusts removed
½ cup chopped candied fruits
1¾ cups whipping cream, lightly whipped

Heat the milk with the sugar in a saucepan, stirring, until it just begins to boil. Remove the pan from the heat. Beat the egg yolks and slowly whisk in the hot milk. Pour the mixture back into the pan and cook over low heat, stirring constantly with a wooden spatula, until the custard thickens enough to coat the spatula, 18–20 minutes. Remove the pan from the heat and crumble in the gingerbread. Stir the mixture until the gingerbread melts.

Set the pan in a bowl of ice water and stir the custard occasionally until cool. Stir in the candied fruits. Transfer the mixture to an ice-cream maker and freeze it according to the manufacturer's directions until partially set. Add the cream and continue to freeze until set.

If the ice cream freezes rock hard, let it soften slightly in the refrigerator for 15–30 minutes before serving.

RESTAURANT LE BEFFROY

15 RUE BEFFROY, ROUEN, TEL 35 71 55 27

Once I bumped into Odile Engel at the bustling fish market in Caen. What was Madame Engel doing in Caen at six in the morning, far from her restaurant in Rouen? "It feels good just to be in the Pays d'Auge," she said.

Having moved from Beuvron-en-Auge, Madame Engel still returns twice a week to where the fish is freshest. She is a fanatic about fish, stroking it and worrying about it. On a slow day at her one-star restaurant Le Beffroy, she frets, "No one wants my beautiful fish."

When Odile Engel first earned her Michelin star in 1987, she felt trapped by the responsibility. "I thought I had lost my freedom," she says. "I did not know what to do." The Michelin inspector suggested that she keep doing things in her own way. Eventually she relaxed back into her cooking.

At Le Beffroy, Madame Engel cooks and her daughter and husband wait tables. But she feels pressure to make her restaurant, housed in a 17th-century landmark, more refined. One restaurant guide plainly told her to replace her menu, hand-written daily, with a printed card, and commented: "Rouen is not the countryside." Yet she dislikes being tied down. "It all depends," she says. "Are the fish biting today?"

GRATIN DE MOULES AU CIDRE

Mussels in Cider Sauce

Odile Engel's style of cooking is a mixture of homespun and cuisine du marché, *the term chefs use for personal cooking based on what is available in the market.*

Mussels in Cider Sauce typifies this spirit. Plump local mussels are steamed open, then gratinéed with a sauce made from the mussel liquor, Norman crème fraîche, and farm cider. Madame Engel sums up her philosophy: "I do the kind of cooking I like to eat."

SERVES 4
2qt mussels, scrubbed and bearded
1 shallot, finely chopped
1 cup dry hard cider
1¼ cups crème fraîche
freshly ground black pepper
1tbsp snipped fresh chives, to garnish

Combine the mussels and shallot in a large saucepan. Cover, set over high heat, and cook the mussels, stirring once or twice, just until they open, 3–5 minutes. Remove the pan from the heat. When the mussels are cool enough to handle, remove the mussel meat from the shells and set aside; discard the shells.

Strain the mussel liquor. Put half of the liquor in a saucepan with the cider and crème fraîche and simmer, stirring from time to time, until it thickens, 5–10 minutes. Add pepper to taste.

Preheat the broiler.

Divide the mussels and cider sauce evenly among four heatproof soup plates. Put the plates on the broiler rack and cook about 3 inches from the heat until the tops are lightly browned, 3–4 minutes. Serve at once, sprinkled with chives. Pass crusty bread for mopping up the sauce.

TURBOT AU BEURRE DE CITRON

Turbot in Lemon Butter Sauce

Odile Engel's love for the food of her adopted Normandy is evident in every dish at her restaurant. She prepares local ingredients without fuss, as this lighthearted and flavorful dish illustrates. It is simply a matter of stewing a few vegetables while sautéing fresh fish. For the sauce, she whisks lumps of unsalted butter into tart lemon juice.

SERVES 4
20 spring onions, trimmed to 2½in
½lb carrots, quartered lengthwise and cut into 1½-in lengths
1 cup shelled fresh or frozen, thawed green peas
5tbsp unsalted butter
1¾lb turbot or other white fish fillets
salt and freshly ground white pepper

FOR THE SAUCE
juice of 1 lemon (about 3tbsp)
10tbsp unsalted butter, cut into pieces
salt and freshly ground white pepper

Cook the onions, carrots, and fresh peas, separately, in boiling salted water until tender, 3–5 minutes, then drain. Put them in a frying pan, with the thawed frozen peas if using, and 2 tablespoons of the butter. Toss the vegetables in the butter with salt and pepper to taste until heated through. Keep them warm.

Clarify the remaining butter: Melt it over low heat, skim off the froth, and let cool to tepid. Pour the butter into a bowl, leaving the milky sediment at the bottom of the pan. Heat the clarified butter in a large frying pan.

Sprinkle the fish fillets with salt and pepper, add to the butter, and cook, turning once, until opaque throughout, 3–5 minutes in all. Drain the fish on paper towels and keep it warm.

For the sauce, bring the lemon juice just to a boil in a small heavy saucepan. Add a little salt and pepper. Gradually whisk in the butter over very low heat. The butter should soften rather than melt completely. The sauce will be frothy and lemony. Taste it and add salt and pepper if needed.

Spoon the sauce onto warmed plates. Arrange the fish on the plates, surrounded by the vegetables. Serve immediately.

CRÈME DE CRESSON AUX MOULES

Watercress Soup with Mussels

Watercress flourishes in the Pays de Caux, its roots washed by the streams that pour into the English Channel. This colorful soup, from the Auberge du Val au Cesne near Yvetot, combines the peppery green with sweet mussels and, just before serving, cream to smooth out the pungent flavor. The contrast of orange mussels set off by the deep green soup is especially appealing. (Illustrated left)

SERVES 4
1qt mussels, scrubbed and bearded
2 cups dry white wine
1 onion, finely chopped
leaves from 1 stalk of celery, finely chopped
1⅓lb bunch of watercress, stems removed
1 boiling potato, peeled, quartered, and thinly sliced
¾ cup crème fraîche
freshly ground black pepper

Combine the mussels, wine, onion, and celery leaves in a large saucepan. Cover the pan and set it over high heat. Cook the mussels, stirring once or twice, just until they open, 3–5 minutes. Remove the pan from the heat. When the mussels are cool enough to handle, take the mussel meat from the shells and set aside; discard the shells.

Strain the mussel cooking liquid into another saucepan. Add the watercress and potato, cover the pan, and bring the liquid to a boil. Reduce the heat to low and simmer, covered, for 20 minutes.

Purée the soup in a food processor or work it through a food mill. Return the soup to the pan and add the crème fraîche and reserved mussels. Heat through gently, season to taste, and serve.

HUITRES AU SABAYON DE POMMEAU

Oysters with Pommeau Sabayon

This new but quintessentially Norman dish features two native specialties: oysters and pommeau, the apple apéritif. The rich pommeau sabayon combines with the briny oysters for a delicious mouthful. At a pinch, Calvados could replace the pommeau. *(Illustrated on page 39)*

SERVES 4 AS A FIRST COURSE
12 large oysters in the shell
fresh seaweed or sea salt (optional)
1 egg yolk
1½tbsp *pommeau*

Scrub the oyster shells. Open an oyster, then free it from the shell by loosening the muscle in the top and bottom shell; discard the flat top shell. Repeat with the remaining oysters. (You can ask your fish merchant to do this for you, but not more than 2 or 3 hours before serving the dish.) Leave the oysters in the bottom shell and set them on a bed of crushed ice to prevent them from tilting. Chill.

Just before serving, preheat the broiler. Cover the plates with a thick bed of fresh seaweed or sea salt, if using. Arrange the oysters, in their shells, on an oven rack.

In a large heatproof bowl, beat the egg yolk with a hand-held electric mixer or a whisk until creamy, about 30 seconds. Beat in the *pommeau*. Set the bowl over a pan of simmering water, making sure the water does not touch the bowl. Continue beating at high speed until the sabayon holds soft peaks, 3–5 minutes.

Spoon about 1 teaspoon of the sabayon over each oyster and broil them until tinged with brown, ½–1 minute.

Transfer the oysters to the prepared plates, or oyster plates, and serve them immediately.

SOUFFLES AU FROMAGE

Individual Cheese Soufflés

Marie-Claude Quesnel claims that there is nothing special about her cheese soufflés. "Just eggs from my chickens and our butter," says this Norman farmwife. Yet her version seems lighter than most, and better. These proportions will make four little soufflés to serve as a first course or side dish. If you like, double the quantities and bake in a 6-inch soufflé dish to serve as a main course.

SERVES 4
3tbsp unsalted butter
1tbsp flour
½ cup milk
3 eggs, separated
1 cup grated Gruyère cheese
salt and freshly ground white pepper

Preheat the oven to 425°F.

Generously butter four ¾-cup individual soufflé dishes or ramekins.

In a heavy saucepan, melt the butter over low heat. Whisk in the flour and cook 30 seconds without letting it color. Pour in the milk, whisking, and bring to a boil. Season liberally with salt and pepper. Simmer the sauce, whisking often, for 10 minutes. Off the heat, whisk in the egg yolks, one by one, then the cheese.

Whisk the egg whites with a pinch of salt until they hold firm peaks. Whisk one-third of the egg whites into the cheese mixture, then fold this lightened cheese mixture gently but thoroughly into the remaining egg whites.

Pour the soufflé mixture into the prepared dishes; it should not completely fill them. Set the dishes on a baking sheet and bake until the soufflés are brown and the mixture no longer wobbles, 20–25 minutes. Serve immediately.

SALADE PAYSANNE ANNE-MARIE CAVELAN

Endive Salad with Tomatoes, Corn, and Duck Cracklings

Like other farmwives in Normandy today, Anne-Marie Cavelan raises ducks for foie gras, confit, and the fat duck breasts called magrets. *She renders the duck fat, too, and saves the cracklings to garnish this salad.*

This unusual salad is one of those between-season dishes, when garden tomatoes are still ripening on the windowsill and the first Belgian endive appears in the market.

The salad abounds with contrasting textures and flavors: crunchy bread, tender potatoes, sweet corn, and rich cracklings, all mixed with slightly bitter endive. If you don't want to fuss with cracklings, substitute 3 ounces of sliced bacon, cut across into fine strips and sautéed. Add the bread at the last minute so it stays crisp.

SERVES 4
1 boiling potato
1½ cups bread cubes
2 or 3 heads Belgian endive, sliced crosswise on the diagonal
1 tomato, chopped
2tbsp duck cracklings (see right)
½ cup cooked fresh or frozen, thawed corn kernels

FOR THE DRESSING
2tbsp red wine vinegar
6½tbsp vegetable oil
salt and freshly ground black pepper

Put the potato in a saucepan of salted water and bring to a boil. Simmer until the potato is tender, about 15–20 minutes, then drain. When the potato is cool enough to handle, peel it and cut it into ½-inch cubes.

Heat the broiler. Toast the bread cubes under the broiler, turning once, until golden, 1–2 minutes. Set aside.

Make the dressing: Whisk together the vinegar and salt to taste until the salt dissolves. Whisk in the oil and pepper until smooth.

Combine the potato, endive, tomato, duck cracklings, and corn in a salad bowl. Add the dressing and toss the salad until it is evenly coated. Taste and adjust the seasoning. Add the bread cubes just before serving.

GRATTELONS DE CANARD

Duck Cracklings

Cracklings are the bits that emerge when fat and skin are cooked slowly. Cooks in southwest France have long treasured these grattelons, *which add texture and richness to dishes. Now that foie-gras farming has been introduced to Normandy, these crunchy bits have begun to appear in Norman cooking, too.*

Cracklings can be made with whatever quantities of duck fat and skin you collect, keeping the general proportions given here.

MAKES 2TBSP
4oz (½ cup) duck fat
2oz duck skin, thinly sliced

Combine the duck fat and skin in a frying pan and set over low heat. Cook gently, stirring occasionally, until the unmelted bits of fat and the skin are golden, about 45 minutes.

Drain the cracklings, and save the flavorful fat to enrich soups and stews, or to fry potatoes.

SALADE DE COQUILLES SAINT-JACQUES

Warm Scallop Salad with Cress and Vegetables

Gilles Tournadre does not offer a regional menu at Gill, his restaurant in Rouen, until April or May, the tourist season. "When people come to my restaurant," he explained, "they expect food they cannot find at their neighborhood bistro."

Out of Gill's kitchen comes some of the most spectacular cooking in Normandy, such as this salad. It's a variation of vegetables à la grecque, *with sweet scallops, fruity nut oil, and peppery cress. Here, I have freely adapted Monsieur Tournadre's original recipe, making a more simplified version.*

SERVES 4 AS A FIRST COURSE
1tbsp olive oil
1 small onion, finely chopped
1 large clove garlic, thinly sliced
pinch of cayenne pepper
½tsp sugar
1 bay leaf
¼tsp crushed coriander seeds
½ cup dry white wine
½ cup chicken stock, preferably homemade
1 small turnip, peeled and cut into ¼-in dice
½ red bell pepper, seeded and cut into ¼-in dice
½ small zucchini, skin and outside flesh only, cut into ¼-in dice
2tsp hazelnut oil
12 scallops
salt
garden cress, to garnish

Heat the olive oil in a small saucepan. Add the onion and sauté it until translucent, 2–3 minutes. Add the garlic and cook it until fragrant, about 1 minute. Stir in the cayenne, sugar, bay leaf, coriander, white wine, and stock. Bring just to a boil, then reduce the heat, cover, and simmer this court-bouillon gently for 10 minutes.

Strain the court-bouillon and return it to the pan. Add the diced turnip and a little salt and cook gently, covered, for 10–12 minutes. Add the diced bell pepper and zucchini and continue cooking until the court-bouillon reduces to a light glaze, 5–7 minutes longer. The vegetables should still be slightly crunchy.

Remove from the heat and let cool to lukewarm, then stir in the hazelnut oil. Taste for seasoning, adding more salt, cayenne, or hazelnut oil until the sauce is as pungent as you like. (The mixture should be slightly less seasoned than for traditional vegetables *à la grecque*.) Keep warm.

Set a nonstick frying pan over moderate heat. When the pan is hot, add the scallops and cook them, turning once, until they are nearly opaque throughout, 2–3 minutes.

To serve, arrange 3 scallops on each plate. Spoon some of the tepid vegetable mixture around the scallops. Scatter cress sparingly over the vegetables and serve immediately.

BELOW A decorative house serves as a backdrop to a weekly market near Dieppe. The architecture in Seine-Maritime reflects the building materials on which it sits. Houses, churches, dovecotes, and even walls display variegated geometric designs in flint, brick, and limestone.

MAQUEREAUX MARINES AU CIDRE

Mackerel Marinated with Cider and Aromatic Vegetables

Unlike most versions of maquereaux au cidre *where the mackerel is fully poached, here the fish, almost raw, marinates in a well-seasoned court-bouillon. This way it retains its rich flavor and produces a finer-tasting dish.*

The recipe was given to me by Claude Havard, who guides visitors through the cidermaking process at the Duché de Longueville cidrerie in Anneville-sur-Scie. It is simple to prepare as a first course or a luncheon dish.

SERVES 4 AS A MAIN COURSE
1 onion, thinly sliced
1 carrot, thinly sliced
a large sprig of fresh thyme
2 bay leaves
2 cups dry hard cider
4 mackerel fillets (total about 1lb),
skin on
$\frac{1}{4}$ cup cider vinegar
20 black peppercorns, crushed
salt
1tbsp snipped fresh chives, to garnish

Combine the onion, carrot, thyme, bay leaves, cider, and a little salt in a saucepan. Bring to a boil, then reduce the heat and simmer this court-bouillon 20 minutes.

Meanwhile, score each fillet on the skin side, making several diagonal cuts about $\frac{1}{8}$ inch deep. Arrange the fillets, skin side down, in a heatproof dish just the size to hold them.

Pour the hot court-bouillon over the fish and add the vinegar and peppercorns. Let the court-bouillon cool to room temperature, then chill the fish, covered, for 48 hours.

To serve, arrange the fish on a platter or plates. Moisten the mackerel with some of the court-bouillon and vegetables and sprinkle with chives. Serve at room temperature.

SOLE DIEPPOISE

Sole Fillets with Mushrooms and Cream

Simone Monneron has lived all over the world, from Indo-China to Britain. She now lives in Paris, in the posh sixteenth arrondissement. *But, she insists, "*Je suis Dieppoise.*"*

Her grandfather was a marin-armateur *(ship-owner) in Dieppe whose three or four trawlers regularly unloaded their catch, mostly sole and mackerel, at the fish market there before 1914.*

Simone spent her childhood in Dieppe, and she remembers eating cream with everything. "In those days," she says, "we had cream with fish, cream with vegetables, cream with chicken." She shared with me the recipe for one of those memorable creamy dishes.

SERVES 4
4 Dover or gray sole (each about 1lb),
cleaned, filleted, and skinned, skin and
bones reserved
2 shallots, finely chopped
$\frac{1}{4}$lb mushrooms, chopped
1 cup fish stock made with the sole skin
and bones, or dry white wine
salt

FOR THE SAUCE
2tbsp unsalted butter
1tbsp flour
$\frac{1}{4}$ cup crème fraîche
fresh lemon juice to taste
salt and freshly ground white pepper

Fold the fish fillets in half, skinned-side inside. Butter a frying pan, add the shallots, fish, and mushrooms, and sprinkle lightly with salt. Pour in the stock or wine and press a piece of buttered foil on top. Bring the stock slowly to a simmer, then reduce the heat to low and gently poach the fish until it is opaque throughout, 5–7 minutes.

Remove the fish and mushrooms with a slotted spoon and drain them on paper towels, then carefully transfer them to a dish. Cover and keep them warm while preparing the sauce. Strain the fish cooking liquid into a measuring cup.

For the sauce, melt half the butter in a heavy

1lb mixed firm white fish fillets, such as
monkfish, John Dory, turbot
2 shallots, finely chopped
$\frac{1}{2}$ cup dry white wine
$\frac{1}{2}$ cup fish stock made with the sole skin and
bones, or more dry white wine
1qt mussels, scrubbed and bearded
$\frac{3}{4}$ cup crème fraîche
2 egg yolks
2tbsp unsalted butter, cut into pieces
salt and freshly ground white pepper

*ABOVE The scales for the daily catch, St-Aubin.
LEFT Poached Fish Fillets and Mussels in
Cream Sauce (far left), and Oysters
with* Pommeau *Sabayon (right), page 35.*

NAGE DE POISSONS FINS, FAÇON DIEPPOISE

*Poached Fish Fillets and Mussels in
Cream Sauce*

Here "façon dieppoise" refers to the vast assortment of seafood sold at the Dieppe fish market. Gilbert Plaisance, chef-owner of Les Galets in Veules-les-Roses, says that this dish needs at least three different kinds of fish to earn its name. In season, scallops are nice, too.

Monsieur Plaisance poaches the fish in stock, steams open some mussels, and then prepares a sauce by reducing the cooking liquid with cream. At the end he whisks in egg yolk and a chunk of butter. (Illustrated above, far left)

SERVES 4
**1 Dover or gray sole (about 1$\frac{3}{4}$lb), cleaned,
filleted, and skinned, skin and bones
reserved**

saucepan over low heat. Whisk in the flour and cook 30 seconds without letting it color. Pour in the fish cooking liquid, whisking, and bring it to a boil. Whisk in the crème fraîche and a little salt, then reduce the heat and simmer the sauce, skimming regularly, about 10 minutes. Reduce the heat to very low and whisk in the remaining butter. It should soften rather than melt completely. Add a few drops of lemon juice and season to taste.

Arrange the fish and mushrooms on a warmed platter or plates. Pour the sauce over the fish and serve immediately with steamed potatoes sprinkled with chopped parsley.

Cut all the fish fillets into 2-inch pieces on the diagonal. Butter a frying pan, add the shallots and fish, and sprinkle lightly with salt. Pour in the wine and stock and press a piece of buttered foil on top. Bring slowly to a simmer, then gently poach the fish until opaque throughout, 3–5 minutes. Remove the fish and drain on paper towels, then transfer to a dish. Cover and keep warm. Strain the fish cooking liquid into a small saucepan.

Put the mussels in a large saucepan, cover, and set over high heat. Cook the mussels, stirring once or twice, just until they open, 3–5 minutes. Remove the pan from the heat. When the mussels are cool enough to handle, remove the mussel meat from the shells and set aside; discard the shells. Strain the mussel liquor into the fish cooking liquid.

For the sauce, bring the cooking liquid to a boil, then lower the heat and simmer, skimming regularly, until it reduces to about $\frac{1}{4}$ cup. Blend 2 tablespoons of the crème fraîche into the egg yolks. Add the remaining crème fraîche to the saucepan and simmer, skimming regularly, until the liquid reduces to about $\frac{3}{4}$ cup. Whisk a little of the sauce into the egg yolk mixture and then whisk this mixture into the sauce in the pan, over very low heat. Whisk in the butter so that it softens rather than melting completely. Adjust the seasoning. Add the mussels to the sauce to warm them.

Arrange the fish on a warmed platter or plates. Pour the sauce and mussels over the fish and serve.

CANARD NICOLE MAUGARD

Broiled Duck with Mustard and Green Peppercorns

When asked about his favorite duck dishes, Robert Maugard says, "Oh, we don't have time to cook." If pressed, however, this poultryman to France's great chefs confesses to liking this recipe, prepared by his wife, Nicole. "We had it today for lunch," he says, adding as a warning, "It is not restaurant cooking." Nicole Maugard's broiled duck is an unfussy dish, designed for working families. (Illustrated right)

SERVES 4
1 duck (about 4½lb)
2tbsp Dijon mustard, or to taste
1 cup crème fraîche
2tsp drained green peppercorns in brine, or to taste

Cut the legs off the duck and trim any excess skin. Cut out the wishbone, then make a slit the length of the breast on one side of the breastbone. Cut and scrape the breast meat from the rib cage until it is free. Sever the joint connecting the wing to the carcass and trim any excess skin. Repeat for the other breast. Preheat the broiler.

Prick the skin all over and put the pieces on the broiler rack, skin upward. Broil about 3 inches from the heat, 10 minutes. Turn them over, brush with half the mustard, and broil until the juice runs pink when a breast is pricked, 7–10 minutes.

Meanwhile, combine the crème fraîche, green peppercorns, remaining mustard, and a little salt in a heavy saucepan. Simmer, stirring occasionally, until thickened, 5–10 minutes. Taste and add more mustard, peppercorns, or salt if you like.

Transfer the duck to a warmed platter or plates, pour over the sauce, and serve.

PINTADE AU CIDRE

Roast Guinea Fowl with Cider

Serge and Marie-Claude Quesnel raise lambs, calves, chickens, and squabs for a living, but on the weekend they open their farmhouse in Goupil-lières to eaters with a yen for granny's cooking. Furnished with an armoire *and a buffet in the Bray style, the dining room here provides the perfect setting for the regional food.*

For this recipe, constant basting with melted butter and cider produces a moist, brown bird. The rich cooking juices provide a simple sauce. With her roasted guinea fowl, Madame Quesnel serves apple slices sautéed in butter, and Individual Cheese Soufflés (see page 35).

SERVES 4
1 guinea fowl (about 3½lb), trussed
1 stick unsalted butter, cut into pieces
1½ cups dry hard cider
salt and freshly ground black pepper

Preheat the oven to 425°F.

Put the guinea fowl in a roasting pan just the size to hold it. Sprinkle it inside and out with salt and dot with the butter. Pour the cider around it. Roast the bird, basting every 10 minutes, until the juice runs clear when an inner thigh is pierced, about 50–60 minutes.

Remove the bird to a carving board with a juice catcher and set it aside to rest, covered loosely with foil, for 10 minutes.

Meanwhile, set the roasting pan over high heat and simmer the cooking juices to concentrate the flavor. Season to taste.

Remove the trussing strings from the bird and carve it. Arrange the pieces on a warmed platter or plates. Pour any juices from the bird into the reduced cooking juices and pour over the bird. Serve immediately.

LEFT Bottled cider from Normandy. A delicious brew whether drunk from a glass or added to the pot, as in Roast Guinea Fowl with Cider.

POULARDE A LA CREME DE POIREAUX

Poached Chicken with Leeks and Cream

The cooking at the Auberge du Val au Cesne is solid and traditional, yet strays from the hum-drum with a handful of this or that collected at the farmers' market. In this recipe, leeks lend a subtle flavor to classic chicken in cream sauce, creating a new dish but saving the mellowness of the original. Plain boiled rice is the usual partner, but try fresh pasta, too, for absorbing the abundant, leek-infused sauce.

SERVES 4
1 chicken (about 3½lb), trussed
2 carrots, thinly sliced
2 onions, quartered and studded with
2 cloves
2 leeks, white and light green parts only,
thinly sliced
a large branch of fresh thyme
2 bay leaves
2qt water
salt

FOR THE SAUCE
3tbsp unsalted butter
¼ cup flour
4 leeks, white and light green parts only,
cut into julienne strips
¾ cup crème fraîche
salt and freshly ground white pepper

Put the chicken, carrots, onions, leeks, thyme, bay leaves, water, and a little salt in a deep flameproof casserole just the size to hold all the ingredients. Bring to a boil, then reduce the heat, cover, and gently poach the chicken ¾–1 hour. Remove the chicken from the casserole and strain the liquid.

For the sauce, melt the butter in the casserole over low heat. Whisk in the flour and cook 30 seconds without letting it color. Pour in all the poaching liquid, whisking, and bring to a boil. Reduce the heat and simmer the sauce, skimming regularly, until it reduces to 3 cups, ¾–1 hour.

Cook the leeks in boiling salted water until tender, 3–5 minutes, then drain. Cut the chicken into serving pieces. Add the pieces to the sauce with the leeks and crème fraîche and simmer gently until the chicken is heated through, about 15 minutes. Adjust the seasoning.

Transfer the chicken and sauce to a warmed serving dish and serve.

LES CAUCHOISES

Applesauce Tartlets

The queue stretches out the door of the Demanneville bakery in Dieppe, waiting to buy regional specialties such as Douillons *(see page 61),* mirlitons *(see page 28) and* Cauchoises *– double-crusted tartlets filled with applesauce and sprinkled with sugar.*

Demanneville's Cauchoises *appear with a hole cut out of the upper crust, but at home when making these pastries, I tend to leave them whole. If you like, cut a 1½-inch round in the upper crust once the tartlets have baked.*

SERVES 6
10oz best-quality puff pastry dough
1¼ cups Applesauce (see right)
1 egg, beaten to mix
1½tbsp sugar

Sprinkle six 4-inch round tartlet molds with water and arrange them close together on a work surface. Roll out half the dough on a floured surface to a rectangle ⅛-inch thick. Wrap the dough around the rolling pin, then unroll it over the molds, letting it drape loosely into them. Press the dough into the molds with a floured ball of dough. Roll the pin over the tops of the molds to cut the dough. With your fingers, press the dough up the sides. Spread applesauce in each shell.

Roll out the remaining dough to a rectangle ⅛-inch thick. Lay the dough over the molds and roll the pin over the tops to cut the edges. Seal the top and bottom crusts with a fork. Chill the tartlets until the dough is firm, at least 15 minutes.

Preheat the oven to 425°F and put in a baking sheet to heat.

Brush the tartlets generously with beaten egg, not using all the egg, and sprinkle them with the sugar. Cut four slits in each tartlet lid. Bake them on the hot baking sheet until the pastry starts to brown, about 10–15 minutes. Reduce the oven temperature to 350°F and continue baking until the tartlets brown, 15–20 minutes longer. Serve hot or at room temperature.

COMPOTE DE POMMES

Applesauce

Simone Coty first taught me the value of the wizened apple. In her home, a pile of apples always sat on the sideboard, just outside the kitchen. One day I noticed the apples, neglected, had begun to wither. Some even had spots. I gathered the aging fruit, expecting to discard them, when Madame Coty stopped me. "What are you doing with those apples?" she asked. "It is a waste to throw them out." That night after our cheese, we had delicious compôte, made with the offending apples.

Here apples are cooked slowly, with the skins still on, but without water, sugar, or cinnamon. What you end up with is apple essence, the basis of a hundred apple recipes and equally wonderful all on its own.

MAKES 1QT
3½lb unpeeled apples, quartered and cored

Cut any large pieces of apple in half. Leave the skin on, but cut away any bruised spots.

Put the apples in a large, heavy pot (cast iron works well). Cover the pot and set it over the lowest possible heat. Cook the apples, stirring occasionally, until they are very soft and falling apart, 1–1¼ hours. If the apples begin to catch and burn at the start of cooking, reduce the heat even more and add a little water. Work them through a food mill to remove the skins.

GATEAU AU YAOURT

Yogurt Cake

Most chambres d'hôte *in France provide, along with a bed, an ordinary breakfast of baguette, jam, and a pot of coffee. But what a pleasure the morning meal is in Nicole Loisel's home in the hamlet of Ecosse near Manneville-la-Goupil. Here, this cake is almost always set out among the other breakfast things.*

A French yogurt container serves as the basic measure in this practical recipe, which calls for one pot of yogurt, two pots of sugar, three of flour, and so on. Madame Loisel suggests decorating this cake with jam or a chocolate-cream filling as a change from plain. For an evening meal, I like to serve it still warm, with a fresh fruit salad laced with Calvados. (Illustrated right)

SERVES 8–10
½ cup plain yogurt
1 cup granulated sugar
1½tsp vanilla sugar
2 eggs
2 cups flour
1tbsp baking powder
3½tbsp vegetable oil

Preheat the oven to 425°F. Butter a round 9-inch cake pan.

Combine the ingredients sequentially, one by one, beating well after each addition. Pour the batter into the prepared pan and bake until the cake is golden and a skewer inserted in the center comes out clean, 20–25 minutes. Remove from the oven and cool on a rack. To serve, unmold the cake and cut it into wedges.

Nicole Loisel's breakfast Yogurt Cake, photographed on the grounds of the Château Miromesnil.

TRUFFES A LA BENEDICTINE

Benedictine Truffles

At the end of the Benedictine tour in Fécamp, there is a bar and a cheery winter garden decorated with old-time posters. It is a pleasant spot for sampling the house liqueurs and edible gifts made with Benedictine, such as these irresistible morsels. At home, serve them with after-dinner coffee to friends who also appreciate immoderate luxury.

MAKES ABOUT 40
¾ cup crème fraîche
10oz bittersweet chocolate, chopped
¼ cup Benedictine, or to taste
unsweetened cocoa powder, for dusting

FOR THE COATING
8oz bittersweet chocolate, broken into pieces
2tsp vegetable oil
¾ cup unsweetened cocoa powder

Bring the crème fraîche just to a boil in a heavy saucepan. Remove from the heat and add the chopped chocolate, stirring until the mixture is smooth. Stir in the Benedictine. Taste this ganache and add more Benedictine if you like. Pour the ganache into a baking dish and chill it until it is firm, 1–2 hours or overnight.

Dust your hands with cocoa powder to discourage sticking. Scoop out the firm ganache with a teaspoon and shape it into balls about the size of a cherry by rolling them between the palms of your hands. Transfer them to a tray lined with wax paper. Chill them until firm, ½–1 hour.

For the coating, put the chocolate and oil in a

OPPOSITE Café Benedictine and Benedictine Truffles.

heatproof bowl and set over a pan of hot, not boiling water (the base of the bowl should not touch the water). Set aside to melt for 5 minutes, then stir until the mixture is satiny.

Sift the cocoa powder onto a tray. Take about 10 truffles from the refrigerator, keeping the remaining truffles chilled until ready for dipping. Drop a truffle into the melted chocolate, rolling it until evenly coated. Lift it out of the chocolate with a fork, letting the excess chocolate drip back into the bowl, then add it to the tray of cocoa. When you have dipped about 5 truffles, roll them in the cocoa until well coated, then leave them to finish drying on a tray lined with wax paper. Repeat with the remaining truffles. Set each truffle in a paper candy case and chill them.

Take the truffles from the refrigerator about 10 minutes before serving them.

CAFE BENEDICTINE

Even if you despise herbal liqueurs, and reject them as better for gargling with than drinking, you will still probably like this brew – Benedictine mixed with strong coffee and topped with whipped cream. For fans of Benedictine, the pleasure is all the more sweet.

The French have the perfect receptacles for drinking such beverages – mazagrans, tall and thick handleless cups, which keep coffee hot.

SERVES 4
½ cup whipping cream
1tbsp confectioners' sugar, sifted
½ cup Benedictine
3 cups strong, hot coffee

Whip the cream with the sugar until it holds soft peaks. Pour 2 tablespoons of Benedictine into each cup and add the coffee. Top each cup with a dollop of whipped cream and serve.

CLAFOUTIS AUX POMMES

Apple Clafoutis

The first time I sampled this pudding was one January night when Anne-Marie Cavelan agreed to take in four weary travelers. When we arrived at the Boucourt farm near Bénesville, Madame Cavelan had prepared a fire in the stone hearth. Decorative plates hung around the room, displayed on dish racks.

She offered us what she had, the same straightforward food that her own family eats, including this homey baked custard. It is fragrant with apples and vanilla, and takes only minutes to prepare. All you need is a sprinkling of confectioners' sugar to dress it up.

SERVES 4
¼ cup flour
⅓ cup granulated sugar
2 eggs
¼tsp vanilla extract
⅔ cup milk
1lb apples, peeled, cored, and thinly sliced
confectioners' sugar, for sprinkling

Preheat the oven to 400°F.

Butter a 1-quart baking dish.

Whisk together the flour, granulated sugar, eggs, and vanilla extract. Gradually whisk in the milk, but do not make the custard frothy.

Arrange the apple slices, slightly overlapping, in the bottom of the baking dish. Pour the custard over the apples. If the apples float, gently press them into the custard.

Bake the clafoutis until the custard sets, 20–25 minutes. Let it cool slightly on a rack and serve it warm or at room temperature. Sprinkle the top with confectioners' sugar just before serving.

top A wisteria-covered house in the Marais-Vernier. A visit to this village, set on the edge of the Seine estuary, is a step back in time.

above Forestland in Eure. The region has 230 hunting clubs, and in season over 27,000 hunters take to the woods of Lyons-la-Fôret, Bord, Brotonne, Beaumont-le-Roger, and Evreux.

right The climax of the cider year comes with apple-picking season, September to December, when small hills of apples accumulate outside farmhouses and barns, for pressing.

EURE

Eure is the understated countryside that most travelers rush through on the way to more fashionable parts of Normandy, such as Honfleur and Deauville. Eure may lack cachet, but along the Seine or one of its tributaries it offers ancient beech forests, fields of hay and wheat, pasturing cows, and poplar-lined riverbanks straight out of a Monet painting. Eure's prairie-like terrain, cut into three parcels by the Seine and Risle rivers, recalls the chalk plateau in neighboring Seine-Maritime. Yet, with no fishing ports and no shingle beaches, this is not the Pays de Caux.

Although the area is not celebrated for many regional specialties, you know you are at a Norman table because of the ever-present apples, rabbit and poultry, and glistening sea and river fish – all sauced with good butter, thick cream, cider, and Calvados.

One cheesemaker here produces Cormeillais, similar to Neufchâtel from the Pays de Bray to the east. Another makes a Pavé Normand, a version of the Pavé d'Auge produced in Calvados to the west. In the transitional Eure, an open country of fields and meadows yields to the humid wooded land of Camembert cheese and Calvados du Pays d'Auge.

THE VEXIN NORMAND

The Vexin Normand is wedged between the Andelle and Epte rivers, on the right bank of the Seine. The Vexin's farms are wedged between fields of wheat that sweep across the flat country here almost to the farm door.

Wheat-growing season is the time for unpacking a picnic on a cliff overlooking the Seine. When the fields of wheat in the Vexin are cut to stubble, then the forests come alive. In the morning, mushroom seekers forage among the beech trees in the Lyons forest where the dukes of Normandy once hunted. They cart baskets of their wild treasures to market under the 18th-century timber frame at Lyons-la-Forêt. This market town is also famous for a pâté, the *pâté de Lyons* prepared with chicken livers, pork, and port wine.

Hunting remains a popular sport in the Lyons forest even now. A stop at the *charcutier* in Lyons, Au Pâté de Lyons, will show you how local cooks turn the hunter's bag into tasty terrines and pâtés.

The Vexin's châteaux and farm museums afford a glimpse of a vanished way of life. In Boury-en-Vexin, the château's imposing cooking chamber once had three open chimneys: one for heating as well as hearths for grilling and roasting, which suggest the style of cooking in the 17th century. The

ABOVE The windmill in Hauville. Unlike water-mills, windmills can be built right in the heart of the matter, eliminating the need to transport the freshly harvested wheat.
LEFT Sweeping fields of grain typify Eure.

majestic kitchen also displays blue glass from Caen, across the Seine in Calvados, and an array of copper utensils that overshadows the stock at even major kitchenware shops.

But the Vexin's most-visited spot is neither a castle nor a farm. It's a *maison bourgeoise* with a lily pond. Ever since Claude Monet's house and garden in Giverny (he also lived a few miles upstream at Vétheuil) were restored to look much as they did in the artist's time, travelers have been making pilgrimages to this village.

It is worth the slowdown at the entrance to stroll in the footsteps of this great Impressionist. As you walk in Monet's garden, twisting and turning with the pathways, you come upon the very sunlit scenes he captured in his paintings. Geysers of flowers spurt out of their beds and the peach stucco house looms in the background. In May, azaleas, peonies, irises, and tulips are all in full bloom. Yet the garden seems smaller, lesser in life than on canvas; finally, it is merely the raw material shaped by Monet's imagination.

If most visitors are lured by the lily pads and their artistic associations, cooks enjoy Monet's sunny dining room, drenched with yellow lacquer on walls and ceiling, and the blue-and-white-tiled kitchen with its expansive iron range and gleaming copper pots.

Monet's home continues to inspire even today. His kitchen sparked a lavishly illustrated cookbook that evokes an alluring way of life, and the luminous blue and yellow colors spurred the Limoges porcelainmaker, Haviland Parlon, to design a pattern of china named "Monet."

Just a few miles downriver, bestriding the Seine, lies Vernon. This sizable residential town, good for ambling past timber-and-brick dwellings, hosts a cherry fair in June.

Besides cherries, Vernon is linked with watercress. This green appears on the town's coat of arms along with the more common fleur-de-lis. One explanation for the symbol is this: Louis IX became parched one day while hunting in the Vernon forest. When no drink could be found, a watercress salad was delivered in its place. The dehydrated King found this offering so revitalizing that he made up his mind to pay tribute to both plant and place. Myth has it that Louis designed Vernon's crest himself, marrying the thirst-quenching salad to the royal family's heraldic emblem.

THE ROUMOIS, LE NEUBOURG, AND EVREUX

The crowd leans forward on their benches to watch Jean-Louis Buhler rolling and folding a piece of dough. "What is he making now?" asks one spectator. The bread-baking room is already filled with a dozen varieties of shaped dough waiting to be baked in the wood-burning oven.

The door of the bread oven stands open so the smoke from the beech wood – collected next door in the Brotonne forest – can rise out of the chimney placed in front of the oven. When the stones turn white hot, after about $1\frac{1}{2}$ hours, Monsieur Buhler will sweep the coals out of the front of the oven, then swab the hot stones with *la dame blanche*, a wet cloth wrapped around the end of a pole. Only then is the oven ready to receive his array of regional breads.

The first Sunday of each month from March to November, Jean-Louis Buhler, a professional baker in Pont-Audemer, comes to nearby La Haye-de-Routot to fire up the 1830s' bread oven. Here he shapes and bakes half-forgotten regional breads in front of a curious crowd more used to *baguettes* from an electric oven.

*TOP The Japanese bridge at Giverny
Retracing the artist's steps.
ABOVE Giverny's lily pads.
During his years here, Monet created a garden
that became his muse.
LEFT A sweep of flowers leads the eye to Monet's
house, where a serene kitchen
and dining room have inspired many cooks
over the years.*

RIGHT It's a good year for cider apples. In the bad years, freezing temperatures and dry weather in spring will nip budding apples and yield a dismal crop in the fall.

BELOW A Norman bread oven, recognizable by the characteristic beehive bulge at the back. Although few of the ovens still function, they remain as valuable remnants of Normandy's gastronomic traditions. Look for them throughout the five départements.

But bread-baking in La Haye-de-Routot is only the tip of the iceberg concerning the revival of customs in the Roumois, the plateau on the left bank of the Seine bordered in the west by the Risle river. Since 1974, when the Ministry of the Environment created the Parc Naturel Régional de Brotonne, defenders of Normandy's heritage have been rescuing and restoring everything from bread ovens and windmills to local cider apples and a blacksmith's forge.

This regional park crosses *département* boundaries to include in its fold the *route des fruits* (see page 28) in Seine-Maritime and portions of the Pays de Caux around Caudebec.

In La Haye-de-Routot you learn about the importance of the baker at a time when each villager ate 2 pounds of bread every day. (Today consumption has dropped to $4\frac{1}{2}$ ounces per person.) Each village in the Roumois kept two or three bakers employed. The larger farms had their own bread ovens. Villagers paid the baker with a kind of credit card. Each time loaves were "bought," a notch was carved in the villager's payment stick, noting the weight of bread and number of loaves. Accounts were settled once a month, every four months, or annually, corresponding to when the farmer received cash at markets, seasonal fairs, or the yearly harvest.

Though not the most beautiful example, the La Haye-de-Routot bread oven typifies those in Normandy. It features a separate roof, built of red-brick shingles and supported by stilts. The oven huddles against the cold and rain under the shielding roof. The top of the clay oven itself resembles a shaven crown. Elsewhere in France, the top of the oven, covered with shingles, doubles as a roof.

Where would the bakers be without flour for their bread? Though we don't think of Normandy as a land of windmills, the hamlet of Hauville, just down the road from La Haye-de-Routot, once counted five of them. In Hauville, a medieval stone windmill has been restored and still grinds grain when it is blustery enough.

In Sainte Opportune-la-Mare, a community that lies at the mouth of the Seine, the "Apple House" (see the Visitor's Guide) also keeps tradition afloat in this part of the world. Here, a conservatory-orchard features fifty varieties of local cider apples as well as dessert apples, such as Bénédictine, named for the order of monks that once encouraged the fruit's cultivation. The wonderful cooking apple, the Rever, which sadly is being replaced by more common apples, grows here, too.

Inside, displays explain the art of cidermaking (see page 56). Each variety of cider apple has its special attributes and weaknesses, and cidermakers look for a balance of qualities to make a well-rounded cider. Sharp apples lend a taste of freshness and protect the mixture against disease. Bitter apples give body. Sweetish apples are sugar-rich and boost alcohol content. All cider apples benefit from marriage with one or more types. This is why it is so hard to make a satisfactory single-variety cider. Even so-called vintage ciders include small amounts of juice from other apples (see page 21).

The entire burg of Marais-Vernier (which goes by the same name as the marsh here) conjures up old Normandy. Nothing has changed in centuries. Sheep and their young nibble grass in the haven of apple orchards, and guinea fowl scratch in barnyards where mixed farming carries on in the time-honored way. Every year on the first of May, the cattle here are still branded on the horns before they are let loose in communal marshland.

Sitting at the mouth of the Seine, Marais-Vernier has geography to thank for its character. Originally a bend in the Seine, dammed up with mud and peat, the Vernier Marsh was eventually drained and a dike was built along the river. But this reclaimed marshland discouraged the kind of industry that grows upon terra firma.

EARTHY CALVADOS

While Calvados from the Pays d'Auge enjoys a special appellation d'origine contrôlée *all to itself, ten other areas across Normandy benefit from the simpler* appellation réglementée. *Everything else is just plain* eau-de-vie de cidre. *Calvados from Avranchin, Calvados, Cotentin, Domfrontais, Mortainais, Pays de Bray, Pays du Merlerault, Perche, Vallée de l'Orne, and Pays de la Risle all have definite geographical flavors, depending on the soil and blend of cider apples and, sometimes, cider pears. These ten Calvados are produced using the single distillation method, resulting in a more pungent, rustic bouquet than that of Calvados from the Pays d'Auge, which has a double distillation. Calvados from the Pays de la Risle in Eure, though less famous than Calvados from the Pays d'Auge, is still much appreciated locally. Note that the quality of Calvados depends as much on the vintage and the maker's skill as on the appellation.*

To the south, the Neubourg plain and Evreux countryside constitute a monotonous, meadow-like landscape with large-scale grain and dairy farms. Le Neubourg is the site of the *comice agricole*, where every Palm Sunday the region's most important agricultural fair takes place. But even in this setting of serious farming and discreet scenic charms, frivolity and creativity still flourish.

Thousands of pieces of smashed plates are artfully embedded in the outside wall of number 80 rue du Bal-Champêtre in the town of Louviers. This naive mural by 84-year-old Robert Vasseur brings the whole *quartier* to life.

The wall is only a sample of what Monsieur Vasseur has accomplished. Inside he has covered every bit of the garden, the garage, the sheds, the house, and each room – even the toilet – with discarded plates, shattered mirrors, and scallop shells. And he can tell you the provenance of each pieced-together dish, whether it's Rouen, Brittany, or fifties' pottery from eastern France. Is this marquetry, recycling, or eccentricity? Whatever it is, the House of Broken Dishes is a 40-year labor of love.

THE LIEUVIN AND PAYS D'OUCHE

Claude Tréhet's *fromagerie*, just off the place Victor-Hugo in Pont-Audemer, looks like a cheese museum with its displays of wooden butter and cheese molds and cheese-draining cups. But his selection of raw-milk farm cheeses from Normandy, plus small-production cheeses from around France are not facsimile. They are fresh and alive.

Why bother with the neighborhood *fromagerie* when you can buy cheese in any supermarket? "The real professionals are in the cheese shops," says Robert Jollit, who ran this shop before turning it over to Monsieur Tréhet. "Supermarkets sell the pasteurized, packaged variety of cheese."

Efforts such as the creation of the Parc Naturel Régional de Brotonne help sensitize people to local history. But those time-honored traditions that have not already been handed over to museums, such as the art of aging cheese, are steadily being eroded.

Monsieur Jollit talked about the profession of the *affineur*, or cheese-ager, compared to the cheesemaker: "It is another job entirely." Farmers used to bring their freshly made cheese to sell at the market to grocers. It was the grocer who tended each cheese as it matured, and sold it in his shop along with chocolate, salt, coffee, and other household staples.

The merchant devoted solely to aging and selling cheeses is a relatively recent arrival and is already threatened. Courses in cheesemaking at agricultural colleges do not promote *affinage* anymore. This last but crucial step in cheesemaking requires special cellars – a dry one for goat's milk cheeses and a moist one for cow's milk cheeses. Also, it demands time and human touch. In the vacuum created by disappearing customs, new practices are evolving. Today the separate professions of cheesemaker and ager are collapsing into one as there are few *affineurs* like Monsieur Tréhet left. The job of ripening cheeses *à point*, to perfection, is falling to cheesemakers.

Despite the pull toward new and better, Pont-Audemer, with its criss-crossing canals and inevitable "Venice of Normandy" tag, has managed to keep much of its old character. In the past, textile mills and tanneries flourished along the Risle river here. One former tannery, now an inn called the Auberge du Vieux Puits (see pages 60–61), still stands with its original half-timbered frame as a reminder of 17th-century life.

*FAR LEFT AND LEFT Robert Vasseur, creator of the
"House of Broken Dishes" next to his handiwork.
The project began when he decided to glue
salvaged dishes on the inside of a cement sink to
make cleaning easier for his wife.
A detail shows discarded mussel and scallop shells
surrounding a dish fragment.
BELOW A view of Les Andelys and the Seine from the
ruins of Château Gaillard, the latter built
by Richard the Lionheart to bar
the French from Rouen.*

LONG-LIFE PAIN BRIE

*Odette Bouteiller, who runs a bed-and-breakfast
on her farm near Pont-Audemer, always has a loaf
of pain brié on hand. "It is ten kilometers [six
miles] to the nearest town, you know," she told me.
"I only get fresh bread when I have overnight
guests. I keep pain brié for us."
Boulangers throughout Normandy still bake
this long-keeping bread, in oval or round loaves.
They slash long bow-like cuts in the shaped
risen dough to allow it to expand during baking
and give a decorative finish.
Kneaded with little water, the crumb is denser
than baguette, giving it a shelf life of eight to ten
days. Once the dough was compressed in a
brié, a contraption to force out air
pockets – hence its name.
In Beuzeville, another fan of pain brié,
Madame Quesney, buys it instead of rye bread
to serve with seafood. "I like it buttered," she says,
"with those tiny gray shrimp from Honfleur."*

FROMAGERIE QUESNEY

*In the face of modern-day inspections, analyses,
and regulations, the Quesney family in Beuzeville
still has some old-fashioned ideas about
cheesemaking. They make Pont-l'Evêque,
Pavé Normand (a variation of the Pavé d'Auge),
and crème fraîche.*

*Their truck picks up the milk – still in churns –
from 22 producers once a day. By comparison, in
industrial dairies, milk is collected every two days;
thousands of gallons of milk are pumped from
farmers'' holding tanks into the truck and then
pumped again into vats at the dairy. Here the milk
flows by gravity or is pumped very slowly, without
"breaking it," as cheesemakers like to say.
At the Quesney dairy, the crème fraîche is also
made the time-honored way. Milk is poured into
basins and left, undisturbed, for 24 hours,
until a nubbly cream crust forms.
Madame Quesney likes to spoon
a dollop of it onto fresh strawberries:
"It is like natural whipped cream."*

Also, Pont-Audemer's bakers have kept alive a piece of gastronomic history: the *mirliton de Pont-Audemer*, said to have been invented in 1340. This rolled buttery wafer is filled with chocolate and praline cream, and the ends are dipped in bittersweet chocolate.

Here you also find a good version of *pomme calvados*. This gooey apple-inspired confection of sponge cake and meringue is layered with Calvados buttercream and swathed in reddish-colored almond paste. Green almond-paste leaves complete the apple illusion. The best look like large marzipan apples. In the worst examples, you miss the apple connection.

Outside Pont-Audemer, on the Lieuvin plateau west of the Risle river, signs of old Normandy contrast with the new. Pollarded trees with thick trunks and branches shooting out like a punk haircut still serve as hedges and cow parks. But the cow stock no longer contains only *la vache normande* with her tell-tale brown "spectacles." Today, those good milkers – the Fresians – complete the herd. And most of their milk goes to the Nestlé factory near Pont-Audemer.

Other traditions carry on but become muddled. Some Norman bakers insist that *douillons* (see page 61) traditionally use pears, while similar pastries called *bourdelots* (see page 103) require apples. Yet, confusingly, I found *douillons* prepared with apples wherever I went.

And while a few cheeses, such as La Bouille and Monsieur in Seine-Maritime, die out, brand new cheeses appear on the cheese platter. At the markets in this region, you see one that resembles Neufchâtel. This oval cheese with a downy rind is Cormeillais, created by Michel Cauvet.

On his farm in Saint-Pierre-de-Cormeilles, southwest of Pont-Audemer, Monsieur Cauvet began making this cheese in 1973. The Cauvet family had been in the cheese business for generations, but Michel Cauvet wanted to do something unique. He is the only maker of Cormeillais, and his creamy, fresh, raw-milk cheese is worth sampling even if its history is recent.

Another new specialty is the *pâté de truite de Bernay*, a cold trout pâté made with cream and whole eggs. It is the creation of the Confrérie des Goules à Truites de Bernay, a gastronomic order here. "Every year in September or October we have a contest," explains Jacques Dubois, the grand master of the order. "Bernay's *charcutiers*, they are artists. They decorate the pâté like a miniature stage set with rivers, bridges, and fishermen." Trout streams surround this town. In fact, the whole Eure *département* is an angler's paradise with 385 official miles of fishable rivers and streams and no fewer than 50 fishing clubs.

Along with food contests, food festivals also help promote Norman gastronomy. Like the fishing ports of Dieppe and Saint-Valéry-en-Caux, the small market town of Lieurey celebrates the early-winter arrival of shoals of herring off the Normandy coast with a yearly festival.

But Lieurey, south of Cormeilles, is landlocked. According to legend, this curious custom dates back to when a shipment of the fresh fish arrived one November from the coast, but transportation for the onward journey floundered. Lieurey's village fathers turned the stalled fish to profit by hastily organizing a great herring auction on the spot.

The country south of the Lieuvin, the Pays d'Ouche, lacks the rich alluvial deposit that makes the rest of the Eure such an important dairy and cereal-growing region. Farming here is spotty. But forest land is as well stocked with wildlife as elsewhere in the *département*. In the Pays d'Ouche, the Rallye Malgré Tout organizes the traditional *chasse à courre*, stag hunting with horses and hounds, in the Beaumont-le-Roger forest. Man against nature – the thrill of the chase, whether it is stag, wild mushrooms, or fish – is one ancient custom that modernity cannot stamp out.

ABOVE Cormeillais cheese. I was surprised to find this oval cheese with a downy rind in Eure, far from the Pays de Bray where one would expect its home to be.
"I didn't like the local cheeses," says Michel Cauvet, the creator of Cormeillais.
He had special oval molds made, perfected the cheesemaking and ageing, and voilà! – a new cheese.
Monsieur Cauvet is convinced of its quality. He says: "It's the only cheese I eat."
LEFT Timbered houses line one of Pont-Audemer's canals.

THE ART OF CIDERMAKING

This February morning at Odile Anfrey's bed-and-breakfast, Le Clos Potier in Conteville, is cold— the water from the tap outside has frozen to an icicle— but we all bundle up for a walk to the farm's 17th-century apple press and the chance to buy a few bottles of cider to take home. There Madame Anfrey, her hair clipped in a bun, her feet stuck into blue Wellington boots, confides the secret of farm cider. "Never make cider during a full moon," she warns. "It will not turn out right."

Agricultural experts say the same thing, only it sounds like this: "Low pressure and changing barometric conditions encourage the formation of carbonic gases and discourage impurities from rising to the top of apple juice, holding them in suspension."

Nature observed provides most answers to good farm cider. Such as how do you know when it is time to harvest the apples? The rule of thumb farmers use is when half the fruit is on the ground.

But apples that are ripe enough to fall on the ground are not yet ripe for cidermaking. Except for early apples, which are pressed as soon as they are picked, apples mature in a loft – two to three weeks for middle apples and four to six weeks for late apples.

When are the apples ready for pressing? Your nose will tell you even before you climb the ladder to the apple loft. A pungent smell of ripening apples pervades the air. Also, the texture of the fruit changes. If you squeeze an apple, you'll leave a thumb print.

Whether cider is made on a farm like Le Clos Potier or in a factory, the same procedure applies. Ripe apples are washed, then crushed. This mush of apple pulp is left to oxidize, then the pulp is pressed to extract the juice. The juice is clarified and left to ferment. When the fermentation is almost complete, the cider is bottled.

For rudimentary cidermaking, there's the circular auge *fitted with a stone wheel like the one at Madame Anfrey's farm. A horse walks around and around the trough, pulling the wheel over the apples. For tradition's sake, a few farmers still use this method for crushing apples. But most of the* auges *you see in the countryside now are planted with petunias and geraniums.*

Today's crushers are not far removed from the first mechanical ones, which resemble a coffee grinder. Electricity or gasoline drives the modern broyeur *or* moulin à pommes, *however, instead of elbow grease. To press crushed apples for juice, farmers once layered rye or wheat straw with the apple pulp. Now small cidermakers drape burlap over wooden frames and shovel on the apple pulp. They wrap the burlap around the pulp like a package, repeating this operation to make 14 to 16 layers. In an old screw-type press like Madame Anfrey's it takes 24 to 36 hours to press one ton of pulp, yielding about 250 gallons of juice. A farmer using a hydraulic press takes one hour to press the same amount.*

Next the juice is transferred to casks where, after a few days, a thick layer of impurities rises to the top. The clear juice is siphoned off and moved to barrels for natural fermenting in its own yeasts.

Odile Anfrey's cider – like all farm cider – is a cloudy yellowish mixture quite unlike the clear industrial brew. It has a bitter after-taste and there is sediment in the bottle. The flavor and quality varies from one cidermaker to another and from season to season, again in contrast to the predictable drink of big cider manufacturers. It also continues to fizz in the bottle, so if you don't know if your cidermaker is an attentive student of nature, beware explosions.

ABOVE Simon and Yvette Salmon, from Caumont-sur-Orne, pear picking in the Bocage. Monsieur Salmon uses a gaule *to shake the tree branches and dislodge the fruit. Apple harvesting is done in the same way.*

LEFT An auge, *or circular trough for crushing apples, filled with cider kegs and jugs. This* auge *is fitted with two stone wheels that are pulled over the apples to crush them and extract their precious juice.*
BELOW La motte – *the pile of layered crushed apples and jute mats in place for pressing. The foamy juice collects around the sides.*
BELOW LEFT A row of industrial cider bottles sealed with metal caps. Only farm cider and the best quality industrial cider are closed with a cork.

CIDER TALK

The language of cidermaking is packed with regional dialect and technical jargon. These definitions of common terms should help to demystify the process.

AUGE: *Circular or rectangular trough for crushing apples.*

BROYAGE: *Crushing the apples.*

BROYEUR: *Mechanical apple crusher.*

CIDRE: *Legally, the beverage made from the fermented juice of fresh apples or mix of apples and pears, with or without the addition of water, and with a maximum alcoholic content of 5°.*

CIDRE A LA PRESSION: *Pasteurized draft cider pepped up with gas.*

CIDRE A LA TIREUSE: *Now rare, the traditional, foamless cider drawn from a barrel for everyday drinking.*

CIDRE BOUCHE: *Bottled cider. Now common, it was once called the Champagne of ciders because only the best cider was bottled. It was drunk on special occasions.*

CIDRE BRUT: *Dry cider. Term borrowed from Champagne usage, which lends prestige and poetry to ordinary dry cider.*

CIDRE DEMI-SEC: *Semisweet cider.*

CIDRE DOUX: *Sweet cider.*

CIDRE EN TONNEAU: *Cider drawn from a barrel.*

CIDRE FERMIER: *Farm cider.*

CIDRE MITOYEN: *Drink of half cider, half water.*

CIDRE MOUSSEUX: *Cider whose sparkle comes exclusively from natural fermentation.*

CIDRE PUR JUS: *First-pressing cider.*

CIDRE SEC: *Dry cider.*

CIDRERIE: *Cider factory.*

CROC: *Long pole, in local jargon, for shaking tree branches and dislodging fruit.*

CUVAGE: *Leaving the crushed apples to oxidize, which boosts the amount of juice during pressing and gives body and a deeper color to the cider.*

DEFECATION: *Naturally occurring. Impurities from apple juice rise to the top of the mixture, leaving limpid juice.*

FERMENTATION: *Transformation of sugar in apple juice to alcohol and gas.*

GADE, GATE, GADAGE, GRUGETTE, GRUGEOIR: *Circular or rectangular trough for crushing apples in the Bocage.*

GAULE: *Long pole, in local jargon, for shaking tree branches and dislodging fruit.*

GLUE, GLUI: *Straw bed, in local jargon, once layered with crushed apples and pressed to force out juice.*

GROS BERE: *First-pressing cider, in local jargon.*

GROS CIDRE: *First-pressing cider, in local jargon.*

MARC: *Crushed apples. Once pressed for cider this is often fed to animals or sold to pectin factories.*

MONTAGE DU MARC: *Layering the crushed apples and woven straw or jute mats for pressing.*

MOQUE: *Traditional cider mug.*

MOTTE: *Mound of layered crushed apples and woven straw or jute mat in place for pressing.*

MOULIN A POMMES: *Mechanical apple crusher.*

MOUT: *Freshly pressed apple juice.*

PELLE A POMMES: *Apple shovel.*

PETIT BERE: *Second- or third-pressing cider, in local jargon, with low alcohol content. Or cider cut with water.*

PETIT CIDRE: *Second- or third-pressing cider, in local jargon. Or cider cut with water. It is this low-alcohol, thirst-quenching drink that workers once quaffed in the field.*

PILAISON: *Crushing and pressing the apples.*

POIRE: *Perry or pear cider.*

POIRE A POIRE: *Perry or cider pear. Any pear too sour to eat.*

POMME A CIDRE: *Cider apple: any too sour to eat.*

POMME A COUTEAU: *Dessert or eating apple.*

POMME DE TERRE: *Potato.*

POMME EN L'AIR: *Dessert or eating apple. A pomme that grows above ground or "in the open air" as opposed to buried in the earth like a pomme de terre.*

POMME FRUIT: *Dessert or eating apple.*

POMMEAU: *Apple apéritif. Freshly pressed apple juice and Calvados or eau-de-vie de cidre aged together in oak. It was awarded an AOC in 1991.*

PRESSOIR: *Place where cider is made on the farm. Also, the apple press itself.*

PRESSOIR A LONGUE ETREINTE: *Long-grip screw press.*

PRESSURAGE: *Pressing the crushed apples.*

PULPE: *Crushed apples.*

RAPAGE: *Crushing the apples.*

RASIERE: *48-liter (over a bushel capacity) apple basket in eastern Normandy, measured heaping.*

REMIAGE: *Pressing the crushed apples, mixed with water, for a second time. Second pressing.*

SERRAGE: *Pressing the crushed apples.*

TOUR A PILER: *Circular or rectangular trough for crushing apples.*

VINAIGRE DE CIDRE: *Cider vinegar.*

CIDER APPLES

TOP ROW, LEFT TO RIGHT:
  Charge-Souvent; A la Faux; Carnette
MIDDLE ROW, LEFT TO RIGHT:
  De la Banque; Mettais; Tête de Brebis
BOTTOM ROW, LEFT TO RIGHT:
  De Cheminée; Gros Moussette; Medaille d'Or

AUBERGE DU VIEUX PUITS

6 RUE NOTRE-DAME-DU-PRÉ, PONT-AUDEMER, TEL 32 41 01 48

A sign swings from its wrought-iron bracket outside the Auberge du Vieux Puits in Pont-Audemer. In June, crimson roses frame a doorway of this cosseted hotel-restaurant still with its 17th-century timber shell. And there is a lovely outdoor garden around a weeping willow, too.

Inside, the burnished stone floors show the passage of generations of travelers. One snug dining room contains a collection of antique glass decanters and lamps made from shiny yellow-copper kettles. In cold weather a fire crackles in the hearth. Upstairs is like another restaurant with light filtering through mullioned glass.

Although the auberge lost its Michelin star for a period, today the food shows the same care and attention lavished on the decor. The menu reads like a hymn to the Norman table, with perfectly prepared regional food that is neither stodgy nor trendy. Who could ask for anything more?

POT AU FEU DU MAREYEUR AUX PLEUROTES

Fish and Oyster Mushrooms in Buttery Broth

This fish merchant's "pot-au-feu" – really an elegant fish stew – is a generous blend of salmon, sole, brill, and scallops in a savory broth of oyster mushrooms and carrots. If you like, add steamed broccoli florets for color. Set out soup spoons for scooping up every drop.

SERVES 4

10tbsp unsalted butter, cut into pieces
2 shallots, finely chopped
2 cloves garlic, finely chopped
$\frac{1}{4}$lb oyster mushrooms, cut into
$\frac{1}{2}$-in pieces
$\frac{1}{2}$ cup dry white vermouth
4 carrots, quartered lengthwise and cut
into 1$\frac{1}{2}$-in lengths
1$\frac{1}{2}$lb mixed fish fillets, such as salmon, sole,
and brill, or other flatfish, equal weights
of each

4 scallops
salt and freshly ground white pepper
fresh chervil sprigs, to garnish

FOR THE BROTH
1¼lb fish skin and bones, rinsed
2 shallots, thinly sliced
2 carrots, thinly sliced
1 leek, white and light green parts only,
thinly sliced
a bouquet garni
1qt water
salt

For the broth, combine all the ingredients in a saucepan. Bring to a boil, then reduce the heat and simmer, skimming regularly, for 20 minutes. Strain the broth, return it to the saucepan, and bring it back to a boil. Reduce the heat and simmer, skimming often, until it reduces by a quarter, 10–15 minutes.

Meanwhile, in a heavy saucepan, melt 2 tablespoons of the butter over moderate heat. Add the shallots and cook until translucent, 2–3 minutes. Stir in the garlic and cook 1 minute. Add the mushrooms and a little salt and sauté in the butter over moderately high heat until the mushrooms lose all their moisture, about 5 minutes. Stir in the vermouth, scraping up any browned pan juices.

Add the reduced broth and bring to a boil. Reduce the heat to low and simmer until reduced by half, 15–20 minutes.

Meanwhile, in a saucepan, combine the carrots, 1 tablespoon butter, a little salt, and water barely to cover. Bring to a boil, then reduce the heat and simmer until the carrots are tender, 7–10 minutes; drain if necessary.

Gradually whisk the remaining butter into the reduced broth, over very low heat so the butter doesn't melt completely but softens smoothly. (This is a concentrated broth rather than a sauce and will not coat a spoon.) Add the carrots, and

taste and adjust the seasoning. Keep the broth warm in a water bath.

Season the fish and scallops with salt and pepper. Steam the fish until opaque throughout, 3–7 minutes, depending on the fish.

For the scallops, set a nonstick frying pan over moderate heat. When the pan is hot, add the scallops and cook them, turning once, until they are nearly opaque throughout, 2–3 minutes.

To serve, ladle the broth into warmed soup plates. Put a scallop in each plate. Divide each fish into four portions and arrange it in the broth. Garnish with chervil sprigs, if you like, and serve.

DOUILLON NORMAND A LA POMME

Baked Apple in Flaky Pastry

What makes these pastries remarkable at the Auberge du Vieux Puits, Jacques Foltz explained, is the choice of apple. He uses the local Rever (also spelt Revert) – butter-yellow with a pink blush – grown in the nearby Marais Vernier. These apples are nothing special eaten raw, but when cooked they turn sweet and drip flavor. Unfortunately, this variety grows only in this corner of Normandy.

Of all the douillon recipes I sampled, this one is the best and easiest. You core and peel the apples,

then roll them in cinnamon sugar and bake them, swaddled in pastry. The addition of crème fraîche and apricot jam before serving is pure genius. If you use medium-sized apples, you will need slightly more dough to make larger pastry cases.

SERVES 4
7tbsp sugar
¾tsp ground cinnamon
4 small cooking apples, cored and peeled
½lb best-quality puff pastry dough
1 egg, beaten to mix
¼ cup crème fraîche, or to taste
3tbsp apricot jam, or to taste

Combine the sugar and cinnamon in a deep dish and roll the apples in this mixture. Spoon some of the cinnamon sugar into the core of each apple.

Roll out the dough on a floured surface to a square ⅛ inch thick. Cut the dough into four 6-inch squares and set an apple on each. Brush the dough around the apple with beaten egg. Bring the dough up to enclose each apple and pinch together the edges.

If you like, turn the *douillons* seam-side down and decorate them with leaves made from the dough trimmings. Chill the *douillons* until the dough is firm, at least 15 minutes.

Preheat the oven to 425°F and put a baking sheet into the oven to heat.

Brush beaten egg over the dough and set the *douillons*, seam-side down, on the hot baking sheet. Bake them until the pastry begins to brown, about 15 minutes. Reduce the oven temperature to 350°F and continue baking until the pastry is brown and the apples are very tender when pierced with a knife, 10–15 minutes longer.

Remove the *douillons* from the oven and set each on a plate. With a knife, cut a slit in the top of each pastry and spoon crème fraîche and apricot jam over the top, letting them drip down the sides. Serve immediately.

OEUFS AU CIDRE

Poached Eggs in Cider Sauce

At the Ferme-Auberge de l'Eglise near Damville, Madame Guérin prepares a Norman version of the Burgundian classic oeufs en meurette *– using hard cider in place of red wine. I love the way the egg yolk spills into the sauce and mixes with the mushrooms and bacon. And the country bread is just right for soaking up the sauce. All this needs is a tossed green salad to complete the meal.*

An egg poacher will remove any trauma from poaching eggs. Be sure the yolks remain liquid: to test, poke them gently with a finger.

SERVES 4 AS A MAIN COURSE
2 cups dry hard cider
2 cups chicken stock, preferably
homemade, or water
1 onion, thinly sliced
1 carrot, thinly sliced
a large bouquet garni
5tbsp unsalted butter
¼lb small mushrooms, quartered
3-oz slab bacon, sliced into
short, thin strips
4½tbsp flour
8 eggs
2tbsp vinegar
4 large slices of country bread
2tbsp crème fraîche
salt and freshly ground white pepper
1tbsp chopped fresh parsley

Combine the cider, stock, onion, carrot, and bouquet garni in a saucepan and bring to a boil. Reduce the heat to low and simmer, skimming regularly, until this cider stock reduces by half, ¾–1 hour, then strain it.

Meanwhile, melt half the butter in a frying pan. Add the mushrooms with a little salt and pepper and toss them in the butter over moderately high heat until they lose all their moisture, about 5 minutes; remove. Fry the bacon gently until golden, about 5 minutes; drain on paper towels.

Melt the remaining butter in a saucepan. Whisk in the flour and cook 30 seconds without letting it color. Pour in all the reduced cider stock with a little salt, whisking, and bring to a boil. Add the mushrooms and bacon. Reduce the heat to low and simmer the sauce, skimming occasionally, about 20 minutes.

Meanwhile, poach the eggs: Fill a sauté pan two-thirds full of water, add the vinegar, and bring to a boil. Break 4 eggs, one at a time, into a patch of bubbling water. Regulate the heat so the water barely simmers, and poach the eggs until the white sets but the yolk is still soft, 3–4 minutes. Remove the eggs with a slotted spoon to paper towels. Poach the remaining eggs.

To serve, toast the bread. Whisk the crème fraîche into the sauce and taste for seasoning. Set a piece of toast on each warmed plate. Arrange 2 eggs on each piece of toast and spoon the sauce over them. Sprinkle parsley over the top and serve.

RILLETTES DE SAUMON

Salmon Rillettes

The texture of these fish "rillettes," from the hotel-restaurant Les Cloches de Corneville, resembles that of their namesake. The taste, however, is infinitely finer and the preparation much easier.

The salmon is poached in a court-bouillon, then blended with herbs, whipped cream, and lemon juice. A small amount of gelatin holds the mixture together without turning it into a typical fish loaf. Garnish plates with lettuce leaves tossed in a fruit vinegar dressing, if you like, and serve the rillettes with toasted country bread.

SERVES 10
1 onion, thinly sliced
1 carrot, thinly sliced
a bouquet garni
2 cups water
2 cups dry white wine
1¼lb salmon fillet, skinned
1tsp crushed black peppercorns
1tsp unflavored gelatin
juice of 1 lemon
½ cup whipping cream
½ cup snipped fresh chives
½ cup chopped fresh parsley
salt and freshly ground white pepper

Combine the onion, carrot, bouquet garni, water, and a little salt in a large sauté pan. Bring to a boil, then reduce the heat and simmer this court-bouillon 15 minutes. Add the dry white wine to the court-bouillon and continue simmering another 15 minutes.

Add the fish and peppercorns and bring the liquid back to a simmer. Reduce the heat to low, cover, and poach the fish until it is opaque throughout, about 5 minutes.

Remove the fish with a slotted spoon and drain on paper towels, then transfer it to a bowl. Let it cool completely, then flake it with a fork. Discard the court-bouillon.

Sprinkle the gelatin over the lemon juice in a small pan and set it aside to swell to a spongy consistency, about 5 minutes. Melt the gelatin over low heat, then remove from the heat and leave it until tepid, stirring occasionally.

Whip the cream with a little salt until it holds soft peaks. Combine the flaked salmon, herbs, and gelatin mixture, then fold in the whipped cream. Season to taste.

Sprinkle a 5-cup terrine mold with water. Pack the salmon mixture into the mold. Cover and refrigerate until firm, at least 3 hours. Slice the rillettes for serving.

SALADE ODETTE

Salad of Lamb's Lettuce with Beets, Corn, and Tuna Fish

Odette Bouteiller lives with her husband Jacques on a 25-acre farm not far from Pont-Audemer. The Bouteillers are now officially retired, but they have not stopped working. "That would be death for me," says Monsieur Bouteiller, who still cares for a few dairy cows and sheep, a mule, and a goat. They both pamper their paying guests, now that their seven children are grown. During my visit to her farm, Madame Bouteiller prepared this salad. (Illustrated right)

SERVES 4–6
1 cooked beet (about 7oz), cut into ½-in cubes
½ cup cooked fresh or frozen, thawed corn kernels
6oz canned tuna fish, drained
1½oz lamb's lettuce (mâche) or other salad leaves
2 hard-cooked eggs, quartered

FOR THE DRESSING
1tbsp red wine vinegar
½tsp Dijon mustard
¼ cup vegetable oil
salt and freshly ground black pepper

Make the dressing: Whisk together the vinegar and a little salt until the salt dissolves. Whisk in the mustard, oil, and pepper to taste until smooth.

Combine the beets, corn, and tuna in a bowl. Add the dressing and toss until evenly coated. Adjust the seasoning.

Arrange the lettuce around the edge of a platter. Pile the beet mixture in the center, spreading it to the border of greens. Set the egg quarters on the lettuce around the platter and serve.

ENDIVES GLACEES

Glazed Belgian Endive

I will always be grateful to Les Cloches de Corneville in Corneville-sur-Risle for reminding me how delicious glazed endive is. And how easy. This is a quick vegetable to serve with any roast.

SERVES 4
**4 heads of Belgian endive, halved
lengthwise
2tbsp unsalted butter
1½tsp sugar
3tbsp chicken stock
salt and freshly ground black pepper**

Steam or boil the endive halves until they are tender, about 5 minutes; drain if needed.

Melt the butter in a large frying pan over moderately high heat and add the cooked endive with a little salt. Sauté the endive until they are golden brown all over. Take care with the browning or the dish will have a disappointing pallor.

Sprinkle the sugar over the endive and cook until it begins to caramelize. Add the stock and simmer until it reduces to a glaze, coating the endive. Season to taste and serve hot.

SALSIFIS ET POMMES A LA CREME

Creamy Salsify and Potatoes

At the Monday market in Pont-Audemer, one farmer displays a gallery of near-extinct vegetables: spiky cardoons, Jerusalem artichokes, and black stick-like salsify. Once reserved for families still practicing the cooking of hard times, these vegetables are now popular with chefs.

SERVES 4
**10oz boiling potatoes
juice of 1 lemon
1¼lb black salsify (oyster plant)
1 cup crème fraîche
grating of nutmeg, or to taste
3tbsp unsalted butter
½ cup fresh bread crumbs
salt and freshly ground black pepper**

Peel the potatoes and cut into 1-inch pieces of about the same width as the salsify. Put them in a pan of salted water, cover, and bring to a boil. Simmer until tender, 15–20 minutes, then drain.

Meanwhile, add the lemon juice to a saucepan of water. Rinse the salsify if it is very sandy, then peel it. (Wear rubber gloves to prevent the dark peel from staining your hands.) Cut it into 1-inch cylinders and add to the acidulated water. Cover and bring to a boil. Simmer until tender, 15–20 minutes, then drain.

Combine the salsify, potatoes, crème fraîche, nutmeg, and a little salt in a saucepan. Simmer, stirring occasionally, until the crème fraîche thickens, about 10 minutes. Taste and add nutmeg, salt, or pepper if required. Spoon into a gratin dish.

Preheat the broiler. Melt the butter and stir in the bread crumbs. Sprinkle the crumbs evenly over the vegetables and broil about 3 inches from the heat until lightly browned, 5–7 minutes.

TURBOT A LA CREME D'OSEILLE

Poached Turbot with Sorrel Sauce

The daily fish dish at La Toque Blanche in Conches-en-Ouche is a safe bet. My turbot was fresh, perfectly cooked, and mildly tangy. This recipe has more sorrel than the original but you could halve the amount for a more subtle sauce.

SERVES 4
**1 onion, thinly sliced
1 carrot, thinly sliced
a bouquet garni
2 cups water
2 cups dry white wine
1⅔lb turbot fillets or other white
fish fillets
2tbsp unsalted butter
½lb sorrel, shredded
1 cup crème fraîche
salt and freshly ground
black pepper**

Combine the onion, carrot, bouquet garni, water, and a little salt in a large sauté pan. Bring to a boil, then reduce the heat and simmer this court-bouillon 15 minutes. Add the dry white wine to the court-bouillon and continue simmering another 15 minutes.

Add the turbot or other white fish and bring the liquid back to a simmer. Reduce the heat to low, cover, and poach the fish until it is opaque throughout, about 5 minutes. Remove the fish with a slotted spatula and drain on paper towels, then transfer it to a dish. Cover and keep warm while preparing the sauce.

Bring the court-bouillon back to a boil, then lower the heat and simmer, skimming off any scum regularly, until it reduces to about ¼ cup, about 5–7 minutes; strain the court-bouillon.

Meanwhile, melt the butter in a saucepan. Gradually add the sorrel, stirring, and a little salt. Cook over moderate heat, stirring often, until the leaves wilt and the liquid evaporates, 5–7 minutes. Add the reduced court-bouillon and the crème fraîche and simmer, stirring often, until the sauce is well blended and heated through, 2–3 minutes. Season the sauce to taste.

To finish, spread the sorrel sauce on a warmed platter or plates. Arrange the fish on the sauce and serve at once.

TRUITE A LA CREME

Trout with Bacon in Cream Sauce

An angler works an intimate stream in the Eure, keeping a respectful distance from other fisher-men. He spends the morning casting and reeling, snagging a trout or two. When the last fish is dragged from the water, he heads home with his catch for a lunch of truite à la crème.

In this version, the fish are pan-fried in bacon fat and the browned bits in the pan are scraped up and simmered with cream, then flavored with lemon juice. (Illustrated left)

SERVES 4
¼ **cup vegetable oil**
¼-**lb slab bacon, sliced into**
short, thin strips
4 **trout (each about ½lb), cleaned,**
with heads on
½ **cup flour**
1 **cup crème fraîche**
2tbsp **lemon juice, or to taste**
salt and freshly ground white pepper
1tbsp **snipped fresh chives**

Heat the oil in a large frying pan or two smaller ones. Add the bacon and fry it gently until golden, about 5 minutes; drain on paper towels.

Sprinkle the fish inside and out with salt and pepper and dredge them in the flour. Fry the fish in the pan over moderately high heat until golden on both sides, 6–8 minutes in all. Drain the fish on paper towels, then transfer them to a warmed platter or plates and keep warm.

Pour off any fat from the frying pan. Add the crème fraîche to the pan with the bacon and simmer, scraping up the browned pan juices, until the crème fraîche thickens, 5–8 minutes. Stir in the lemon juice and season to taste. Pour the sauce over the fish and sprinkle with chives.

COQUELETS AUX GROSEILLES

Squab Chickens with Red Currants

Monsieur Bachet, chef at La Toque Blanche, likes to cook squab chickens with tart red currants. Instead of adding crème fraîche to mellow the berries though, which turns the sauce a borscht-like pink, I prefer to use unsalted butter. The golden chickens in a pool of scarlet berries makes a stunning presentation. With them, serve a potato gratin and buttered green beans, or sautéed oyster mushrooms. (Illustrated above)

SERVES 4

1½pt fresh red currants
4 squab chickens (each about 14oz)
1 stick unsalted butter, cut into pieces
1 cup chicken stock, preferably homemade
sugar to taste (optional)
salt and freshly ground black pepper

Preheat the oven to 425°F.

Comb the red currants off the stems with a fork. Sprinkle them with salt and pepper. Push about half the currants into the body cavities of the birds and truss them.

Put the birds in a roasting pan just the size to hold them. Sprinkle them with salt and dot with the butter. Roast, basting every 10 minutes, until the juice runs clear when an inner thigh is pierced, 30–40 minutes. Remove the birds to a carving board and set them aside, covered loosely with foil, to rest 10 minutes.

Meanwhile, add the stock and remaining red currants to the roasting pan and bring to a boil, scraping to dissolve the browned roasting juices. Boil until the liquid is reduced by half and the currants are tender, 5–7 minutes. Taste and add salt, pepper, or sugar, if needed.

Remove the strings from the birds. Arrange them on a warmed platter or plates and spoon the sauce around them. Serve any remaining sauce separately in a sauceboat.

LAPIN A LA MOUTARDE AU CALVADOS

Rabbit with Mustard and Calvados

Odile Anfrey, the irrepressible mistress of Le Clos Potier, seems to be everywhere at once: in the courtyard greeting visitors as they arrive at her bed-and-breakfast near Conteville, at the farm's 17th-century cider press giving a tour, or in the living room with a map of the surrounding countryside recommending day trips.

From her kitchen comes farm cooking, based on local ingredients. For her Rabbit with Mustard and Calvados, she cleverly swathes the lean meat in caul fat. This gauzy web of fat protects and bastes the meat while it roasts and also adds a hard-to-define extra something. With the rabbit, serve buttered noodles.

SERVES 4
¼lb caul fat
1 rabbit (about 3lb), cut into serving pieces
2tbsp Dijon mustard, or to taste
7tbsp Calvados
1 cup crème fraîche
salt and freshly ground black pepper

Preheat the oven to 425°F.

Rinse the caul fat in several changes of cold water, then gather it into a ball. Gently press out most of the water between the palms of your hands. Do not wring it. Carefully open the caul fat on a work surface, stretching it slightly.

Smear a piece of rabbit with mustard and set it on one corner of the caul fat. Wrap the piece of rabbit in caul fat, cutting the fat to fit. Set the rabbit piece, seam down, in a flameproof baking dish just the size to hold all the pieces comfortably. Repeat with the remaining rabbit pieces, using about half the mustard in all.

Roast the rabbit, basting every 10 minutes, until it is golden and tender, ¾–1 hour.

Skim off the fat, leaving the browned roasting juices. Set the flameproof baking dish over low heat on top of the stove.

Heat the Calvados in a small pan and light it. (It will flare up so take care.) Pour the Calvados over the rabbit and baste it until the flames subside. Remove the pieces of rabbit to a warmed serving dish and keep them warm.

Add the crème fraîche and remaining mustard with a little salt to the baking dish, scraping up the browned roasting juices. Simmer the sauce, stirring from time to time, until it thickens, 5–8 minutes. Taste the sauce and add more mustard, salt, or pepper, if needed. Pour the sauce over the rabbit and serve.

SAUTE D'AGNEAU DE L'EGLISE

Lamb Stew with Turnips

At least half of the ingredients served at a ferme-auberge must be home-raised or -grown for it to earn the "ferme-auberge" label. At the Ferme-Auberge de l'Eglise, this includes poultry, eggs, and lamb, pastured in the valley along the Iton River.

Lamb Stew with Turnips is a hearty dish. At the Eglise farm the meat and vegetables are cooked until they are falling apart. But if you like, reduce the cooking time, braising the meat until it is very tender but still in large chunks.

This is a dish to prepare ahead, and chilling the stew makes degreasing easy. With the lamb, serve boiled potatoes.

SERVES 4
1¾lb boneless lamb for stew, cut into 2-inch cubes
¼ cup vegetable oil, more if needed
1lb turnips, peeled and quartered or cut into eighths, depending on size
2 onions, sliced
2 cloves garlic, sliced
2tbsp flour
3 cups water
a large bouquet garni
salt and freshly ground black pepper

Season the pieces of meat with salt. Heat the oil in a sauté pan or wide, shallow flameproof casserole just the size to hold the meat and turnips in a single layer. Add pieces of meat to the oil and lightly brown them all over, then remove them. Add the turnips to the casserole and cook them over moderate heat until they are lightly browned, 5–7 minutes; remove the turnips. Add the onions and garlic to the casserole and lightly brown them, too, stirring occasionally.

Remove any fat from the casserole. Sprinkle the flour over the onions and cook until it browns lightly, 1–2 minutes. Stir in the water, scraping up the browned pan juices. Return the meat and turnips to the casserole, tuck in the bouquet garni, and bring to a boil. Reduce the heat to low, cover, and simmer until the lamb and turnips are very tender, about 2 hours.

Skim off any fat. Taste and adjust the seasoning and serve.

TARTE AUX POMMES ODILE ANFREY

Odile Anfrey's Apple Tart

Every counter and table top in Odile Anfrey's restored 250-year-old farmhouse holds some treasure from the barn or flea market. In the dining room, an old wooden apple shovel leans against a heavy standard and, in the corner, the family cat lies, stuffed, eerily curled up on a chair.

Join the communal dining table here for this favorite apple tart. With apricot jam and apple sauce in the bottom, a wheel of apple wedges, and an almond cream topping, it is irresistible.

SERVES 8
10oz best-quality puff pastry dough or Pâte Brisée (see right)
3tbsp unsalted butter
2lb firm apples, cored, peeled, and each cut into 8 wedges
2tbsp sugar
2tbsp apricot jam
$\frac{2}{3}$ cup applesauce, preferably homemade (see page 42)

FOR THE TOPPING
3tbsp sugar
1 egg
3tbsp crème fraîche
3tbsp ground almonds
2tbsp Calvados

Sprinkle a 10-inch tart pan with water. Roll out the dough on a floured surface to a round $\frac{1}{8}$ inch thick. Line the tart pan with the dough. Chill the tart shell until firm, at least 15 minutes.

Preheat the oven to 400°F.

Prick the tart shell all over with a fork about every $\frac{1}{2}$ inch. Line the shell with a double thickness of aluminum foil, pressing it smoothly against the dough. Bake the tart shell 15 minutes. Remove the foil and continue baking until the pastry just begins to brown, for about 5–10 minutes. Remove the tart shell, and put a baking sheet in the oven to heat.

Melt the butter in a large frying pan. Add the apples and sugar and cook until the apples are tender and golden on all sides, 10–15 minutes. Remove them to a plate as they are done.

Melt the jam and brush it over the bottom of the tart shell. Spread the applesauce in a thin layer over the jam. Arrange the apples on the applesauce in three concentric rings, working toward the center. Whisk together the topping ingredients and pour over the apples.

Bake the tart on the hot baking sheet until a knife inserted in the center of the filling comes out clean, about 20–30 minutes. If the pastry browns too quickly, cover it with aluminum foil.

Serve the tart hot.

PATE BRISEE

Buttery Pastry Dough

MAKES ONE 10-IN TART SHELL
1$\frac{3}{4}$ cups flour
pinch of salt
1 stick unsalted butter, cut into pieces
1 egg yolk
3–4tbsp cold water

Whizz the flour and salt in a food processor until mixed. Add the butter and process until the mixture resembles coarse crumbs. Add the egg yolk and 3 tablespoons of water and process just until the dough holds together when you pinch it with your fingers. Add another tablespoon of water if the dough is still dry. Transfer the dough to wax paper, flatten it into a disk, wrap well, and chill until firm, at least 1 hour.

CHARLOTTE AUX POMMES AU COULIS DE FRAISES

Apple Charlotte with Strawberry Sauce

The Nuttens farm stands next to the Reuilly church, not far from Eure's capital, Evreux. Behind the old white farmhouse, assorted barns, and tractor sheds, lie the fields. They are planted with wheat, corn, and a few apple trees, enough for Lucien Nuttens to supply his family with cider and Calvados.

This pudding of stewed apples folded with whipped cream in a case of ladyfingers is Marie-Thérèse Nuttens' specialty. When I sampled it in her home, everyone at the table, including family and overnight guests, wanted seconds.

Not only can the charlotte be made a day ahead, it tastes even better the next day. Several hours chilling time dramatically improves the taste and it firms up the charlotte, too, so try to make it at least in the morning if you plan to serve it for the evening meal.

Try this charlotte also with pears or peaches or whatever fruit is at its peak. (Illustrated right)

SERVES 8
1$\frac{1}{2}$lb aromatic apples, peeled and sliced
1 cup whipping cream
1tbsp confectioners' sugar
$\frac{1}{2}$tsp vanilla extract
$\frac{1}{2}$ cup water
$\frac{1}{4}$ cup Calvados
about 30 ladyfingers

FOR THE SAUCE
1pt fresh or frozen, thawed strawberries
confectioners' sugar to taste

Put the apples in a heavy saucepan, cover, and cook over low heat, stirring occasionally, until they are very soft and falling apart, 25–30 minutes. Add a little water, if needed, to prevent the apples from catching and burning. Cool, then chill well.

Whip the cream with the sugar and the vanilla extract until it holds stiff peaks. Chill the cream until ready to use.

Combine the water and Calvados in a deep dish. Dip a few ladyfingers in the Calvados mixture just to moisten. Cut each cookie in half crosswise and trim each half into a long triangle resembling a flower petal. Arrange the cookie triangles in a flower shape, rounded sides down, in the bottom of a 1½-quart charlotte mold. Use as many cookie triangles as will fit comfortably, without overlapping. Fit the trimmings into any gaps.

Moisten more ladyfingers in the Calvados mixture and stand them upright, rounded sides out, around the side of the mold, packing them as closely together as possible. Trim the cookie tops level with the top of the mold, if necessary.

Fold together the chilled apples and the whipped cream. Fill the mold with this mixture.

Dip more ladyfingers in the Calvados mixture and cover the apple filling completely with them, cutting to fit if necessary. Gently press the cookies into the filling. Chill until ready to serve.

For the sauce, purée the strawberries in a food processor. Add sugar to taste. Work the purée through a fine strainer if you want to remove the seeds. Chill the sauce.

To serve, run a knife around the charlotte to loosen it and turn it out onto a platter. Pour the strawberry sauce around the charlotte and over the top, letting it drip down the sides.

TOP *A window on the rural architecture of the Pays d'Auge, whose wooded valleys straddle Calvados and Orne.*
ABOVE *A sampling of cider apples. Each variety contributes special qualities to the finished product.*
RIGHT *The new cider, carefully packed for shipping. Cider keeps only 12 to 18 months.*

CALVADOS

When most people think of Normandy, they are conjuring up Calvados. A rural kingdom of meadows, half-timbered barns, cows, and cider apples. Calvados. The Bayeux tapestry. Calvados. Omaha and Juno Beaches. Calvados. High rollers and horse-racing. All Calvados.

Everywhere in Normandy you see farm butter and cream, hand-crafted cheese, and apple brandy. But Calvados boasts no fewer than five Norman staples designated with an *appellation d'origine contrôlée* lauding their rare qualities.

Pont-l'Evêque cheese received its AOC in 1976, Livarot in 1975. The orchards here also produce the one *eau-de-vie* in Normandy with its own appellation, "Calvados du Pays d'Auge."

West of the Pays d'Auge, in the Bessin, lies butter and cream territory. The crème fraîche from around Isigny is the lone French cream with an AOC. Isigny butter is one of only two with an appellation. (The Charentes-Poitou on the Atlantic coast also produces an AOC butter.) Calvados is Normandy, at heart.

THE COTE FLEURIE AND THE COTE DE GRACE

It is the first hot, sunny Sunday in May and the fish merchants at the Trouville fish market are in a sour mood. "Are you here to ogle or buy?" one stallholder shouts to no one in particular. "How about some gray shrimp?"

The *crevettes grises* in question are visibly torpid. Unlike the sun-worshipers who traipse along without buying, the shrimp wilt in searing heat.

At the open market set up farther along the boulevard Fernand-Moureaux, farmers, *charcutiers*, and cheesemongers are crammed among stands of cheap clothing. The fishwives have been pushed to the concrete wall that backs onto the Touques river. Every now and then a shopper darts through the crowds like a thief, clutching a blue plastic bag with Dover sole or flounder.

Even when it sizzles here on the Fleurie Coast (from Trouville to Cabourg) and Côte de Grace (from Trouville to Honfleur), this span of sandy beach is *not* the epitome of chic. Mom unpacks the lunch she has prepared for her family. Children fly kites or poke in the sand for clams. The flesh fair at Cannes is not for these friendly northern beaches.

Those searching for a lunchtime buzz in Trouville have booked at Les Vapeurs across from the fish market. The *maître d'hôtel* here warns you not to bother claiming the table if you're late. At 12:30 pm the tables on the sidewalk begin filling. The first customers order *crevettes grises* and Mussels in Cream Sauce (see page 87) to start. Sole or flounder *meunière*, sautéed in butter with lemon juice (also page 87), will follow.

It is Deauville on the other side of the Touques River that lures the fashionable set. On the fourth Sunday in August, Deauville hosts the Grand Prix horse race. At other times there are more races, the yearling sales, and polo matches. Even when you buy a jar of apple jelly at the open-air market here, the farmer may wrap it in last week's *Paris-Turf*, the racing paper. He also breeds horses.

Besides a diet of equestrian fare, Deauville offers designer clothes shops, a regatta scene, golf, a casino, and *les planches*. As you stroll on this boardwalk, you pass Belle Epoque hotels and houses in brick and stucco. On the sea side, rows of matching umbrellas planted on the beach give it the look of a parade of guardsmen in full regalia.

If Deauville's old-world flair has long drawn the glamorous, Honfleur, with its historic port, timbered Eglise Sainte-Catherine, and narrow slate-gray houses, has exerted a legendary tug on painters. Boudin, Courbet, Monet, Daubigny, Jongkind, and Braque all came to work here. Today, galleries line the quays, and a new generation of artists sets down its own vision of Honfleur.

But Honfleur is not just a pretty town. It is also a real fishing port. Here shrimp fishermen deliver *crevettes grises*, still wriggling, to market. In other shrimp ports, where the distribution network is less developed, the *crevettiers* cook the shrimp on board so they will keep.

Eating the tiny *crevettes grises* calls for fingers not forks. Some shrimp fanciers painstakingly peel them until a mouthful of tails accumulates. But the common way of consuming them is to break off the head and pop the shrimp, shell and all, into your mouth. It's like munching peanuts. Between bites, don't forget buttered bread and a sip of dry white wine.

THE PAYS D'AUGE

For Monsieur Touzé, who still makes farm cheese in Vieux-Pont-en-Auge, cheesemaking is like motherhood. "Only a mother suspects when her child is not his usual self," he says. "A cheesemaker can have a formula, but if he doesn't have cheese sense, if he doesn't know when something is not right or how to remedy a problem, he'll never make a good *fromager*."

The traveler who comes to the beaches of Calvados is likely to miss the traditional Pays d'Auge found in country villages like Vieux-Pont. Come in late April or early May, when the pear and apple trees are in blossom, and spend a day driving the small lanes, pausing at cheese farms like Monsieur Touzé's as well as thatch-roofed cottages with cider for sale and at Calvados distilleries.

In addition to Pont-l'Evêque cheese (see pages 80–81), Monsieur Touzé makes Pavé d'Auge. This square chunky cheese resembles Pont-l'Evêque but it is bigger. It takes five to six quarts of milk to make one Pavé d'Auge and only three and a half litres quarts to make a Pont-l'Evêque. Yet this slight difference means that the larger cheese takes longer to drain, requires more salt, and ages longer. The finished Pavé d'Auge (which does not have an AOC) simply tastes different.

Cheese aside, the wooded valleys of the Pays d'Auge have given their name to a favorite local dish, *Poulet Vallée d'Auge* (see pages 88–89). It appears on menus throughout the region, but the name carries only an inkling of what you can expect.

TOP Lunchtime at an outdoor café in Honfleur.
ABOVE A plate of moules à la marinière *savored at a fishing port on the Côte de Grace is one of the pleasures of the Calvados coast.*
LEFT Kodachrome-colored umbrellas under a cloudy sky evoke the sophistication and panache of Deauville and its sister towns along the coast. Doffing their caps to Paris, whence come so many of this area's visitors, the coastal resorts make a fascinating contrast to the countryside inland.

ISIGNY BUTTER AND CREAM

When European food quotas in 1984 threatened cream and butter production around Isigny-sur-Mer, local dairymen struck back to protect their gastronomic heritage, and livelihoods. Instead of blocking roads, they lobbied the government to slap an official appellation on their celebrated crème fraîche and butter.

The AOC, granted in 1986, certifies that the milk for this butter and cream comes from pastureland extending less than 22 miles around Isigny, including Bayeux in Calvados, and stretching to Montebourg and La Haye-du-Puits in neighboring Manche. It must be processed in creameries here, too. By law, both the butter and cream are pasteurized.

What makes these dairy products unique is their buttercup-yellow color – bouton d'or – and their taste (see also page 76). Rich in iodine and mineral salts, they reflect their homeland: low-lying marshes regularly flooded by the coastal rivers Aure, Vire, Taute, Douve, and Merderet.

ABOVE Isigny also produces an AOC Camembert with the milk that goes to make its famous butter and cream.

*ABOVE A rabbit hutch on a Normandy farm.
LEFT A signboard advertises apples, pears, and their deliciously alcoholic derivatives. Norman cider- and Calvadosmakers are rightly proud of their inherited tradition.
BELOW Geese waddle into an old barn. Previously more typical of other regions of France, the lucrative foie gras industry is a new and thriving one for Normandy.*

In its simplest form, the chicken is roasted and the pan deglazed with Calvados and crème fraîche. Some cooks prefer to sauté the chicken, then flame it with Calvados and moisten it with chicken stock or cider. Finally, the cooking juices are reduced with cream. Sometimes onions, mushrooms, or apples sautéed in butter join the platter as a garnish. Veal and pork chops often stand in for chicken, or even fish. In any event, the dish spotlights the abundance of fine ingredients here.

As in the rest of the European Community, there is too much milk here, so dairy farmers have been told to diversify. Happily, this has led to the renewal of at least one old specialty. Twice a week at the Ferme des Pâtis in Mery-Corbon west of Lisieux, Odile Gasson simmers the milk from her 35 cows with sugar to make *confiture de lait*, a sweet spread with a caramelized flavor. Madame Gasson and her husband, Jean-Marie, started making the *confiture* in 1987. They could have made yogurt or Camembert. "We felt like doing something different," Madame Gasson explains.

Madame Gasson remembered the sticky spread from when her grandmother used to make it. But the recipe had not been prepared in two generations. "I looked in old cookbooks," she says. "I started with two litres of milk on my kitchen stove. Who knew if today people would take to it?" Once Madame Gasson had a result that met her standards, she presented it at a local fair. To her surprise, people did enjoy it. Even some who don't like milk liked her *confiture de lait*. Encouraged by this reaction, Madame Gasson increased her output. Today she makes 10,000 jars a year.

Because it is an all-natural, homemade product, it turns out differently every time. The finish can be shiny or mat. It depends on the milk. Once in a while the sugar is drier than usual or moister. Now and then the *confiture* crystallizes, like honey. "It's still good to eat," she says. "But the texture isn't as good. I'm looking for something silky smooth." And like honey, the taste is sugary-intense on its own. It's luscious spread on crêpes and topped with whipped cream, or poured over vanilla ice cream. It's delicious stirred into *fromage blanc* or yogurt, too.

The humid earth in the valleys of the Pays d'Auge, which makes ideal pasturage for the region's cows, is also the best soil for apple trees. A signed *route du cidre* links cidermakers from Cambremer to Beuvron, and Beaufour to Bonnebosq.

Some of the farmers here are lobbying for a *cidre du Pays d'Auge* AOC. By garnering an appellation, they hope to hold their own in the cider industry. The seal would legally establish that this locality produces a natural, select cider. It would define the varieties of authorized apples, restrict the yield in the orchards, disqualify pasteurization, prohibit the use of fruit concentrate, and ban pepping up the cider with gas.

While cidermakers are just embarking on their struggle for recognition, the Calvadosmakers here can now enjoy the fruits of their pains to upgrade "*calva*" to Calvados, and Calvados to Calvados du Pays d'Auge AOC. *Calva* was the clear 70° distillate as it emerged from the still. It was this that was routinely poured into coffee to make *café-calva*. It also triggered the Norman Prohibition, which quashed the automatic privilege of cider growers to distill their own potent brew.

Today's rehabilitated Calvados is blended, aged, and watered down with pure rain or distilled water to produce a 40 to 45° proof spirit of the highest quality. Cooks flame young Calvados and add it to stews or use it, sparingly, as a flavoring. Hosts offer older Calvados as a "*trou normand*," a shot gulped between the courses of a lengthy meal. In restaurants, the famous *trou* often takes the form of a slushy Calvados sorbet. The best Calvados receives all the ceremony of a fine Cognac and caps a celebratory feast among friends and family.

MODERN LIVAROT

When I visited the Graindorge cheesemaking factory in Livarot, the first thing I was asked was my shoe size. Before entering the factory, I was dressed as if to perform surgery: lab coat, cap to cover my hair, and rubber boots. Cleanliness is a serious matter for this family-run business, which is the largest maker of genuine raw milk Livarot. So workers here slosh through walkways of soapy water and gain entrance to the cheesemaking room by washing their hands, which unlocks the door. Also for reasons of hygiene, Graindorge does not offer tours to sightseers. But anyone interested in the cheesemaking process can visit the Musée du Fromage in the town (see the Visitor's Guide).

Since farm Livarot virtually disappeared, Graindorge has perpetuated the tradition of this pungent, elastic, reddish disk with its stripes of paper or sedge. With factories such as Graindorge producing such high-quality Livarot, we can feel hopeful about the survival of authentic regional cheeses.

NORMAN APERITIFS

*Marie-Thérèse Clouet, who runs a table d'hôte at
her farm in western Normandy, offers her
guests an apéritif and asks:
"Can you guess what this is?"
The fruity and effervescent drink recalls a kir
royale, made with crème de cassis and
Champagne. But, instead, it is cassis and pear
cider. Madame Clouet calls it a "kir normand."
While this local kir appears in homes and family
restaurants,* pommeau, *the other favorite apéritif,
features more on menus of good restaurants.
It has also become a popular flavoring in cooking,
like Calvados. This wasn't always so.
Until recently,* pommeau *was a homey drink,
retrieved from the cellar when a neighbor
stopped by. Today astute
marketing has boosted* pommeau's *status.*
Pommeau *is made by blending freshly pressed
apple juice with Calvados or cider eau-de-vie.
Before it is bottled,* pommeau *is aged in
wood casks, which imparts both its
amber color and oaky taste.*

CAEN AND THE BESSIN

The sky is still ashy gray at 6 this October morning when Chef Michel Bruneau arrives at the Caen fish market in his van. With its wave-like and other nautical motifs, the market looks as if it might house a swimming pool or maybe an aquarium. Inside, fish merchants pad across the wet yellow-tiled floor in rubber boots. Monsieur Bruneau, chef-owner of the two-star La Bourride in Caen (see pages 82–3), heads off to greet his suppliers. In front of him on polished granite counters, a dizzying array of fish is arranged in polystyrene boxes.

Caen, the capital of Lower Normandy, sits in fertile countryside with vast open fields. This plain marks the western border of the rolling Pays d'Auge and stretches down through Argentan in the Orne. Though set inland on the Orne river, Caen receives the best of the catch from the seaports along the Côte de Nacre, the Bessin coast to the west.

A tour of the *criée* or fish market turns up mussels and oysters from Courseulles and Isigny, octopus, flounder, red mullet, whelks, skate, sardines, *équilles*, a shimmering eel-like fish, two different kinds of crab, blue lobsters, their claws bound with green rubber bands, *pétoncles* (small scallops), cockles, live *bouquet* shrimp, and *langoustines* from Scotland.

In five minutes, Monsieur Bruneau has done his shopping. Occasionally, he snaps up the catch even before the boats dock – fishermen with a choice haul radio their wives from the Channel, and the wives ring the chef with the news.

Caen offers an open-air farmers' market on Fridays, on the preserved Place Saint-Sauveur not far from Caen's citadel. (Some 80 percent of the city was destroyed during Allied bombing in 1944.) Also near the citadel are the rue Sainte-Pierre and rue Saint-Jean, two lively shopping streets.

But among foodies, Caen is best known for its tripe *à la mode de Caen* (see page 78). Every year since 1952, in October or November, the Confrérie de Gastronomie Normande has convened to bestow its trophy, the *tripière d'or*, on one plate of tripe. The best *tripe à la mode de Caen* have a chickeny taste and a texture and succulence similar to that of perfectly cooked squid.

To the west of Caen, on the Côte de Nacre, fishing ports thrive next to remembrances of war: rusting coastal defence fortifications and cemeteries for the war dead of all nationalities. This is the Bessin, pastureland with a low green horizon. The local architecture changes from the timber-framed houses of the Pays d'Auge to creamy-colored stone buildings.

Here the cow, or *la vache normande*, is queen. Some of the finest crème fraîche and unsalted butter in France comes from the marshland around Isigny and the Baie des Veys (see page 74). In this lowland between Bayeux and La Haye-du-Puits in the Manche to the west, farmers produce 10,000 to 12,000 tons of cream and butter a year. The seasonally flooded grass is high not only in iodine and mineral salts but also carotene, which gives the butter and cream its soft yellow color.

Traditionally, farmers simply let the cream rise to the surface of the milk, then skimmed it off. To make crème fraîche, the cream was left to ripen naturally. In the Bessin, a cream sauce is literally that – cream heated and seasoned with salt – not a sauce enriched with cream.

Alternatively, dairymen churn the fresh cream to make butter. Isigny butter is olein-rich, high in the liquid part of fat, which gives this butter its unctuous texture. Part of this wonderful butter is bought up by the local confectionery industry to be used in their famous caramels. A lot of Norman candy features butter and cream. Most are forgettable. But do not miss the caramels from Isigny.

LEFT *The fish market at Caen offers a true cornucopia of foods from the sea. Chef Michel Bruneau at La Bourride (see pages 82–83) told me that only the bulk catch is set out in plain view – the choice catch is kept hidden away for special clients.* BELOW *The morning's milk. A truck from the local dairy will soon pass to collect the churns, filled with the milk that has made Norman food products famous worldwide.*

CALVADOS DU PAYS D'AUGE

Entering a Calvados distillery in the Pays d'Auge, you are struck by the heady aroma of apples. Here, in a few select cantons in Calvados and Eure, cider is distilled not once but twice in the onion-domed copper stills called alambics *charentais, or* à repasse. *During the first heating, a light spirit 25° proof collects. This* brouillis *or* petite eau *rests until enough is collected for a second heating. In the second stage, called* repasse, *the spirit is distilled to obtain the* bonne chauffe, *or final product, 65° to 70° proof. This clear* eau-de-vie *is transferred to new oak casks for several months where it takes on an amber hue and subtle flavors. To prevent the taste from becoming woody, the Calvados is then moved to older casks for further aging. Calvados houses blend old and young spirits to make their individual styles. The youngest spirit determines the age under which the Calvados is sold.*

LA TRIPE A LA MODE DE CAEN

"There are no calves' feet in tripe à la mode de Caen,*" says Annick Collette, who runs a butcher shop in Courseulles-sur-Mer. She is winner of the 1989* tripière d'or, *the traveling trophy awarded for the world's best* tripe à la mode de Caen.

"It is not an improvised dish," she continues.

Four kinds of beef tripe, cow heel, aromatic vegetables, and a bouquet garni simmer in their own juices for 24 hours. And the pieces of tripe are cut just so – in uniform squares. The best tripe à la mode de Caen *is rich but not heavy, fragrant with carrots and leeks, and not at all fatty.*

Critics of gastronomic tournaments argue that winners prepare a special recipe for the competition and an inferior one for customers. But Madame Collette is adamant: "It is the same tripe."

BELOW *Traditional earthenware* tripières *for making* la tripe à la mode de Caen.

THE BOCAGE

Emile Roussel became a baker because his parents had set their hearts on one butcher, one mechanic, and one baker in the family. "I didn't have any choice," says Monsieur Roussel. "That's the way things worked then."

At 13 he was apprenticed to a local baker to learn the trade. He worked hard and eventually opened his own bakery in Clinchamps-sur-Orne, a village in his native Suisse Normande.

This strip of country follows the Orne river where it curls through deep gorges south of the Bessin in the Orne valley. In this northeastern section of the Bocage, blackberry, wild rose, and sloe bushes edge the secondary roads. On the infrequent farms, a few chickens and cows strut in the barnyard and pastures, and every house has a well-stocked vegetable garden.

Despite the achievement of his own shop, Monsieur Roussel looked for a change from baking routine. He thought of the *brasillé* of his childhood, the "poor man's cake" made in the Bocage. In the old days, bakers prepared it with bread dough and folded in lard or margarine. It was eaten hot out of the wood-fired oven, sprinkled with sugar.

Madame Roussel didn't share her husband's fond recollection of the pastry. When as a girl she moved with her family from Brittany to Normandy, she longed for a taste of *brasillé*. She had watched people buy the pastry every Sunday and was filled with curiosity. But accustomed to the butter-rich cakes of Brittany, she hated *brasillé* when she finally tasted it.

In 1978, Monsieur Roussel began experimenting with the unpalatable cake, replacing the bread dough with one more like brioche, and folding it with butter. He added almond cream and dusted the top with confectioners' sugar. Today he makes 1,000 of the foot-long pastries a week. The most popular day for buying *brasillé* is still Sunday.

Locals serve the up-to-date version of *brasillé* for breakfast or at teatime. A slice of the cake is also popular with *teurgoule* (see page 91), also known as *terrinée*. There was a time when farmwives carried their earthenware terrines filled with the ingredients for this creamy rice pudding to the baker's. In his stone oven still hot from bread-baking, the pudding bubbled slowly, for hours, until the milk, sugar, and rice reduced and softened to a delicious mash.

South and west of the Suisse Normande is the center of the Calvados Bocage, and Vire is its hub. While this corner has no legally praised specialty, the *andouille de Vire* (see page 79) here is as famous as the Calvados in the Pays d'Auge.

This *andouille* is sometimes mistakenly called a tripe sausage. But as it is not made with the stomachs of ruminants but, rather, pig stomach and intestine, it is more properly labeled a chitterling sausage. Waverley Root once described the *andouille* as shaped like a bludgeon. It makes a rather short club as it measures only 8 to 10 inches.

Unlike most sausages prepared with more or less finely chopped meat, the meat for *andouille de Vire* is cut into narrow strips and crammed into sausage casings. Several small *andouilleries* in Vire still make a traditional, lean sausage using no preservatives and no coloring (the black results from the smoking).

Starting a meal with an hors d'oeuvre of spicy *andouille de Vire* – cut into very thin slices and served with country bread and good butter – is one of the enduring pleasures of the Bocage. Oh yes, and remember to uncork a chilled bottle of cider.

ANDOUILLE DE VIRE

*Bernard Lesbaude lives above the factory outside
Vire where he has been in charge of
making Danjou* andouille *for longer than he
cares to say. He knows all there is to
know about this famous sausage.
"It takes pork stomach and two kinds of intestine to
make* andouille de Vire," *he explains. Monsieur
Lesbaude meticulously washes them, then cuts them
into strips. Next morning they are stirred
in vats with salt and white pepper and left to
marinate ten days.
The seasoned strips are packed into casings
and hung above smoldering beechwood
six to ten weeks.
After this, the smoky sausages are soaked in water
two days to remove excess salt,
and then are tied and poached.
That is when the sausages change color from
brown to black.
Living above the store, with his hand in the making
of these sausages every day, does Monsieur
Lesbaude still enjoy eating it?
"Certainly," he says. "I know my* andouille."*

FARM CHEESES

At 7:30 in the morning, the sun is just beginning its ascent when a cowherd, Jean-Pierre Poulbes, finishes milking his herd of 80 cows. The animals leave the barn slowly, in no apparent hurry to regain the green October pastures of the Pays d'Auge. But soon they are out of sight, scattered in the fields of Vieux-Pont.

At 8 o'clock, the cheesemaker, Patrick Bove, arrives at this farm near Lisieux. He hooks a milk-filled cistern to his tractor and tows it to Le Bôquet, the Touzé farm and dairy down the road.

After Patrick has set to work, Michel Touzé shuffles in to see how things are coming along. As his athletic cheesemaker begins another grueling day making Pont-l'Evêque and Pavé d'Auge, Monsieur Touzé comments: "You cannot survive this kind of life unless you are passionate about what you do."

OPPOSITE, TOP Rolling the curd crumbs to draw off whey.
OPPOSITE, LEFT CENTER Batches of curds in the mold, with a tub of curdled milk and tools for cutting it.
OPPOSITE, BELOW LEFT Pont-l'Evêque aging in the cheese cellar.
THIS PAGE, RIGHT Monsieur Touzé's Pavé d'Auge.
FAR RIGHT Livarot cheese. Today virtually all of it is made in dairies. Its AOC confines production to five cantons surrounding the town of Livarot.
RIGHT, CENTER Pont-l'Evêque, a staple on cheese boards throughout Normandy.
RIGHT, BELOW Camembert, France's favorite cheese.

In the steamy dairy, Patrick pours last night's milk, reheated to body temperature, and this morning's still-warm milk– 225 gallons in all– into tubs. Then he adds enough rennet to curdle this unskimmed milk, which takes about 45 minutes. "I cannot tell you exactly how much I add," he says. "I gauge it by eye."

Once the curd forms, he pushes a wire affair, which looks like a giant deep-frying basket, into a batch, gives it two quick turns, then moves on to the next tub. Then he stabs the mixture with a ski pole-like tool. Cutting the curd into small pieces helps the whey to drain and makes a firmer cheese. But to judge whether the curds are ready for draining, he plunges in his arms up to his elbows and churns them.

When the curds are ready, Patrick dips a bucket into one tub, fills it with curds, and tips it into a tray lined with cheesecloth. He fills the tray with the curds of one tub and lets them drain about five minutes. Then he lifts up the corners of the cheesecloth and rolls the curd crumbs back and forth to draw off more whey.

The curds, which resemble cottage cheese now, are scooped into a rectangular mold. Patrick kneads and packs the curds into the mold with his knuckles. He then presses in a stainless-steel divider, which makes the mold look like an oversized ice cube tray.

He flips the mold over onto a board lined with plastic mesh; the cheese takes its corrugated look from this mat. And on to the next tub of curds.

The cheeses are then moved to a cool saloir. This is the realm of Carole Poulhes, the cowherd's wife. Here Madame Poulhes turns each cheese daily and moves all of them around the room in sequence so at all times she knows how old each cheese is by where it sits.

On the fifth or sixth day, she salts the square cheeses and moves them to the aging cellar. There she shelves them like books on wood planks because they dry better that way. After a week she pats labels on the Pont-l'Evêque cheeses (the Pavé d'Auge takes longer to age) and wraps them in wax paper. Now they are ready for the shops, where they will take another week to ripen.

After a lifetime of cheesemaking, Monsieur Touzé still finds that overseeing the making of Pont-l'Evêque and Pavé d'Auge brings him pleasure. "We had a rough life," says Monsieur Touzé, "but we were happy anyway. People had an understanding of things that maybe we have lost today."

LA BOURRIDE

15–17 RUE DU VAUGEUX, TEL 31 93 50 76

Wherever I went in search of "Normandy Gastronomique" I was told: "You must speak to Michel Bruneau at La Bourride in Caen. He'll tell you. He knows."

Monsieur Bruneau is the dean of Norman chefs, the godfather of countless gastronomic bands, a goad in the side of food critics, the publisher of La Lettre de la Bourride, *a quirky newsletter.*

With a profile like this, it is surprising that the man is so modest. But this diffidence belies rigorous standards. At the butcher's, Monsieur Bruneau hangs back – until he is served. Then he springs to life, lunging after the butcher, inspecting the meat. "It is important to have a good relationship with your suppliers," he says, "so they know what you want, why you are so demanding."

La Bourride is charmingly rustic, with a monumental fireplace two stories high. And the cooking amply lives up to the promise of creative regional dishes. In the words of Michel Bruneau: "Vive la Normandie gourmande!"

TOP Michel Bruneau, chef at La Bourride, selects a Normandy lobster during his daily pre-dawn visit to the fish market at Caen.
Such commitment to the freshest and the best is what sets his restaurant apart.
ABOVE Veal Shanks Braised in Cider.

JARRETS DE VEAU AU CIDRE

Veal Shanks Braised in Cider

Michel Bruneau agrees that the quantity of cider here does seem a lot for four servings. The four- or five-day wait before tasting looks excessive, too. "We tried it with less cider and a shorter resting time," the chef explained, "but the result was ordinary. This dish is special."

The recipe yields four generous portions, so if it is part of a multi-course meal it will serve six or eight. To increase the amount of sauce, add ⅔ cup cooking liquid for each additional serving and simmer until all the liquid reduces by two-thirds. Also, add 2 tablespoons butter per person to finish the sauce. Try this with Gratin of Creamy Salsify and Potatoes (page 64). (Illustrated left)

SERVES 4–6
4 veal shanks (each about 1¾lb)
1 onion, thinly sliced
1 carrot, thinly sliced
1 celery stalk, thinly sliced
2 apples, sliced with skin
4qt dry hard cider
7tbsp cider vinegar
10tbsp unsalted butter, cut into pieces
salt and freshly ground black pepper

Combine the veal shanks, onion, carrot, celery, apples, cider, and a little salt in a flameproof casserole just the size to hold all the ingredients. Cover and bring to a boil, then simmer gently until the meat is tender, about 1½ hours. Cool to room temperature, then chill 4 or 5 days.

To finish, remove 2½ cups of the cooking liquid to a saucepan and add the vinegar. Bring to a boil, then lower the heat and simmer, skimming regularly, until reduced to scant 1 cup. Gradually whisk in the butter over very low heat so it softens to form a smooth sauce. Season.

While the sauce is simmering, gently reheat the veal in the remaining cooking liquid. Drain the veal shanks and transfer them to a carving board with a juice catcher. Carve the meat off the bone in thin slices. Spoon some of the sauce on warmed plates and arrange slices of meat on top. Serve at once, with the remaining sauce.

SORBET GRANITE A LA POMME VERTE

Green Apple Sorbet

It is no surprise that Michel Bruneau, champion of the Norman harvest, has developed a recipe that makes the most of the apple. His recipe works like a charm, with Calvados added at the end. This sorbet can be made with any sweet apple. Each variety will produce its own delicious flavor. (Illustrated right, as served at La Bourride with a selection of miniature desserts)

MAKES ABOUT 1QT
1¼lb Granny Smith apples
juice of 1 lemon
1½ cups sugar
1¼ cups water
Calvados, for sprinkling

Core the apples and halve them, but leave the skin on. Cut the apples into very thin slices – a food processor is useful for this. Add the lemon juice at once to discourage browning and toss the apples until they are evenly coated with the juice. Freeze this mixture overnight.

The next day, combine the sugar and water in a small saucepan and heat gently, stirring, until the sugar dissolves. Pour this hot sugar syrup over the frozen apples, then scoop the clumps of apples into a food processor. Work the mixture until it becomes smooth. Transfer this purée to an ice-cream maker and freeze according to the manufacturer's directions. (If you don't have an ice-cream machine, freeze the purée until almost firm, then whizz it in the food processor before freezing again until solid.)

If the sorbet freezes rock hard, let it soften slightly in the refrigerator before serving, 15–30 minutes. Scoop the sorbet into bowls and sprinkle with Calvados, adding as much as you like.

SOUPE DE POISSONS ET ROUILLE AU BEURRE

Fish Soup with Garlicky Butter

In his fish soup, Chef Michel Choplin, of the Hostellerie du Moulin du Vey in Clécy, draws on Mediterranean ingredients – extra-virgin olive oil, bulb fennel, garlic, and saffron threads. The mixed sea fish and vegetables are simmered together to produce a flavorful broth that is strained and then puréed with fresh cod fillet.

Monsieur Choplin adds a Northern touch to the garlicky spread, which he calls rouille, *by replacing part of the olive oil with Normandy butter. At the table, guests spread little toasts with the "*rouille,*" sprinkle them with freshly grated Gruyère, and add them to their bowl of soup.*

SERVES 4

**7tbsp extra-virgin
olive oil
2lb white sea fish, cleaned and
cut into 1-in steaks,
heads reserved
½lb onions, thinly sliced
½ bulb fennel, thinly sliced
¼lb leeks, white part only, thinly
sliced
4 cloves garlic, crushed
¼-lb tomato, cut into 8 wedges
2qt water
½tsp fennel seeds, crushed
a bouquet garni
pinch of saffron threads
5oz cod fillet, cut into 1-in pieces
40 thin slices of baguette, toasted
1 cup grated Gruyère cheese
sea salt
freshly ground white pepper**

FOR THE ROUILLE

**1 slice white bread, crusts discarded,
soaked in milk and squeezed dry
2 cloves garlic
pinch of saffron threads
3tbsp extra-virgin olive oil
10tbsp unsalted butter, cut into pieces**

Heat the oil in a large saucepan. Add the fish steaks and heads, sprinkle with salt, and sauté over moderately high heat until opaque, about 10 minutes total. Remove and set aside.

Add the onions, fennel, and leeks to the pan with a little salt and stir until evenly coated with the oil. Cover and cook over low heat, stirring occasionally, until tender, 7–10 minutes. Push the vegetables to one side, then add the garlic and tomato and cook, stirring, 5 minutes.

Replace the fish in the pan and add the water, fennel seeds, bouquet garni, saffron, and a little salt. Bring to a boil and boil, stirring to break up the fish, for 15 minutes. Lower the heat and simmer gently, partially covered, until the broth reduces by half, about 45 minutes. Skim the broth regularly, but leave behind the threads of saffron that float to the surface.

Meanwhile, make the *rouille*. Work the bread, garlic, saffron, and a little salt and pepper in a food processor. With the blades turning, add the oil in a thin stream. Add the butter and blend until smooth. Check the seasoning. Pack this *rouille* into a small serving bowl and chill it until it is firm but spreadable.

Strain the fish broth, pressing on the solids to extract all the liquid. Discard the solids. Return the broth to the saucepan, add the cod, and bring to a boil. Reduce the heat to low, cover, and simmer 10 minutes. Purée the cod with some of the broth in a food processor, then return it to the remaining broth and reheat to simmering. Season to taste.

Serve the soup in a warmed tureen or soup plates. Pass the *rouille*, toasts, and cheese separately.

VELOUTE DE LEGUMES

Creamy Vegetable Soup

Here is an uncomplicated and satisfying recipe from La Rançonnière, a fortified farm near the D-Day beaches. Old-world generosity pervades this farm-hotel. Dinner is served in a cathedral-like room, heated at one end by a monumental stone fireplace. The menu reads like an advertisement for Norman markets. It features Isigny oysters, free-range chickens, and this vegetable soup. Because the soup is prepared with water rather than stock and is simmered only briefly, the flavors of the vegetables and the tart crème fraîche remain pure and bright.

SERVES 4

**7tbsp unsalted butter
1 small carrot, finely chopped
1 small turnip, finely chopped
1 boiling potato, peeled and finely chopped
1 tomato, peeled, seeded, and chopped
a small handful of green beans, cut into
½-in pieces
5 cups water
1 cup crème fraîche
salt and freshly ground black pepper**

Melt the butter in a saucepan. Add the vegetables with a little salt and stir until evenly coated with the butter. Cover and cook over low heat, stirring occasionally, until tender, 7–10 minutes.

Add the water to the vegetables and bring to a boil. Lower the heat and simmer gently, uncovered, for 30 minutes.

Purée the soup in a blender or food processor. For extra smoothness, work the purée through a fine strainer. Return the soup to the pan and add the crème fraîche. Heat gently, then check the seasoning and serve in warmed soup bowls.

TARTE PAYSANNE AU LIVAROT

Livarot Cheese Tart

With a brioche-like dough (enriched with an egg and butter) and dabs of crème fraîche, this tart tastes like a well-to-do peasant's idea of cheese pizza. If Livarot conjures up smelly socks for you, note that its flavor is in fact disarmingly mild and fruity. You can cut the rind off the cheese if you like, but it gives a pleasant, crunchy texture when baked. Make sure you remove the five paper or sedge stripes if you do leave on the rind. (Illustrated right)

SERVES 8
1 cup milk
1 package active dry yeast ($\frac{1}{4}$oz)
6tbsp unsalted butter
2 cups flour
$\frac{1}{2}$tsp salt
1 egg, beaten to mix
$\frac{1}{2}$ Livarot cheese (8oz), rind removed and cut into thin slices
2tbsp crème fraîche
salt and freshly ground black pepper

Scald the milk in a small saucepan, then remove from the heat and let it cool to tepid. Sprinkle the yeast over the milk and set aside to dissolve, about 5 minutes. Reserve 1 tablespoon of the butter; melt the rest and let cool. Butter and flour a 10-inch round cake pan or baking dish.

Sift the flour with the salt into a large bowl and make a well in the center. Add the melted butter, yeast mixture, and egg. With your fingertips, stir the central ingredients together, gradually drawing in the flour to make a smooth dough. It will be very soft, almost soupy. Using your cupped hand, knead the dough, by slapping it against the side of the bowl, until it is elastic, about 5 minutes.

Transfer the dough to the prepared pan. Cover and let it rise in a warm place until doubled in bulk, 1–1$\frac{1}{2}$ hours.

Preheat the oven to 375°F and put a baking sheet in the oven to heat.

Knock the air out of the risen dough, then cover it with the cheese slices. Spread the crème fraîche on top; it will cover the cheese only in patches. Season generously with salt and pepper and dot the top with the reserved butter.

Set the cake pan on the hot baking sheet and bake until the tart is puffed and golden, 30–40 minutes. Serve it at once.

LANGOUSTINES AU BEURRE D'ISIGNY

Langoustines in Orange Butter Sauce

Union Isigny-Sainte-Mère is a giant dairy co-operative based in Isigny-sur-Mer and the largest one in France to work with unpasteurized milk. Despite its industrial size, ISI boasts four AOC products favored for their quality: butter and cream d'Isigny, Camembert, and Pont-l'Evêque.

This buttery recipe is inspired by one offered to me by Monsieur Prou, the butter and cream spokesman here. Cloud-like langoustines simmer in a fragrant court-bouillon, which is reduced and flavored with orange juice, and then thickened with Isigny butter to make a sauce. While nothing tastes quite like langoustines, jumbo shrimp, or tiger prawns are also good prepared this way. (Illustrated left)

SERVES 4

1 onion, thinly sliced
1 carrot, thinly sliced
a bouquet garni
2 cups water
2 cups dry white wine
24 raw *langoustines*
3tbsp orange juice
1½ sticks unsalted butter, cut into pieces
½lb spinach, stems removed
salt and freshly ground white pepper

Combine the onion, carrot, bouquet garni, water, and a little salt in a large sauté pan. Bring to a boil, then reduce the heat and simmer this court-bouillon 15 minutes. Add the wine and continue simmering another 15 minutes.

Add the *langoustines* and bring the liquid to a simmer. Reduce the heat to low, cover, and poach the *langoustines* 3–4 minutes. Remove the *lan-*

MOULES A LA CREME LES VAPEURS

Mussels in Cream Sauce

Les Vapeurs (illustrated left) is a sophisticated brasserie in the oceanside town of Trouville-sur-Mer. It is packed here on weekends, with locals and Parisians dining on platters of these steaming-hot mussels, fresh gray shrimps from the fish market across the road, and perfect sole or Carrelet Meunière (see right). Gérard Bazire's recipe for Mussels in Cream Sauce makes four generous servings. With a basket of good bread and white wine, it's a meal in itself.

SERVES 4
2 shallots, finely chopped
½ onion, finely chopped
½ cup dry white wine
3tbsp distilled white vinegar
1 stick unsalted butter, cut into pieces
4qt mussels, scrubbed and bearded
2 cups crème fraîche
¼ cup chopped fresh parsley
freshly ground black pepper

Combine the shallots, onion, wine, vinegar, and butter in a large saucepan. Set the pan over high heat and cook, stirring, until the butter melts. Add the mussels, cover, and cook, stirring once or twice, just until the mussels open, 3–5 minutes.

Take the pan from the heat. With a slotted spoon, transfer the mussels to a warmed serving dish or soup plates. Keep warm.

Discard half the mussel cooking liquid from the saucepan. Add the crème fraîche to the remaining liquid in the pan and bring to a boil. Reduce the heat to low and simmer this sauce 2 minutes to concentrate the flavor. Add the parsley, stir to mix, and season to taste.

Pour the sauce over the mussels and serve.

CARRELET MEUNIERE

Golden Plaice Sautéed with Butter and Lemon Juice

Plaice didn't used to thrill me. The fillets fell to shreds when cooked and tasted like wet cotton. That was before I sampled the Carrelet Meunière at the brasserie Les Vapeurs in Trouville. This plaice arrives straight off the boats docked in the Touques river, facing the brasserie. It's like a different fish – firm and sweet-tasting.

Sole, of course, is the classic fish prepared à la meunière. But cooking plaice in this way, dipped in flour and pan-fried in butter, makes the most of its delicate flavor.

SERVES 4
1 stick unsalted butter, cut into pieces
2tbsp vegetable oil
4 plaice or flounder (each about 10oz),
skinned, cleaned, and heads removed
¼ cup flour
juice of 1 lemon
salt and freshly ground black pepper
parsley sprigs, to garnish

Heat the butter and oil in a large frying pan over moderately high heat. Meanwhile, season the fish with salt and pepper and dredge them in the flour, patting to discard the excess.

Add two fish to the pan and brown them, 2–3 minutes on each side. Reduce the heat to moderately low and continue cooking the fish, turning once, until the flesh is opaque next to the bone, 5–7 minutes. Transfer the fish to a warmed platter or plates and keep warm. Cook the remaining fish.

Pour the lemon juice into the pan, bring to a boil, and simmer this sauce 1 minute to concentrate the flavor. Season to taste.

Pour the sauce over the fish and serve immediately, garnished with parsley sprigs.

goustines with a slotted spoon and drain on paper towels. Transfer them to a dish, cover, and keep warm while preparing the sauce.

Bring the court-bouillon back to boil, then lower the heat and simmer, skimming regularly, until reduced to about ¼ cup, 5–7 minutes.

Strain it into a small heavy saucepan. Add the orange juice and bring to a boil. Gradually whisk in 10 tablespoons of the butter over very low heat so it softens to form a smooth sauce rather than melting completely. Season to taste and add more orange juice if you like: The sauce should be fruity.

Melt the remaining butter in a saucepan over moderately high heat. Add the spinach with a little salt and cook, stirring, just until it wilts.

Spoon the sauce onto warmed plates. Arrange the *langoustines* and spinach on top and serve.

PINTADE FARCIE A LA SUISSE NORMANDE

Guinea Fowl with Apple Stuffing

The old water wheel still turns at the Moulin du Vey in Clécy. In fine weather umbrella-shaded tables are set up on the terrace overlooking the gurgling Orne river. Here you can enjoy food based on locally popular ingredients, such as this guinea fowl, in which boned pieces of the bird are filled with an apple stuffing flavored with Calvados.

For a speedy version of the recipe, use four boneless chicken breast halves, plus an additional $3\frac{1}{2}$oz of chicken meat for the stuffing.

SERVES 4
1 guinea fowl (about 3lb)
4tbsp unsalted butter
1 cup rich chicken stock, preferably homemade
1 cup dry hard cider
1tbsp crème fraîche
$1\frac{1}{2}$tsp *pommeau*, or to taste
3 firm apples, peeled, cored, and each cut into 8 wedges
salt and freshly ground black pepper

FOR THE STUFFING
1tbsp unsalted butter
1 small apple, peeled and cut into $\frac{1}{4}$-in dice
1tbsp crème fraîche
$1\frac{1}{2}$tbsp Calvados, or to taste

Cut the legs off the guinea fowl and trim any excess skin. Cut and scrape the meat off the leg bones in one piece. Remove any sinews.

Cut the breast meat and wings off the carcass. Trim excess skin. Cut the wing meat off the bones; separate the fillets from the breast.

For the stuffing, melt the butter in a small frying pan, add the diced apple with a little salt and pepper, and cook, stirring occasionally, until tender and golden on all sides, 4–5 minutes. Let cool completely.

Work the guinea fowl wing meat and fillets in a food processor with the crème fraîche, Calvados, and a little salt and pepper until puréed. Beat in the cooled apple dice by hand. Sauté a small piece of this stuffing in a frying pan, taste it, and adjust the seasoning of the remaining mixture. Chill until firm, about 1 hour.

Preheat the oven to 425°F.

Lay one guinea fowl breast half flat on a work surface and cut a pocket horizontally in the breast. Repeat for the other breast half. Divide the stuffing among the breast pieces and legs and sew the openings shut with a trussing needle and string or close them with poultry pins. Set each piece of guinea fowl on a square of foil and sprinkle with salt and pepper. Cut half the butter into 4 pieces and put one on each piece of guinea fowl. Wrap up the foil, set the packages on a baking sheet, and bake until a knife inserted in a package comes out hot, 20–25 minutes.

Meanwhile, prepare the sauce and garnish. In a heavy saucepan, boil together the stock and cider, skimming often, until reduced to $\frac{1}{2}$ cup, 12–15 minutes. Add the crème fraîche and simmer the sauce to concentrate the flavor. (The sauce is thin and will not coat a spoon.) Add the *pommeau* with seasoning to taste.

Melt the remaining butter in a frying pan over moderately high heat. Add the apple wedges with a little salt and pepper and cook until tender and golden on both sides, 10–15 minutes.

Unwrap the pieces of guinea fowl and remove the strings or poultry pins. Cut each piece cross-wise into slices. Coat warmed plates with the sauce and arrange a piece of guinea fowl, slices overlapping, on each plate. Arrange the apples in the same way on each plate and serve immediately.

POULET VALLEE D'AUGE

Chicken with Calvados, Cream, and Apples

Poulet Vallée d'Auge may be a typical dish in Calvados, but there is nothing humdrum about this version. Here, chicken pieces are seared and then poached in a court-bouillon, and a sauce is prepared with the cooking liquid, cream, and Calvados. It's a combination of the best I sampled in my travels. (Illustrated right)

SERVES 4
1 chicken (about $3\frac{1}{2}$lb), cut into serving pieces
4tbsp unsalted butter, clarified (see page 33)
1 onion, finely chopped
1 carrot, finely chopped
1tbsp flour
1 cup dry hard cider
1 cup chicken stock, preferably homemade
a large bouquet garni
$\frac{1}{2}$ cup Calvados
scant 1 cup crème fraîche
salt and freshly ground black pepper

FOR THE GARNISH
3tbsp unsalted butter
4 small, firm apples, quartered, cored, and peeled
salt and freshly ground black pepper

Season the pieces of chicken with salt. Heat the clarified butter in a sauté pan just the size to hold the chicken pieces in a single layer, add the chicken, and brown all over. Remove and set aside. Add the onion and carrot to the pan and cook over low heat until the onion is translucent, 3–5 minutes.

Remove any fat from the pan. Sprinkle the flour over the vegetables and cook until it browns, 1–2 minutes. Stir in the cider and stock, scraping up the browned pan juices. Return the chicken to the pan, tuck in the bouquet garni, and bring to a boil. Cover and simmer 15 minutes.

Heat the Calvados in a small saucepan, light it, and simmer until it reduces by half. (It will flare up so take care.) Add the Calvados to the chicken.

Continue cooking the chicken until tender, 10–15 minutes longer. Remove the pieces of chicken and keep them warm.

Bring the cooking liquid to a boil, then reduce the heat and simmer, skimming regularly, until reduced by half. Strain the liquid into a small heavy saucepan. Add the crème fraîche and continue simmering and skimming until the sauce reduces by a third. Season to taste.

Meanwhile prepare the garnish. Melt the butter in a large frying pan over moderately high heat. Add the apples with a little salt and pepper and cook them until they are tender and golden on both sides, 10–15 minutes.

To serve, arrange the pieces of chicken on a warmed platter or individual plates and pour the sauce over them. Surround with the apple quarters and serve immediately.

ANDOUILLE CHAUDE A LA BOVARY

Warm Chitterling Slices with Sorrel Purée

In Bayeux, famous for its extraordinary "tapestry" recounting the invasion of England by William the Conqueror, the hotel-restaurant Lion d'Or turns out classic food with a regional slant.

This recipe – with its literary allusion to Emma Bovary, Gustave Flaubert's tormented heroine – is a wonderful pairing of rich local andouille de Vire sausage and pungent sorrel.

The andouille *is sliced and poached in cider, then arranged on a bed of puréed sorrel and spinach. And what a good idea to set everything on a buckwheat crêpe to mop up all the delicious flavors. Note that the crêpes used here are rather thicker than the usual paper-thin variety – and more absorbent.*

SERVES 4

4tbsp unsalted butter
10oz spinach, stems removed and chopped
6oz sorrel, stems removed and chopped
1¾ cups crème fraîche
pinch of sugar, if needed
7oz *andouille de Vire* or other chitterling sausage
2 cups dry hard cider
salt and freshly ground white pepper

FOR THE CREPES

½ cup buckwheat flour
⅓ cup all-purpose flour
pinch of salt
1 egg
3tbsp milk
3tbsp water

For the crêpes, put the flours and salt in a mixing bowl and make a well in the center. Break the egg into the well and add a little milk. With a whisk, beat the egg and milk to mix. Gradually beat the flour into the central ingredients while pouring in the remaining milk and the water. Let the batter stand at least 1 hour. (Cover and chill the batter if leaving it longer.)

Melt the butter in a saucepan over moderately high heat. Add the spinach and sorrel with a little salt and cook, stirring, just until they wilt. Add half the crème fraîche and simmer, stirring often, until this purée thickens slightly, 8–10 minutes. Check the seasoning and, if the sauce is very acidic, add a little sugar.

In a small heavy saucepan, bring the remaining crème fraîche with a little salt to a boil. Reduce the heat and simmer, stirring occasionally, until the cream has thickened slightly, about 5–7 minutes. Add pepper to taste.

Peel the sausage and cut it on the diagonal into ¼-inch slices. Bring the cider to a boil in a saucepan, reduce the heat, and poach the sausage slices until heated through, 3–5 minutes. Keep them warm in the pan; drain before serving.

Set a 7-inch crêpe pan, lightly brushed with butter, or a nonstick frying pan over moderately high heat. When a drop of batter sizzles in the pan, pour in 3–4 tablespoons of the batter and quickly swirl it around so it covers the bottom of the pan evenly. Cook 1–2 minutes, then flip the crêpe and cook about 1 minute on the other side. The crêpe should be lightly colored on both sides. As the crêpes are done, stack them on a plate. (Crêpes can be made ahead and kept, wrapped in foil, in the refrigerator for a day. Reheat them in a low oven until warmed through.)

To serve, put the crêpes on warmed plates. Spread a quarter of the spinach and sorrel purée on each crêpe. Arrange four slices of the sausage, overlapping, on each plate. Spoon the reduced crème fraîche over all and serve immediately.

POULET A LA NORMANDE

Poached Chicken with Mushrooms

How many hotels can boast of selling their own guinea fowl, chickens, eggs, and rabbits as well as fromage blanc and crème fraîche? At La Rançonnière, a tote board leaning against a fortified wall announces what is fresh from the farm today.

The same home-grown products appear on the daily menu here, transformed into regional favorites such as Poulet à la Normande. There are as many versions of this dish as there are Norman cooks. This one from La Rançonnière is a classic. Serve the chicken with its traditional accompaniment, a dish of steaming rice pilaf.

SERVES 4

1 chicken (about 3½lb), cut into 4 serving pieces
1 carrot, thinly sliced
1 small onion, sliced
1 leek, white part only, thinly sliced
a large bouquet garni
2qt chicken stock, preferably homemade, or water
salt

FOR THE SAUCE

2½tbsp unsalted butter
4½tbsp flour
¼lb mushrooms, halved if large, thinly sliced
2tbsp crème fraîche
salt and freshly ground black pepper

Combine the chicken pieces, carrot, onion, leek, bouquet garni, stock, and a little salt in a sauté pan just the size to hold the pieces of chicken in a single layer. Bring to a boil, then reduce the heat, cover, and gently poach the chicken 50 minutes.

Remove the chicken from the pan, and strain and reserve the poaching liquid.

For the sauce, melt the butter in a heavy saucepan over low heat, whisk in the flour, and cook 30 seconds without letting it color. Pour in 1 quart of the strained poaching liquid, whisking constantly, and bring to a boil. Reduce the heat to low again and simmer, skimming regularly, until the sauce is reduced by half, about $\frac{3}{4}$–1 hour.

Add the mushrooms and crème fraîche to the sauce during the last 5 minutes of cooking. Season the sauce to taste.

To serve, reheat the chicken pieces in the remaining poaching liquid. Drain the chicken and transfer to a warmed serving dish. Pour the sauce over the chicken and serve.

TEURGOULE

Creamy Baked Rice Pudding

The Confrérie de la Teurgoule de Normandie, a serious group of cheerleaders for the native rice pudding, awarded its annual prize to this recipe. It was contributed by Françoise Bruneau, who prepares it at La Bourride in Caen.

Any Norman abroad would feel at home with a spoonful of this in his mouth. Slow cooking thickens and caramelizes the milk and sugar, which serve as a creamy sauce for the soft rice. Resist breaking the brown crust that forms over the rice, as it acts like a lid, preventing the rapid evaporation of the milk and keeping the rice moist during the hours of cooking.

SERVES 8
1 cup sugar
14tbsp short-grain rice
pinch of salt
¼tsp ground cinnamon
2qt whole milk

Preheat the oven to 300°F. Mix together the sugar, rice, salt, and cinnamon in a deep 2½-quart baking dish. Gradually stir in the milk. Put the dish in the oven and bake, undisturbed, until three-quarters of the milk has been absorbed and the rice is very, very soft, about 5 hours. The finished *teurgoule* should have a brown crust and enough lightly thickened liquid to act as a sauce. Serve it at room temperature from the dish.

BELOW Whether it's called Teurgoule *or* La Terrinée, *this is simply the best rice pudding you will ever taste. Its warming heartiness is entirely typical of genuine Norman cooking.*

ABOVE Apple Tart Flamed with Calvados (left), and Pear and Almond Cream Tart (recipes opposite). With such a wealth of fruit trees, and such a tradition of expert growing of many different varieties, the apple or pear tart is bound to be a standby for any Norman cook.

PATE SABLEE

Crumbly Pastry Dough

MAKES ONE 10-IN TART SHELL
$1\frac{2}{3}$ **cups flour**
$\frac{1}{3}$ **cup sugar**
pinch of salt
1 stick unsalted butter, cut into pieces
1 egg yolk
2–3tbsp cold water

Work the flour, sugar, and salt in a food processor for a few seconds until mixed. Add the butter and process until the mixture resembles coarse breadcrumbs.

Add the egg yolk and 2 tablespoons of water and process just until the dough holds together when you pinch it with your fingers. Add another tablespoon of water if the dough is still dry.

Transfer the dough to wax paper, flatten it into a disk, wrap well, and chill until the dough is firm, at least 1 hour.

TARTE FLAMBEE AU CALVADOS

Apple Tart Flamed with Calvados

This must be the purest version of Normandy apple tart, flavored with just apples and Calvados. First you cook the apples in butter and sugar, then arrange them in a sweet pastry case. Halfway through baking, the apples are flamed with the Calvados. I prefer to precook the apples before baking them to ensure a tender filling instead of spongy fruit. (Illustrated opposite, left)

SERVES 8
1 quantity Pâte Sablée (see left)
3tbsp unsalted butter
2lb firm apples, cored, peeled and cut into wedges
$\frac{1}{3}$ cup sugar
$\frac{1}{2}$ cup Calvados

Roll out the dough on a floured surface to a round $\frac{1}{4}$-inch thick. (If the dough is difficult to work with, roll it out between two sheets of wax paper.) Line a 10-inch tart pan with the dough and chill until firm, at least 15 minutes.

Preheat the oven to 400°F.

Prick the tart shell all over with a fork about every $\frac{1}{2}$ inch. Line it with a double thickness of foil, pressing it against the dough. Bake the pastry case 15 minutes. Remove the foil and continue baking until the pastry just begins to brown, 5–10 minutes. Remove from the oven. Reduce the oven temperature to 375°F.

Melt the butter in a large frying pan. Add the apples and half the sugar to the butter, without crowding the pan, and cook until tender and golden on all sides, 10–15 minutes. Remove the apples as they are done to the tart shell, arranging them in three concentric circles, working toward the center.

Bake the tart 20 minutes. Heat the Calvados in a small pan, light it, and pour over the apples. (It will flare up so take care.) Sprinkle the remaining sugar evenly over the top. Continue baking until the sugar caramelizes and the apples are tinged with brown, 15–20 minutes. Serve warm.

TARTE AUX POIRES A LA CREME D'AMANDES

Pear and Almond Cream Tart

Pear and almond cream tarts appear in pastry shop windows throughout Normandy, but it is rare to find one as good as you can make yourself. Taking the time to prepare your own pastry and using fresh pears makes all the difference. (Illustrated opposite, right)

SERVES 8
1 quantity Pâte Sucrée dough (see right)
$3\frac{1}{2}$oz almond paste, cut into chunks
$3\frac{1}{2}$tbsp sugar
$1\frac{1}{2}$tbsp Calvados, or to taste
1 egg
4tbsp unsalted butter, softened
$\frac{1}{4}$ cup flour
$1\frac{3}{4}$lb ripe, firm pears
1 lemon, cut in half

Roll out the dough on a floured surface to a round $\frac{1}{4}$ inch thick. Line a 10-inch tart pan with the dough and chill until firm, at least 15 minutes. Preheat the oven to 400°F.

Prick the tart shell all over with a fork about every $\frac{1}{2}$ inch. Line it with a double thickness of foil, pressing it against the dough. Bake the tart shell 15 minutes. Remove the foil and continue baking until the pastry just begins to brown, 5–10 minutes. Remove from the oven. Reduce the oven temperature to 375°F.

Work the almond paste with half the sugar in a food processor until smooth. Add the Calvados, egg, butter, and flour and process until the mixture is smooth. Taste and add more Calvados, if needed. Spread the mixture in the tart shell.

Core and peel a pear, then sprinkle it with lemon juice and rub it with the cut lemon to discourage it from browning. Halve it lengthwise. Set a pear half, rounded side up, on a cutting board and cut it crosswise into thin slices. Slip a metal spatula underneath and, keeping the slices together, set it on the almond cream, base towards the side of the tart shell. Press the pear gently to flatten the slices a little. Repeat with the remaining pears.

Bake the tart until the almond cream sets, about 30 minutes. Sprinkle the remaining sugar over the top and continue baking until golden, 10–20 minutes. Let cool to room temperature.

PATE SUCREE

Sweet Buttery Pastry Dough

MAKES ONE 10-IN TART SHELL
$1\frac{2}{3}$ cups flour
2tsp sugar
pinch of salt
1 stick unsalted butter, cut into pieces
1 egg yolk
2–3tbsp cold water

Work the flour, sugar, and salt in a food processor until mixed. Add the butter and process until the mixture resembles coarse crumbs.

Add the egg yolk and 2 tablespoons of water and process just until the dough holds together when you pinch it with your fingers. Add another tablespoon of water if the dough is still dry.

Transfer the dough to wax paper, flatten it into a disk, wrap well, and chill until the dough is firm, at least 1 hour.

TOP *Half-timbering filled with cob in Le Pont-d'Egrenne, a Domfrontais village.*

ABOVE *An edible find.* Girolles *are a common sight beneath pine trees in the Andaines forest in the Bocage.*

RIGHT *A basketful of cider pears in the orchard of the Maison de la Pomme et de la Poire, Barenton.*

ORNE

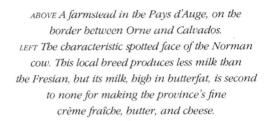

This is undiscovered Normandy, where on a country lane near Domfront you stumble upon a brown and white spotted cow licking her newborn calf. It is the end of the day and she has just delivered on a bed of soft straw in an orchard of apple and pear trees. Near them, in the fading light, another new mother watches over her infant calf, who struggles to stand for the first time.

Here in the Orne, far from the coast (Orne is the only *département* in Normandy not in sight of the English Channel), most farms are still lived in. There are few for-sale signs standing by the mailbox at the driveway entrance.

Unlike Seine-Maritime and Eure in Upper Normandy, which geologically are of a piece and form one sweeping limestone plateau, Orne straddles both sedimentary and granitic Normandy. The landscape and rural architecture change dramatically as you move around the *département*.

Every town here worth its salt has a gastronomic order with competitions for excellence. And every food shop seems to boast an award-winning specialty, from Camembert and *andouillette* sausages to *tripes en brochette* and *bourdelot* pastries.

THE PAYS D'AUGE AND PAYS D'OUCHE

Hundreds of Camembert labels adorn the walls of the Musée du Camembert in Vimoutiers. On close inspection, the labels come from Normandy, naturally, but also from the Loire Valley, the Lorraine, the Pyrénées, the Atlantic Coast, Brittany, Burgundy – every corner of France – and even Denmark and the United States.

Camembert cheese may be made all over the globe, but its home is the village of Camembert. This tiny village stands in the heart of the Pays d'Auge, which reaches from eastern Calvados into the northern Orne. It is just down the road from other brand-name towns like Livarot and Pont-l'Evêque in Calvados. This is quintessential Normandy, with rolling wooded countryside, scattered villages, and isolated farms, with the ever-familiar half-timbered finish and brown-and-white cows.

Near the Camembert museum in Vimoutiers (a few miles north of Camembert), a statue of a Norman dairymaid clasping Camembert cheeses in chipboard boxes honors Marie Harel, the accepted creator of Camembert cheese. But the history of France's preferred cheese is made of less solid stuff than the Vilhonneur-stone statue.

ABOVE A farmstead in the Pays d'Auge, on the border between Orne and Calvados.
LEFT The characteristic spotted face of the Norman cow. This local breed produces less milk than the Fresian, but its milk, high in butterfat, is second to none for making the province's fine crème fraîche, butter, and cheese.

The search for Camembert's originator began as a gesture of thanks. Joseph Knirim, a New York physician, credited the healing of his stomach troubles to a cure of Camembert and Pilsen beer. Wishing to show his appreciation to Camembert's creator, he came to Vimoutiers in 1926. In interviewing village elders, Mr. Knirim was told that a certain Marie Harel, born in Crouttes on April 28, 1761, had lived in Camembert and had lodged with a distant cousin, the abbot Gobert, who was familiar with Brie-making. Madame Harel purportedly created her own version of Brie, and Camembert was born. However, it was not until Marie Harel's grandson, Victor Paynel, presented Napoleon III with a Camembert that France developed a taste for this Norman cheese.

World-famous Camembert thus appeared to have a life story. After this tale had become generally accepted, however, further research turned up contradictory evidence. Documents from 1680 and 1708 were found already mentioning a cheese from Camembert well before Marie Harel was born. In addition, investigation proved that Marie Harel never lived in Camembert at all.

The fact is, we don't know anything about what early Camembert looked like or how it was made. Possibly it was an unrelated cheese by the same name. Also, while Marie Harel never lived in Camembert, she did often visit the Beaumoncel farm in Camembert, where her husband worked. Moreover, a priest who knew how to make Brie did often stop at the Beaumoncel farm, and his counsel apparently allowed Madame Harel to fashion a soft cheese with a downy rind. As for Marie Harel's grandson, according to the Historical Society of Vimoutiers, he was indeed His Majesty's purveyor of Camembert.

Today the village of Camembert counts only two cheesemaking families. Recent arrivals to the profession, they didn't start crafting farm Camembert until the 1980s when dairies could no longer pay them a living wage for the milk from their cows.

Although these small farmers make a pleasant cheese, it does not meet *appellation d'origine contrôlée* standards. Specifically, the homemade version doesn't have the smooth, classic taste of other Camemberts. So the only Camembert cheeses actually made in Camembert are not considered authentic! All AOC Camembert is made in dairies, which produce a high-quality, consistent cheese.

While changing times spurred some farmers to come around again to the traditions of cheese-making, other Normans, wishing to return to the land yet make a living as well, have embarked on new farming ideas.

At the bottom of the Pays d'Auge near Argentan, where undulating countryside levels out to flat pastureland, Alain de Quenetain raises *daguets d'Argentan*, or yearling stags, for their meat.

Monsieur de Quenetain drives to the grassy enclosures on his orange tractor. As he scatters pellets for the deer, he urges them gently to eat. "Come, come," he whispers in English. "Come, come," he says. "I speak to them in English so they will understand. They are English, you know."

Monsieur de Quenetain gave up his work as a geometrician to move to the country. His in-laws already lived in Sevigny at the château, and the Domaine de la Bonnerie next door was available. When he started in 1987, he found that selling the meat was trickier than raising the deer. Today he cannot produce as much as he could sell. Unlike wild venison, the farmed *daguet d'Argentan* can be sold year round. And to extend its shelf life, the meat, still fresh, is vacuum packed.

The stags Monsieur de Quenetain raises are *daguets*, 15 to 27 months old. At this age, the animals shed their first horns. They have not yet reproduced and their meat is still mild and tender. The taste and texture most resembles filet mignon. There is no gaminess and very little fat.

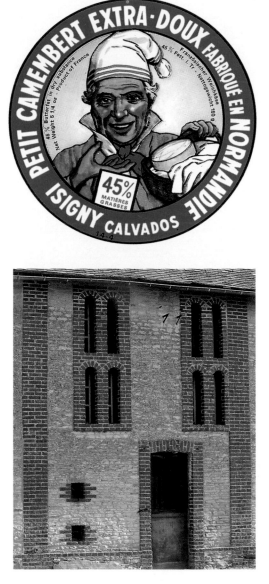

ABOVE *A 19th-century Camembert factory in Vieux-Pont-en-Auge. Its characteristic narrow windows regulate incoming air and shield the interior from sun; one can imagine the cool, shady spaces in which the cheese would be made.*

OPPOSITE, TOP LEFT *Camembert label. Cheese museums in Normandy display thousands of old labels, mirroring the times and local politics.* ABOVE *A poem recounts the history of Camembert, spotted on a poster in the village of Camembert.* ABOVE RIGHT *The process that makes Camembert unlike any other cheese in the world is the requirement, laid down in the AOC regulations, for the curd to be* moule à la louche, *or ladled into the molds, by hand or by machine, in five successive passes.*

CAMEMBERT DE NORMANDIE

With white-washed walls and warm swirling vapors, the salle de moulage *at the Réaux Camembert factory in Lessay resembles a steam room. The workers here, called* mouleurs, *ladle a scoop of wobbly white curd into tall cheese molds, one by one. When the countless molds have received their first scoop, the* mouleurs *begin again. In all, each mold receives five ladles of curd to make a Camembert* de Normandie.

Over 30 million of these supple disks, with a white crumpled surface tinged with rust, a blond interior, and delicate fruity taste, are made each year. Yet, it was not until 1983 that the government bestowed an AOC on France's favorite cheese, protecting it from imposters.

The belated hallmark guarantees that for AOC Camemberts, the uncut curd is moulé à la louche, *or ladled into the molds, in five successive passes, as at Réaux. This ensures an even distribution of butterfat, which naturally rises to the surface. Also, the uncut curd gives the velvety texture that Camembert is famous for. In smaller dairies like Réaux, the ladling is still done by hand, while industrial cheesemakers use machines.*

Another condition for AOC status requires that the cheeses be made with raw milk, that is milk that has not been heated above body temperature, thus preserving all its fragrance and flavor. The milk must come only from Normandy's five départements *and the finished cheese must contain 45 percent butterfat.*

It takes 20 days to make a perfect Camembert. Rennet is added to partially skimmed milk, which curdles it in 5 to 12 minutes, depending on the milk's acidity. The curd is left in vats to firm up for an hour before the workers ladle it into the molds. Once the molds are filled, they are turned and left to drain overnight.

The next day, the fresh cheeses are sprayed with penicillium – which will develop into the characteristic bloomy rind – then salted and turned again. In the drafty, cool hâloir, *white down begins to appear on the cheeses. Workers then turn them again on about the fifth day. After 16 days, some cheesemakers like Réaux wrap up the infant Camemberts and send them out to the shops. Others move the cheeses to a humid cellar, where they age for four or five days on wood planks.*

One category of Camembert lover prefers the cheese demi-affiné, *with a sliver of chalky white running through the center. The opposing school wants theirs* fait à coeur, *or creamy all the way through. However you like your Camembert, it should smell fragrant with no hint of ammonia. It is best kept in its wood-chip box, wrapped in newspaper, in the vegetable drawer of your refrigerator. Unwrap the cheese and let it stand at room temperature for one hour before serving.*

BOUDIN BLANC D'ESSAY

*The Charcuterie Chartier stands on one corner of
the Place Général-de-Gaulle in
Le Mêle-sur-Sarthe. It might be any rural
charcuterie in small-town Normandy.
After years of working for a large caterer in Paris,
Monsieur Chartier came home to the Orne
to establish his own charcuterie, where he sticks to
the business of preparing pork
the old-fashioned way.
His boudin blanc à la mode d'Essay, for instance,
named for the village northwest of here that
sponsors an annual competition for the best white
sausage, contains only lean pork, eggs, and
milk with salt and pepper for seasoning – no bread,
chicken, or veal, and no unorthodox additions
such as apples or truffles. "For me," says Monsieur
Chartier, "à la mode d'Essay means a pure
sausage." It also implies a traditional context.
He prepares the sausage from October to Easter,
the time-honored season for boudin blanc.*

*ABOVE A pigeon house at the Château d'O.
Such solidly built roosting and nesting houses
are a common sight throughout the
Norman countryside, and in many regions there
are signed routes des pigeonniers that will
take the visitor on a tour of the best ones.
ABOVE CENTER Alain de Quenetain raises young deer
on his farm near Argentan for their mild,
tender meat. He is typical of many young,
farmers who are making a living
from untypically Norman occupations.
LEFT In the Perche, a blue coat does duty as a
scarecrow during the cherry season, when birds
can strip the trees of the precious fruit.*

Monsieur de Quenetain has launched the Confrérie du Daguet d'Argentan, and is its grand master. As he puts it: "A town without a gastronomic order is not a real town." Every year in October the *confrérie* mobilizes a culinary contest in Argentan. Here, chefs deliver recipes using, what else – *daguet d'Argentan*.

East of the Pays d'Auge lies the Pays d'Ouche, a plain sprawling from southwestern Eure over to northeastern Orne. The Pays d'Ouche is a less-favored corner of Normandy, but only in comparison to the rich surrounding countryside, where either the soil is intensively cultivated or clay soil and a damp climate make excellent pasturage.

At the weekly market in L'Aigle, however, one of the largest in France, you wouldn't guess the Pays d'Ouche was less endowed. Every Tuesday, under an open sky on the outskirts of town, the livestock market opens at 7:30 am with the sale of bulls. There is no auctioneer. Buyers and sellers cluster next to the steel pens and strike a bargain face to face, man to man.

Meanwhile, in the center of town on the Place Boislandry, the food market gets under way. One of L'Aigle's *charcutiers* offers award-winning *cervelas aiglon*. This lightly smoked, fine-textured pork sausage is flavored with Calvados, thyme, bay leaf, and onion. It is delicious grilled and served with split pea purée and smoked bacon, or poached and set atop a mound of sauerkraut. Each year this *cervelas* is honored during a four day fair held the weekend before Ascension.

On a rotisserie, rows of chickens turn slowly, basting each other with dripping fat. A basket of eggs, two rabbits, and a bucket of dandelion greens on a folding table make a pastoral still life. Crates of cheeping ducklings, chicks, and guinea fowl line the sidewalk.

Trading carries on all afternoon. But by 5 pm the farmers have packed up their home-grown produce, the fish merchants have boxed the fish in ice, and the street is strewn with leek greens, carrot tops, and discarded packing crates. This Norman town has once again found its own sleepy rhythm.

THE PERCHE

It is Wednesday afternoon in Mortagne au Perche, and all is quiet at Le Roi du Boudin Noir, Claude Guillochon's *charcuterie*. The occasional customer wanders in to buy a coil of blood sausage. But on the third weekend in March, when the Confrérie des Chevaliers du Goûte Boudin kicks off the *foire au boudin*, the town swells with visitors and one ton of blood sausage is sold.

Mortagne sits atop a hillock in the northern Perche, a region with a history different from the rest of Normandy. The green and valleyed scenery in southeast Orne resembles the Pays d'Auge. But compared to the charming wood-ribbed houses of the Pays d'Auge, Perche manors look like small fortresses with thick stone walls, turrets, and brown-tiled roofs.

The blood sausage fair in Mortagne began in 1962, and the town claims that the competition held during the fair is France's oldest. Since it first started, 15,000 sorts of blood sausage have passed under the noses of the judges.

On the Friday of the *foire au boudin*, the eliminations begin for the international blood sausage competition. This event is open to all, and visitors join members of the jury at tables, tasting and rating 25 to 30 different sausages per table. At day's end, the number of contestants is whittled down from about 650.

GIFT-WRAPPED BOUDIN

When you are invited to a friend's house for dinner, what do you take? Chocolates? Wine? If you lived in Mortagne-au-Perche, France's blood sausage capital, the answer might be a coil of sausage. "Here people buy boudin noir to give as a present instead of flowers," says Claude Guillochon, charcutier and Mortagne's king of blood sausage.

How do you recognize a good boudin noir? "You can tell by slicing it," says Monsieur Guillochon. The pieces of fat should be evenly mixed with the blood. Also, it must not be dry and crumbly. And the seasoning should be just right, neither too much nor too little. Finally, the best sausage is firm and fills its casing evenly.

He will not reveal the recipe for his own boudin. It is a secret handed down to him by Monsieur Batrel, his former boss and mentor. But he does admit that it is equal parts onion, pork blood, and fat. "The rest," he says, "is savoir-faire."

LEFT Three generations of Calvadosmakers. Roger, Isidore, and Didier Lemorton stand in a cellar doorway at Mantilly near Domfront.
BELOW LEFT Le Pin Stud, the famous horse-breeding center.
BELOW Notre-Dame Cathedral in Alençon's Grande-Rue.
RIGHT Bouchons alençonnais, rolled cookies filled with praline cream, decorate the window of Jacky Pedro's candy store in Alençon.

LEMORTON CALVADOS

To make superior Calvados, one that is smooth, well rounded, with definite character, you must begin with the right attitude: "You have to love what you are doing," says Roger Lemorton (above), Calvadosmaker extraordinaire.
"There are no hours in this business."
Without a doubt, his was the finest Calvados I tasted in Normandy. (Also the best poiré and even the best pommeau.)
Here in Mantilly, farm Calvados is made following the long-standing tradition of the Domfrontais – with a mixture of apples and pears. Some of the pear trees on the Pont-Barrabé farm are 150 years old. There are no temperature-controlled storage sheds here, and Madame Lemorton sticks the labels on the bottles of Calvados herself.
The Lemorton family has been making Calvados for generations. Monsieur Lemorton's father, Isidore, has won countless prizes for his Calvados du Domfrontais. He no longer makes Calvados, but sells the aging stock to Fauchon and La Tour d'Argent in Paris.

On the Saturday the official judges select 30 prize winners, but festivities carry on through Monday with dinner dances, fairground rides, bicycle races, magic acts, and a contest for those interested in swallowing the largest quantity of blood sausage in ten minutes. Phew!

Claude Guillochon sells 330 pounds of blood sausage each week in the winter, less in summer. His business is a family affair. Mother peels the onions for the famous *boudin*, and brothers help out, too. For variety, Monsieur Guillochon makes blood sausage flavored with Calvados, with apples, with chili pepper, and with tongue, as well as smoked.

Besides Mortagne, several other Perche towns honor Norman specialties. Longny-au-Perche fetes its own version of tripe on May Day. It also salutes wild mushroom terrine, made with mushrooms collected in the Perche forests, with a competition in October. Moulins-la-Marche calls itself the capital of brioche, and in April its Confrérie des Ventres à Brioches de Moulins-la-Marche inaugurates a competition for the best brioche in France. The village of Essay hosts a white sausage contest (see page 98) in November. Alençon holds an *andouillette* (see page 103) and white sausage competition each year in October.

Specialty food shops crowd Alençon's cobbled pedestrian streets. Candy stores prepare *pierres de Nôtre-Dame* or *vieux pavés*, domino-sized candies of buttercream dipped in bittersweet chocolate, named for Eglise Nôtre-Dame next door and the paving stones that line the street. *Bouchons alençonnais* are another popular confection featured in window displays. The size of a cork and roughly the same color, these rolled cookies are filled with praline cream.

Countless chocolates take equestrian themes for their decoration: Orne is the home of one of France's most famous horse-breeding centers, Le Pin Stud, and the Percheron horse, a stocky work animal, once prized by Paris transporters for its congenial disposition and strength.

THE BOCAGE

How about tripe for breakfast? With a glass of white wine and coffee doused with Calvados, of course. Beginning at 8 am, Gérard Chatel opens the tasting room next to his *triperie-boucherie-charcuterie* in La Ferté Macé to tripe lovers. They come for steaming hot *tripes en brochette mode fertoise* (see page 102), served with boiled potatoes. "Even people who don't like tripe eat our *brochettes*," says Madame Chatel. "It is not *charcuterie* [pork], you know. Only the best beef tripe."

In this western corner of the Orne, called the Bocage (it extends from Orne north into Calvados and west into the Manche) maze-like hedges planted on high banks divide the rolling landscape. Many people live in remote farms even now, keeping to the old ways. Several habits – like eating tripe for a mid-morning snack while in town – which have faded in other parts of Normandy or have been banished to dusty museums, still carry on in the Bocage.

One well-kept secret in Orne's Bocage is the Andaines Forest. This serene oasis, frequented by mycologists and mushroom gatherers, lies a stone's throw from the spa town of Bagnoles-de-l'Orne. In September and October, the Manoir du Lys (see pages 108–9), set in the forest, organizes mushroom weekends here when Yves Fairier leads guests to stalk wild mushrooms. With his horn-rimmed glasses, lanky frame, and neat gray hair, Yves Fairier looks very much the math and biology teacher he is. Microscopic mushrooms that grow on logs are his special passion.

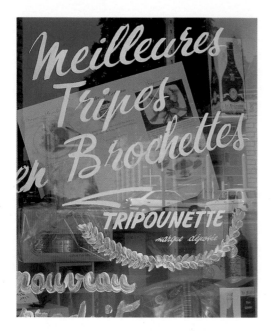

*RIGHT Mushroom hunting in the Andaines forest.
Bright red – and deadly – montre ceps show the
way to a cache of prized cèpe mushrooms.
BELOW Next to their shop (described below left), the
Chatels have a cosy dining room where tripe
fanciers gather in the mornings for a bowl of
award-winning tripes en brochettes.*

TRIPES EN BROCHETTE

*Janine Chatel battles prejudice daily in her shop in
La Ferté-Macé when selling tripes en brochette.
"People think it's dirty," she says, "all that
inner tubing. And gluey. But it is cow-heel that
gives a gluey texture and there is none
of that in our tripe."
In tripes en brochettes mode fertoise, or en paquet
as they are also called, four sorts of beef tripe are
rolled in a fifth kind and secured with a billette –
a special skewer of hazelnut wood (right).
Gérard Chatel gently simmers these tripe
"packages" with aromatic vegetables, herbs, and
white wine. Monsieur Chatel is one of the last tripe-
dressers to use tripières, the squat earthenware
vessels in which the ingredients cook slowly for
14 hours until – voilà, perfection.
Is it worth all the hard work to produce this unsung
dish? Madame Chatel's response is steadfast: "My
husband is happy if people say of him, 'That fellow,
he really makes good tripe.'"*

But wild mushrooms provide good eating as well as hunting. In a morning's foray, you can expect to find pounds of *cèpes*, plus carpets of trumpet-shaped orange *girolles* hiding under pine trees. All the wild mushrooms served at the Manoir du Lys come from the Andaines forest. "Pensioners or people out of work know where to find them," says Franck Quinton of the Manoir du Lys. "They often bring them around to the kitchen."

On the subject of edible wild mushrooms, Monsieur Fairier says, "I have been studying mushrooms for ten years. The more you know, the warier you are."

French druggists warn mushroom chasers to bring their harvest in for identification before eating them. But can you trust the druggist? Monsieur Fairier explains that druggists, charged with being advisers, receive only two days' training. He thinks two years would be more reasonable.

Although Monsieur Fairier adores the mushroom quest, he is timid about eating mushrooms. When he does, he prefers them cooked simply, just sliced and sautéed with butter, parsley, and garlic. "Very little garlic," he specifies.

Another unspoiled patch of the Bocage is found on the *route du poiré* (the perry road), a signed route that meanders from Domfront to Barenton in the Manche *département*. Here, farmers use their tractors like a car, driving them to the nearest village to fetch a loaf of bread and the day's paper.

Along the lanes, A-shaped pear trees alternate with rounder apple trees in mixed orchards. Spring is the time for seeing this area, called the Domfrontais, at its floral best. Pear trees bloom first, before the apple trees. In April, pear trees stand out in all their majesty, graceful branches laden with white flowers. These kings of the Domfrontais orchard live to 200 years of age. They are taller, their trunks straighter and thicker, their canopies fuller than apple trees.

Farmers in the Domfrontais raise a few cows, grow hay, and press the fruit of their orchards. The trees here produce fruit for cider, *poiré*, and Calvados; it is too sour for eating.

Poiré is made in the same way as apple cider (see pages 56–58), but fragile pears are pressed immediately after picking instead of maturing in lofts like cider apples. And perry is naturally clear, almost limpid compared to the average farm apple cider.

Calvados du Domfrontais, like other Calvados *appellation réglementée*, is distilled just once. What sets Domfrontais Calvados apart from the rest is that it is an aged blend of both distilled *poiré* and apple cider.

To the north of the Domfrontais lies the Suisse Normande. Because of different soil make-up, *poiré* here cannot match the finesse of Domfrontais *poiré*. But daffodils grow wild like dandelions by the side of the road and in fields. And instead of half-timbered architecture with ocher-colored cob, rugged brown and gray stone houses built of schist come into view.

The Suisse Normande village of Athis-de-l'Orne is the *bourdelot* capital of Normandy. Here, the Confrérie des Gouste Bourdelots du Bocage Athisien strictly spells out the proper characteristics of this confection. "A *bourdelot* is not a tart," says Raymond Lelouvier, grand master of the *confrérie*. "It is covered top and bottom with pastry."

The *confrérie*'s rules state that a *bourdelot* must include Calville apples, the hard, acidic apples favored for baking in the Bocage, or their equivalent. Each apple, cored, but unpeeled, is cut into eight wedges, and the apples are wrapped in a 1-foot round or rectangular piece of dough: bread dough, puff pastry, pie pastry, or sweet pie pastry. The regulations permit no vanilla or cinnamon, but a drop of Calvados is tolerated.

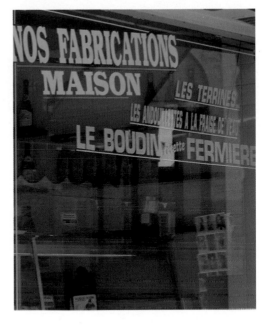

ABOVE A shop advertises charcuterie *from the Perche, including* andouillettes *and blood sausage.*

ANDOUILLETTES D'ALENCON

"Andouillette is not just a little andouille," explains Cécile Ruel, who runs the family charcuterie in Alençon. "They are not at all the same sausage." Cécile and her husband Patrick took over the town's most respected charcuterie – already 95 years old – in 1979, and continued its traditions. Size is only the most obvious difference between these sausages. Andouillettes are made with fraise de veau (veal tripe); andouilles consist of pork stomach and intestine. Andouilles are smoked; andouillettes are not. Also, a layer of waxy fat covers the andouillette, while andouille has no such coating. The best way to eat andouillette is grilled over a fire, with other sausages. Though andouille is wonderful sliced and poached, it is more commonly served cold.

PEARS FOR POIRE

Raymond Joubin arrives by tractor at the pear orchard in Le Pont-d'Egrenne with his wife and son. It is almost noon and the weak October sun has not yet burned through the clouds that hang above this part of the Domfrontais. The wind tosses the tree branches, and ripe fruit drops to the ground with a thump and a thud. The family works quickly and silently. Monsieur Joubin circles the trees, pushing a lawn-mower-like machine that sweeps the fruit off the ground and drops it into a wire basket, while Thérèse Joubin gleans. Alain Joubin swaps the full basket with an empty one, then he tilts the fruit into a wagon. When the Joubins finish the harvest, Alain will haul the pears to a cider press.

Poiré, a delicate pear cider, is little known in France outside Normandy. Though farmers in other parts of the province make perry like the Joubin family, the only sizeable orchards are in the Domfrontais.

BELOW *Alain, Raymond, and Thérèse Joubin collecting cider pears in Le Pont-d'Egrenne.*

CIDER PEARS

TOP ROW, LEFT TO RIGHT:

Fausset; Père Omiot

SECOND ROW, LEFT TO RIGHT:

Domfront; Rouge Vigné; Pomeret

CIDER PEARS

THIRD ROW, LEFT TO RIGHT:

Belle Verge; Petit Roux; Bezie

BOTTOM ROW:

Normandie (Sainte-Marie); Gros Blot

MOULIN DE VILLERAY

VILLERAY, TEL 33 73 30 22

A solid, bourgeois clientele frequents the Moulin de Villeray near Nogent-le-Rotrou, nestled in the rolling, verdant hills of the Perche. They come to carry out that sacred rite: a fine, leisurely meal in the country.

The restaurant here was once the machine room of an old mill, and the water wheel, separated by a glass wall, still occupies one end of the sweeping space. Rough-hewn standards adorned with antique dishes support the beamed ceiling. Across from the water wheel, a fire burns in the raised hearth, offering warmth and a sense of well-being in cold weather. In summer, dining moves outside under airy umbrellas next to the Huisne river.

Christian and Muriel Eelson, newly arrived in 1992, have revitalized this old watermill. Their menu blends lightened regional fare with equally appealing contemporary offerings.

TOURTE DE CANARD ROUENNAIS

Crisp Potato Cake with Broiled Duck

Here is an edible jewel box from François Lagrue, chef at the Moulin de Villeray. In the classic French way, Monsieur Lagrue leaves on the rich duck skin and cooks his duck rare like steak. (But you can cook the duck as you like.) Duck legs on greens are served with potato cases filled with sliced duck breast and wild mushrooms. It's a restaurant recipe for the home cook who likes a challenge.

SERVES 4
FOR THE DUCK AND STOCK
1 duck (about 4½lb)
2tbsp vegetable oil
1 carrot, thinly sliced
2 onions, thinly sliced
a bouquet garni
1qt water
7oz goose or duck fat or 1 cup vegetable oil
salt and freshly ground black pepper

TOP The view through an open window at the watermill.
ABOVE Separate menus for gentlemen and ladies.

FOR THE TOURTES
1 stick unsalted butter
1 shallot, finely chopped
¼lb fresh *girolles* or other wild mushrooms,
cut into ¼-in pieces
2tbsp chopped fresh parsley
1½lb evenly shaped boiling potatoes

FOR THE SALAD
1tsp red wine vinegar
1tbsp vegetable oil
2oz mixed salad greens

Cut the legs off the duck and trim any excess skin. Cut each leg in half at the knee joint. Cut the breast meat and wings off the carcass. Cut the wing from each breast and trim any excess skin. Cut the carcass into pieces.

Heat the oil in a large saucepan over moderately high heat. Add the duck wings and carcass and brown them, turning often, 10–12 minutes; remove. Reduce the heat to moderate, add the carrot and onions, and cook until the onions are tinged with brown, 8–10 minutes. Return the duck wings and carcass to the pan with the bouquet garni and water. Bring to a boil, then simmer the stock, skimming regularly, until it reduces to ½ cup, about 45 minutes; strain.

Meanwhile, melt the goose fat in a large frying pan over low heat. Sprinkle the duck leg pieces generously with salt and cook them gently in the fat, turning occasionally, until the skin is golden and the meat is very tender, 40–45 minutes. Remove the pieces to paper towels to drain. Strain the fat; save it to enrich stews or to fry potatoes.

For the tourte filling, melt 2 tablespoons of the butter over moderate heat in a frying pan. Add the shallot and cook until translucent, 2–3 minutes. Add the mushrooms with a little salt and sauté over moderately high heat until they lose all their moisture, about 5 minutes. Remove from the heat and stir in the parsley.

Melt the remaining butter. Brush the bottom and sides of four 5-inch individual gratin dishes or tartlet molds with butter. Chill the dishes until the butter sets, then butter the dishes again. Brush four butter rounds of the same size on a baking sheet. Chill and butter them again.

Peel the potatoes and cut them crosswise into paper-thin slices. Working from the center and up the sides, arrange a layer of potatoes, with the slices overlapping, in a neat pattern in each gratin dish. Carefully brush the potato slices with butter and sprinkle with salt and pepper. Chill the tourte cases until the butter sets.

Repeat for the butter rounds on the baking sheet to make potato lids for the tourtes.

Preheat the oven to 425°F.

Bake the tourte cases and lids until crisp and golden, about 15 minutes.

While the potatoes are baking, make the dressing for the salad: Whisk together the vinegar and a little salt until the salt dissolves, then whisk in the oil and pepper until smooth.

Preheat the broiler. Score the skin of the duck breast pieces and put them on the broiler rack, skin upward. Broil about 3 inches from the heat for about 10 minutes. Turn them over and broil until the juice runs pink when a breast is pricked, 7–10 minutes. Remove to a carving board and keep them warm, loosely covered with foil.

Reheat the legs under the broiler. Reheat the mushroom mixture. Season the stock with salt and pepper and simmer it briefly. Toss the salad greens with the dressing.

Carefully remove the tourte cases from the gratin dishes and set one on each warmed plate. Spoon in the mushroom mixture. Cut the duck breasts crosswise into thin slices and arrange half a breast piece, slices overlapping, in each tourte. Spoon the reduced stock over the duck breast and cover with the tourte lids. Mound a quarter of the salad greens on each plate and top with a piece of duck leg. Serve immediately.

LA POMME SOUFFLEE, COULIS DE RHUBARBE

Meringue-Filled Apples with Rhubarb Sauce

In this dessert, François Lagrue has combined hot and cold with sweet and tangy: Apple shells are stuffed with apple meringue, then baked and served with apple sorbet and rhubarb sauce.

SERVES 4
12 very small or 4 large apples
3tbsp Calvados
pinch of ground cinnamon
6 egg whites
¾ cup sugar
4 scoops Green Apple Sorbet (optional, see page 83)

FOR THE RHUBARB SAUCE
½lb rhubarb, peeled and cut into
¼-in pieces
⅓ cup sugar
3tbsp water
juice of ½ lemon

TO DECORATE (OPTIONAL)
tiny sprigs of red and white currants
fresh mint leaves

For the rhubarb sauce, combine the ingredients in a saucepan, cover, and cook over moderately high heat 5 minutes. Uncover and continue cooking, stirring occasionally, until the rhubarb is very tender, 5–7 minutes. (Watch the mixture carefully toward the end of the cooking so it doesn't caramelize.) Let cool to room temperature, then purée in a food processor. Chill.

Cut off the top of each apple about an eighth of the way down; save the tops. With a grapefruit knife or melon baller, cut out the insides of the apples, leaving a thin but sturdy shell.

Put the apple tops and insides (cores and seeds, too) in a heavy saucepan and add the Calvados and cinnamon. Cover and cook over the lowest possible heat, stirring occasionally, until the apples are very soft and falling apart, 12–15 minutes. Work through a food mill, then chill thoroughly. Preheat the oven to 425°F.

Beat the egg whites until they hold soft peaks. Gradually beat in the sugar until the meringue holds stiff peaks. Fold in the chilled applesauce.

Spoon the apple meringue into the apple shells, mounding it slightly. Put the apples on a baking sheet and bake until the tops are lightly browned, 12–15 minutes.

To serve, spoon the rhubarb sauce onto plates and spread it to cover the bottom. Set 1 large or 3 small apples on each plate. If you like, set a scoop of apple sorbet on each plate, arrange the currants in the sauce, and decorate with mint leaves.

MANOIR DU LYS

BAGNOLES DE-L'ORNE, TEL 33 37 80 69

At the Manoir du Lys, you can pull on your boots and hunt for cèpes *on an October morning, then sink into a leather armchair and peruse the menu by a glowing fire at night. In this luxurious auberge, set in the Andaines forest, wilderness does not mean roughing it.*

Marie-France and Paul Quinton run their country retreat, just outside the sophisticated bustle of Bagnoles-de-l'Orne, with warmth, style, and informality. Today their 28-year-old son, Franck, also lends a hand.

Franck Quinton apprenticed at restaurants in Paris before joining his father in the kitchen at the Manoir du Lys. Their menu offers celebratory food as well as more down-to-earth fare: foie gras, lobster, game, wild mushrooms, brochette de tripes fertoise, *country ham in cider. Franck is glad to be back in the family fold: "It is so much more exciting to work for yourself than someone else."*

NOISETTES DE DAIM AUX POIRES POCHÉES

Venison with Poached Pears and Spinach

Franck Quinton cooks with the bounty of the Andaines forest. This venison dish, for example, takes advantage of the nearby wildlife. It is deceptively simple. You pan-fry venison steaks and serve them with wine-poached pears and spinach. But the success of the dish depends on the stock (Monsieur Quinton uses game stock), a matter of simmering scraps and bones for hours, skimming regularly. You can prepare the pears a day ahead; gently reheat the fruit in the wine.

SERVES 4

6tbsp unsalted butter
½lb spinach, stems removed
1¼lb venison tenderloin, cut into
12 even steaks
salt and freshly ground black pepper

FOR THE PEARS
1 bottle (3 cups) fruity
red wine
a bay leaf
2 juniper berries, crushed
2 black peppercorns, crushed
2tbsp granulated sugar
4 small pears
juice of ½ lemon
⅓ cup pitted prunes
¼ cup crème fraîche

FOR THE SAUCE
1tbsp brown sugar
2tbsp red wine vinegar
1½ cups rich brown veal stock
juice of ½ orange
salt and freshly ground black pepper

For the pears, combine the wine, bay leaf, juniper berries, peppercorns, and granulated sugar in a saucepan. Heat, stirring, until the sugar dissolves.

Peel the pears, halve them lengthwise, and core them. Rub the pears with lemon juice as you work to discourage browning. Add all the pear halves to the saucepan and bring just to a simmer. Poach the pears until just tender, 8–10 minutes. Remove from the heat but leave the pears in the wine.

Soak the prunes in boiling water to cover for 10–15 minutes. Drain and pat dry. Purée with the crème fraîche in a food processor. Set aside.

For the sauce, boil together the brown sugar and vinegar in a small saucepan until the mixture reduces by half. Stir in the stock and orange juice and simmer the sauce, skimming regularly, until it lightly coats a spoon, 7–10 minutes. Season.

Meanwhile, melt 2 tablespoons of the butter in a saucepan over moderately high heat. Add the spinach and a little salt and cook, stirring, just until the spinach wilts. Keep warm.

Clarify the remaining butter (see page 33). Heat it in a frying pan over moderately high heat. Sprinkle the venison steaks with salt and pepper, add to the pan, and cook, turning once, 3–4 minutes for rare meat, 5–7 minutes for medium.

To serve, reheat the pears, sauce, and spinach if needed. Drain the pears, then set each half, rounded-side up, on a cutting board and cut it crosswise into thin slices. Arrange 2 sliced halves, core-side up, on each warmed plate. Pipe or spoon the prune cream along the core of each pear half. Pile a small mound of spinach near the pears. Pour a little of the sauce next to the spinach. Arrange 3 venison steaks on the sauce.

TARTE DE BOUDIN NOIR AUX POMMES

Blood Sausage and Apple Tart

The combination of boudin noir *and apples in a tart is unexpected but seems to please everyone who tries it – everyone who likes blood sausage, that is. A version of this appears in many of the specialty food shops in Mortagne-au-Perche. (Illustrated left)*

SERVES 8
10oz best-quality puff pastry dough or
Pâte Brisée (see page 68)
10oz firm apples, cored, peeled, and sliced
3 eggs
1¼ cups light cream
1tsp salt
7oz blood sausage, cut into
¼-in slices
freshly ground white pepper

Sprinkle a 10-inch tart pan with water. Roll out the dough on a floured surface to a round ⅛ inch thick and use to line the pan. Chill the tart shell until firm, at least 15 minutes.

Preheat the oven to 425°F and put a baking sheet into the oven to heat.

Arrange the apple slices in the bottom of the chilled tart shell, making three concentric rings and working toward the center. In a bowl, beat the eggs to mix. Whisk in the cream and salt and pepper to taste. Pour this custard over the apples.

Bake the tart on the hot baking sheet until the pastry begins to brown, 10–15 minutes.

Reduce the oven temperature to 350°F. Arrange the slices of blood sausage on top and continue baking until a knife inserted in the center of the filling comes out clean, 20–30 minutes. If the pastry browns too quickly, cover it with aluminum foil. Serve the tart hot.

SALADE PAYSANNE A LA CREME

Cabbage Salad with Ham, Apples, and Potatoes

The Hôtel de la Poste in Domfront is one of those old-fashioned places in the town's high street where locals, traveling salesmen, and the odd tourist gather for a simple meal and a good bottle of cider that will not unbalance the budget. The prix-fixe menu is chalked on a blackboard outside and includes this wintry salad. It is a satisfying mix of shredded cabbage with creamy diced ham, apple, and potato. (Illustrated right)

SERVES 4

1lb green cabbage, shredded
2tbsp cider vinegar
3tbsp vegetable oil
2 small boiling potatoes
2 small apples, peeled and cut into
½-in cubes
6oz cooked ham, cut into
½-in strips
1 small shallot, finely chopped
1 small head leaf lettuce
2tbsp finely chopped mixed fresh herbs,
such as parsley, chives, and tarragon
salt and freshly ground black pepper

FOR THE DRESSING
2tbsp cider vinegar
1½tsp Dijon mustard
3tbsp vegetable oil
1tbsp walnut oil
2tbsp crème fraîche
salt and freshly ground black pepper

Layer the cabbage in a colander, salting each layer generously. Set aside to drain 3–4 hours, then squeeze out the liquid by handfuls. Taste the cabbage: if it is too salty, rinse it and dry in a salad spinner. Whisk together 1 tablespoon of the vinegar, the oil, and pepper to taste. Pour this over the cabbage and toss until evenly coated. Taste and adjust the seasoning. Set aside.

Put the potatoes in a saucepan of salted water and bring to a boil. Reduce the heat and simmer until tender, 15–20 minutes, then drain. When the potatoes are cool enough to handle, peel them and cut them into ½-inch cubes. Sprinkle them with the remaining vinegar.

Make the dressing: Whisk together the vinegar and a little salt until the salt dissolves. Whisk in the mustard, oils, crème fraîche, and pepper to taste until smooth.

Combine the potatoes, apples, ham, and shallot in a bowl. Add the dressing and toss until evenly coated. Taste and adjust the seasoning.

To serve, arrange lettuce leaves on a platter or plates. Pile the cabbage salad in the middle and surround with the potato mixture. Sprinkle the herbs over the top and serve.

CREPES A LA SAUCE CAMEMBERT

Crêpes Filled with Mushrooms, Ham, and Camembert

Once, Norman cheese was reserved for the cheese course – after the main dish and before the fruit. Today it's all over the place in a Norman meal and you are as likely to find it cooked as not. It is sliced and arranged on tarts, chopped and deep-fried for croquettes, folded into dough and sautéed, and, as here, melted to flavor a white sauce that is used to fill crêpes.

Even if your crêpe-making technique is rudimentary, these crêpes from the Ferme-Auberge de Croutles near Vimoutiers will taste better than any you would be served in the average crêperie. Of course, you must use the freshest mushrooms, best-quality ham, and raw-milk Camembert. (Illustrated left)

SERVES 4 AS A MAIN DISH
FOR THE CREPES
1 cup + 2tbsp all-purpose flour
½ cup buckwheat flour
pinch of salt
2 eggs
1 cup milk
½ cup water
2tbsp vegetable oil

FOR THE FILLING
6tbsp unsalted butter
½lb mushrooms, thinly sliced
4 slices of best-quality cooked ham
4½tbsp flour
2 cups milk
1 Camembert (8oz), rind removed, cut into thin slices
2tbsp crème fraîche
salt and freshly ground black pepper

For the crêpes, put the flours with the salt in a mixing bowl and make a well in the center. Break the eggs into the well and add a little milk. Whisk the eggs and milk to mix. Gradually whisk the flour into the central ingredients while pouring in the remaining milk, the water, and oil.

Let the batter stand at room temperature at least 1 hour. (Cover and refrigerate the batter if leaving it to stand longer.)

For the filling, melt half the butter in a frying pan. Add the mushrooms with a little salt and toss them in the butter over moderately high heat until they lose all their moisture, about 5 minutes.

Cut the ham into fine strips or chop it.

In a heavy saucepan, melt the remaining butter over low heat. Whisk in the flour and cook 30 seconds without letting it color. Pour in the milk, whisking constantly, and bring to a boil. Reduce the heat and gently simmer the sauce 10 minutes, whisking occasionally.

Add the cheese and stir until it melts. Add the mushrooms, ham, crème fraîche, and pepper to taste and heat through. Taste the filling and adjust the seasoning. Keep warm.

Set a 9-inch crêpe pan, lightly brushed with butter, or a nonstick frying pan over moderately high heat. The pan is hot enough when a drop of batter sizzles in the pan. Pour in 3–4 tablespoons of the batter and quickly swirl it around so it covers the bottom of the pan. Cook 1–2 minutes, then flip the crêpe and cook about 1 minute on the other side. The crêpe should be lightly colored on both sides. As the crêpes are done, stack them on a plate. (Crêpes can be made ahead and kept, wrapped in foil, in the refrigerator for a day. Reheat them in a low oven until warmed through. If necessary, reheat the filling on top of the stove, without boiling.)

Spread the filling over the crêpes. Fold them in half and in half again to make triangles, and arrange them on a warmed platter or plates. Allow two crêpes per person.

OMELETTE AUX CIVES

Spring Onion Omelet with Parsley

The Bas-Chêne farm in Saint-Victor-de-Reno is the only place I have been offered a real country supper: soup, cive omelet, pork pâté from the cellar, dandelion salad, fromage blanc still in its draining mold, and preserved pears.

Cive, which often goes by other names such as ciboule, appears fleetingly in the market during early spring, before the tender shoots develop into shallots. When briefly sautéed, they turn sweet, making a fragrant filling for an omelet. Scallions make a fine substitute.

SERVES 2
3tbsp unsalted butter
4 scallions with the greens, very thinly sliced on the diagonal
2tbsp chopped fresh parsley
5 or 6 eggs
salt and freshly ground black pepper

Melt 1 tablespoon of the butter in a frying pan. Add the onions with a little salt and pepper and cook gently until translucent, 2–3 minutes. Remove from the heat and stir in the parsley.

To make the omelet, whisk the eggs with a little salt and pepper until mixed. Heat the remaining butter in a 9-inch omelet pan until it stops sputtering. Add the eggs and stir briskly with a fork, pulling the cooked egg from the sides to the center of the pan, until the mixture is almost as thick as scrambled eggs, 15–20 seconds. Sprinkle on the onions. Leave the omelet on the heat until browned on the bottom and still runny on top if you like a moist omelet, or until almost set.

Fold the omelet, tipping the pan away from you and turning the edge with a fork. Half roll, half slide the omelet onto a warmed platter so it lands folded in three. Serve it at once, cutting it in half.

GRATIN DE POMMES AUX POIREAUX

Golden Potato and Leek Gratin

Come November, most of the vegetables in the carefully tended kitchen gardens in the Suisse Normande have been harvested. Only a few rows of leeks remain to enliven the dishes of winter.

Here sautéed leeks are tossed with potato slices and baked with stock. When the stock has been absorbed, cream and cheese are spread over the top and then the gratin is baked until brown and bubbling. This soul-satisfying gratin can accompany fish and poultry dishes as well as meat. (Illustrated opposite, left)

SERVES 4

**½lb leeks, white and light green parts
only**
2tbsp unsalted butter
**1½lb boiling potatoes, peeled and
thinly sliced**
½tsp salt
grating of nutmeg
**1¼ cups chicken stock, preferably
homemade, more if needed**
½ cup light cream
½ cup grated Gruyère cheese

Preheat the oven to 375°F.

Butter a 1½-quart gratin dish.

Slice the leeks in half lengthwise, almost through the root end, and wash them to remove all grit. Thinly slice the leeks crosswise. Heat the butter in a frying pan, add the leeks, and sauté them until translucent, 2–3 minutes.

Combine the leeks, potatoes, salt, and nutmeg in a bowl, tossing to distribute the leeks and spices evenly through the potatoes. Arrange a layer of the potato mixture, slices overlapping, in a neat pattern in the bottom of the gratin dish. Layer the potato mixture until all the ingredients are used. Add enough of the stock just to cover the potatoes.

Bake the gratin until most of the stock has been absorbed, ¾–1 hour. Spread the cream evenly over the potatoes and sprinkle with the cheese. Continue baking until golden, 20–30 minutes.

LAPIN AU CIDRE

Rabbit Braised in Cider with Bacon and Mushrooms

This recipe brings together some of Normandy's best ingredients: farm rabbit, rough cider, smoked bacon, and field mushrooms. I have tasted it made with cidre doux *and* demi-sec, *but I prefer* cidre sec *or* dry cider, *which lends a whiff of fruit without the sweetness. Golden Potato and Leek Gratin (see left) would make a good accompaniment. (Illustrated opposite, right)*

SERVES 4

**1 rabbit (about 3lb), cut into
serving pieces**
**4tbsp unsalted butter, clarified (see
page 33)**
2 shallots, preferably gray, finely chopped
1tbsp flour
2 cups dry hard cider
a large bouquet garni
salt and freshly ground black pepper

FOR THE GARNISH

½lb pearl onions
2tbsp unsalted butter
pinch of sugar
**½lb mushrooms, halved or quartered
if large**
**5-oz slab bacon, sliced into
short, thin strips**
salt

Season the pieces of rabbit with salt. Heat the clarified butter in a sauté pan just the size to hold the pieces of rabbit in a single layer. Add the rabbit and lightly brown the pieces all over, then remove them. Add the shallots to the pan and cook over low heat until translucent, 2–3 minutes.

Remove any fat from the pan. Sprinkle the flour over the shallots and cook until it browns lightly, 1–2 minutes. Stir in the cider, scraping up the browned pan juices. Return the rabbit to the pan, tuck in the bouquet garni, and bring to a boil. Reduce the heat to low, cover, and simmer until the rabbit is tender, ¾–1 hour.

Meanwhile, make the garnish. Blanch the onions in boiling water 1 minute, then drain and peel them. Trim off the roots and stems of the onions carefully so they will not fall apart during cooking. In a saucepan, combine the onions, 1 tablespoon of the butter, the sugar, a little salt, and water barely to cover. Bring to a boil and simmer until the onions are tender and the liquid has evaporated, 10–15 minutes.

Melt the remaining butter in a frying pan. Add the mushrooms with a little salt and toss them over moderately high heat until they lose all their moisture, about 5 minutes; remove. Fry the bacon gently in the same pan until golden, about 5 minutes, then drain on paper towels.

To finish, remove the pieces of rabbit to a warmed serving dish and keep warm. Strain the cooking liquid into a saucepan and add the onions, mushrooms, and bacon. Bring to a boil, reduce the heat, and simmer, skimming regularly, until the sauce will lightly coat a spoon, 10–15 minutes. Taste and adjust the seasoning. Pour the sauce over the rabbit and serve.

*RIGHT Golden Potato and Leek Gratin (left), served
with Rabbit Braised in Cider with Bacon
and Mushrooms: a perfect duo of fine, wholesome
country food, guaranteed to brighten a
dark winter evening and put the world to rights.*

ABOVE A 1926 Calvados from Isidore Lemorton (see page 100) is better reserved for leisurely sipping than flaming.

COTES DE PORC GRILLEES AU CAMEMBERT

Broiled Pork Chops with Camembert

At the grill restaurant in Alençon's Hôtel du Grand Cerf, pork chops are broiled with a topping of Camembert. The cooking in the recipe here produces tender meat that is still slightly pink in the center yet perfectly safe to eat.

Note that in this simple dish the quality of the meat and the Camembert make all the difference. With the pork, serve a few sprigs of peppery watercress, sautéed potatoes, and tomato halves browned under the broiler.

SERVES 4

4 pork chops (1in thick, each about ½lb)
a large pinch of fresh thyme leaves
1 Camembert (8oz), rind removed and cut into thin slices
salt and freshly ground black pepper

Preheat the broiler.

Sprinkle both sides of the pork chops with thyme, salt, and pepper. Put the chops on the broiler rack and cook them, about 3 inches from the heat, for 5–6 minutes. Turn them over and broil another 5–6 minutes.

Arrange the slices of Camembert on the pork chops and continue broiling until the cheese melts, 1–2 minutes. Serve immediately.

CAILLES FLAMBEES AU CALVADOS

Quails with Onions and Calvados

Dominique and François Williams turned their backs on the temptations and pressures of city life to settle in a corner of the Orne and raise quail. I worked with one of their recipe ideas until I came up with a dish that balances quail's game flavor with the sweetness of stewed onions and the thwack of Calvados and cider. With the quail, serve golden pan-fried new potatoes and buttered green beans.

SERVES 4

10tbsp unsalted butter, clarified (see page 33)
1⅔lb onions, thinly sliced
a bouquet garni
8 quails (each about ¼lb)
2tbsp Calvados
1 cup dry hard cider
salt and freshly ground black pepper

Heat half the butter in a heavy flameproof casserole (cast iron works well) just the size to hold the birds. Stir in the onions with a little salt and add the bouquet garni. Cover and cook over low heat, stirring occasionally, until the onions are very tender, about 45 minutes. Remove the onions.

Sprinkle the quails inside and out with salt and tie them with string. Heat the remaining butter in the casserole. Add the birds and lightly brown them all over, then remove them. Spoon the onions back into the casserole and set the quails on top.

Heat the Calvados in a small saucepan and light it. (It will flare up so take care.) Pour the Calvados over the quails. Add the cider and bring the liquid to a boil. Reduce the heat to low, cover, and simmer until the quails are tender, 10–15 minutes.

Remove the birds to a carving board with a juice catcher and set them aside, covered loosely with foil, to rest 10 minutes.

Meanwhile, boil the onions and cooking liquid to concentrate the flavor. Taste and adjust the seasoning. Discard the bouquet garni.

Arrange the onions and sauce on a warmed platter or plates. Discard the string from the quails and set them on the onions. Pour any juices from the birds over them and serve.

PORC ROTI AUX ECHALOTES ET AUX MARRONS

Roast Pork with Shallots and Chestnuts

This recipe practically suggested itself during one autumn trip to the Orne. The country lanes of the Domfrontais were littered with wild chestnuts, and gray shallots were for sale in all the markets. At the same time, butcher shops displayed pork roasts, all neatly tied and tempting.

Since then I have tasted similar meals on farms throughout Normandy. This is my own version of Norman pork roast.

The pork cooks en cocotte, a traditional French way of treating lean meat. It browns in butter in a casserole, shallots are added, a lid is set on top, and the ingredients are left to simmer, gently, until tender. This method produces abundant flavorful juices. For a quicker meal, farmwives often replace the fresh chestnuts with sautéed or mashed potatoes. Buttered winter squash or Brussels sprouts make a seasonal accompaniment for this cold-weather dish.

SERVES 4

1lb fresh unpeeled chestnuts
3tbsp unsalted butter
1¾-lb boneless pork roast, for pot roasting
½lb shallots, preferably gray
1 celery stalk, cut into ¼-in dice
salt and freshly ground black pepper

Make a cut in the rounded side of each chestnut, being sure to cut all the way through the outer skin. Put the chestnuts in a saucepan, cover with water, and bring to a boil over high heat. Remove the pan from the heat and set aside for 5 minutes. Remove the chestnuts, a few at a time, and peel them, making sure to remove both the outer peel and the dark inner skin.

Melt 1 tablespoon of the butter in a flameproof casserole just the size to hold the pork roast. Add the pork and brown it on all sides over moderate heat. Sprinkle with salt, cover the casserole tightly, and reduce the heat to low. Cook gently until the pork is cooked through, 45–50 minutes.

Meanwhile, trim off the tops and root ends of the shallots carefully and make a shallow cross in the base of each to prevent them from falling apart during cooking. Add the shallots to the meat with a little salt during the last half-hour of cooking.

Put the peeled chestnuts in a saucepan, add a little salt, and cover with water. Simmer over low heat until tender, 25–30 minutes. Drain.

Melt the remaining butter in a frying pan, add the celery, and cook over low heat until tender, 3–5 minutes. Add the cooked chestnuts and toss them in the butter until evenly coated. Taste and adjust the seasoning.

Transfer the pork to a carving board with a juice catcher and set it aside, loosely covered with foil, to rest 10–15 minutes. Remove the shallots with a slotted spoon and add them to the chestnuts.

To serve, cut the meat into thin slices and arrange them on a warmed platter. Surround the meat with the chestnuts and shallots. Moisten the meat and chestnuts with a little of the unthickened cooking juices and serve the rest separately.

BELOW In the fall, wild, edible chestnuts (châtaignes) *are a common sight.*

TERRINE DE CREPES A L'ORANGE

Terrine of Crêpes with Orange Caramel Sauce

Sliced, this terrine is a swirl of brown lines set in pale yellow, on an amber ground. To achieve the effect, crêpes are layered with custard sauce in a mold and served with caramel sauce. The crêpes swell and soften, making an elegant pudding.

It comes from La Renaissance, a grand old hotel-restaurant in Argentan, with upholstered chairs, heavy napery, and serious tableware. Still, framed menus and polished butter churns make the setting welcoming. (Illustrated far left)

SERVES 10

FOR THE CREPES

1 cup flour

pinch of salt

1 egg

1 cup milk

½ cup water

3tbsp unsalted butter, melted

1tbsp Calvados

FOR THE EGG CUSTARD SAUCE

3 cups milk

14tbsp sugar

8 egg yolks

2tbsp *pommeau*, or to taste

2 envelopes unflavored gelatin

6tbsp water

FOR THE CARAMEL SAUCE

1 cup sugar

¼ cup water

scant 1 cup orange juice

LEFT Terrine of Crêpes with Orange Caramel Sauce (left) and Apple Terrine with Calvados.

For the crêpes, put the flour and salt in a mixing bowl and make a well in the center. Break the egg into the well, add a little milk, and whisk to mix. Gradually beat the flour into the central ingredients while pouring in the remaining milk and the water. Set the batter aside to stand at least 1 hour. (Cover and chill the batter if leaving it longer.) Just before frying, beat in the butter and Calvados.

Fry the crêpes (see page 113), stacking them on a plate as they are done.

Make the egg custard sauce (see terrine recipe, right). Take the pan from the heat and stir in the *pommeau*. Taste the custard sauce and, if liked, add more *pommeau*. Keep warm.

Sprinkle the gelatin over the water and leave until it swells to a spongy consistency, about 5 minutes. Melt the gelatin over low heat, then let it cool until tepid, stirring occasionally. Stir the gelatin into the warm custard sauce. Set the pan in a bowl of ice water. Stir until it starts to thicken, then remove it from the ice water. Pour a little of the custard sauce into a 1½-quart terrine mold just to cover the bottom. Arrange half a crêpe on top, letting the other half flop over one side of the mold. Pour a little more of the custard sauce on top, then fold over the other half of the crêpe. Continue layering the custard sauce and crêpes in this way until all the ingredients are used, ending with a layer of custard sauce. Cover the terrine and chill it until set, at least 2 hours.

For the caramel sauce, have ready a bowl of cold water. Combine the sugar and water in a small heavy saucepan and heat gently until the sugar dissolves, stirring often. Continue cooking over moderately low heat, without stirring, until the sugar syrup turns a deep amber color. Dip the base of the pan in the cold water to stop the cooking. Pour the orange juice into the caramel. It will sputter so be careful not to get burnt. Return the pan to moderate heat and stir the orange juice thoroughly into the caramel until melted and evenly blended. Cool to room temperature.

To serve, take the terrine from the refrigerator about 10 minutes before serving it. Run a knife around the terrine and turn it out onto a platter. (The terrine will turn out more easily if you dip the mold briefly in hot water.) Cut the terrine into thin slices and arrange them on dessert plates. Pour the caramel sauce around the edge. Pass the remaining sauce separately.

TERRINE DE POMMES AU CALVADOS

Apple Terrine with Calvados

With its taste of apple and buttery caramel, this pudding reminds me of tarte Tatin. But here the caramelized apples are molded in a terrine and set with gelatin.

At La Renaissance, Alain Autin cooks the apples in butter and sugar until they turn a deep brown. Then he layers them with drops of Calvados and bakes them. He serves the terrine cool with a crème anglaise, laced with pommeau. *(Illustrated opposite, right)*

SERVES 10
3tbsp unsalted butter
¼ cup sugar
4½lb small firm apples, cored, peeled, and quartered
1 envelope unflavored gelatin
2tbsp Calvados

FOR THE EGG CUSTARD SAUCE
2 cups milk
⅓ cup sugar
5 egg yolks
1½tbsp *pommeau*, or to taste

Preheat the oven to 300°F.
Butter a 1½-quart terrine mold.

Melt the butter in a large frying pan. Add the sugar and cook, stirring, over moderate heat until the sugar caramelizes. (It will look like boiling paste.) Add the apples and cook, turning them often so they do not stick, until they are tender, 15–20 minutes. Increase the heat to moderately high and continue cooking the apples until they are deep brown, 5–10 minutes longer.

Arrange a layer of apples, rounded side down, in the bottom of the mold. Sprinkle with a little gelatin and Calvados. Continue layering the apples, gelatin, and Calvados until all the ingredients are used, finishing with a sprinkling of Calvados.

Press a piece of buttered foil on top and set the mold in a simmering water bath. Bake 45 minutes.

Remove the terrine mold from the oven and the water bath. Set weights on top (cans of food work nicely) to pack down the contents, and let the terrine cool to room temperature. Then chill the terrine, with the weights, until set, at least 2 hours or overnight.

For the egg custard sauce, heat the milk with the sugar in a saucepan, stirring, until it just begins to boil. Take the pan from the heat. Beat the egg yolks and slowly whisk in the hot milk. Pour this mixture back into the pan and cook over low heat, stirring constantly with a wooden spatula, until the custard sauce thickens enough to coat the spatula, 18–20 minutes. Take the pan from the heat and let cool to room temperature. Stir in the *pommeau*. Taste the custard sauce and, if liked, add more *pommeau*.

To serve, take the terrine from the refrigerator about 10 minutes before serving it and remove the weights and foil. Run a knife around the terrine and carefully turn it out onto a platter. (The terrine will turn out more easily if you dip the mold briefly in hot water.) Cut the terrine into thin slices and arrange them on dessert plates. Pour the custard sauce around the edge. Pass the remaining custard sauce separately.

TOP Fishing nets at Granville.
ABOVE A mud house in Marchesieux, a village in
the Parc Régional Marais du Cotentin.
This park occupies a swampy coastal plain that
extends from the center of the Cotentin peninsula
into eastern Calvados. Its mud buildings
are curious and characteristic.
RIGHT Strings of mussels wrapped around bouchots
in Pirou-Plage, where the growing and harvesting
of seafood is both a skilled business and a way of
life for many generations of fishermen.

MANCHE

ABOVE Views of the extraordinary pinnacle of Mont-Saint-Michel dominate the southern parts of Manche. The famous salt-marsh sheep graze the water-flattened meadows all around.
LEFT Jacques Leterrier's flat-topped brioches cooling on a rack in Le Vast (see page 126).

More than in any other *département* in Normandy, in the Manche, the sea shapes the way people live. Orne is landlocked and Eure has no ports. Seine-Maritime and Calvados have two basic cultures: land and sea. In those *départements*, fishermen and farmers come into contact rarely, only at markets, and then they return to their separate communities.

But in the Manche, or Cotentin as this western peninsula jutting into the English Channel is often called, the sea culture blends with that of the interior. At any point in the Manche you are no more than 30 miles from the sea. Nowhere do the labors of farmers and fishermen overlap more.

Everywhere, diners glory in seafood, poultry, salt-marsh lamb, pork, and *sauce normande* – a white sauce enriched with meat or fish essence. Throughout the Manche, cider is made in the fall, followed by Calvados until late September of the following year.

THE COTENTIN COAST

The sea laps Pirou-Plage at 10 o'clock on this drab June morning, and water spans the horizon. Except for a half-dozen beached tractors and several dories anchored offshore, there is no sign of human life at the water's edge. With 205 miles of coastline on the Cotentin peninsula, the rhythm of the tides affects life here as much as the weather.

Pirou sits on a flat stretch of dune and beach midway up the west coast of the Manche. It doesn't have a harbor. Indeed, the only port between Mont Saint Michel and Carteret is at Granville.

At 12:30 the sky has brightened somewhat and, with the tide high but ebbing, the first boat appears in the distance off Pirou beach. But while still at sea, anchor is dropped near a dory. Fishermen pass baskets of whelks and crabs into the dory, then hop in and chug the short distance to land.

One of the men leaps into the water and wades ashore. He scampers up the beach to a tractor-trailor, then drives it to the dory, backing it right into the water. Now the other fishermen leap off and steer the boat onto the trailer. When the boat is secured they jump in with their cargo, and the tractor drives off, towing its load.

By 1:30 pm the retreating sea reveals the first of the metal oyster tables in the "park," or oyster farm, on the left-hand side of Pirou beach. The tractors that were left on the beach this morning have all been claimed, and now each driver waits his turn to drive up the concrete ramp leading from the seashore into Pirou.

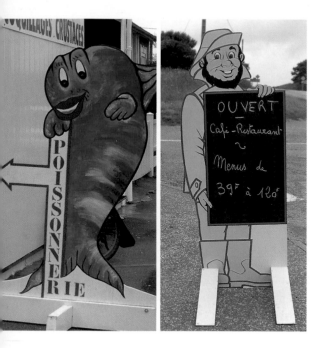

ABOVE The work of local sign painters makes a visit to a restaurant or fish shop almost irresistible.
ABOVE RIGHT In villages where there are no ports, the fishermen bring their dories, loaded with oysters, mussels, whelks, or crabs, close to the water's edge. A tractor is driven into the sea to tow the dory out, so the harvest can find its way to market.
RIGHT The oyster parks at Pirou-Plage.

The crabs and whelks harvested near Pirou will be simmered by cooks in salted water, with or without a bouquet garni, then left to cool and served with homemade mayonnaise. Or they will be added to heaped platters of raw shellfish.

At 2 pm the sun shines brightly on Pirou's oyster and mussel parks. Now that sand flats replace water on the horizon, travel movement switches direction.

Dressed in shorts and waders, shrimp and clam fishermen walk across the squishy beach in twos and threes. Fishing nets and rakes balance over one shoulder. Wicker baskets are slung over the other shoulder and hang down to the hips. These baskets are round on one side and flat on the other, where they jostle against the body.

A procession of tractors rolls past to the now-uncovered parks, mussel growers to the north, oystermen to the south. Norman oysters are not fattened in protected gulfs and estuaries but in the open sea, washed twice a day by the tide.

Some of the oyster tables are as close to the shoreline as 650 feet. Others, holding the youngest oysters, are as far away as 6 miles, where a neap tide covers them most of the time.

The metal tables reach to about your knee. On each table lies a single layer of plastic mesh sacks, called *poches*, filled with oysters. They are strapped to the table with rubber bands. When raised above the sea floor, oysters are less vulnerable to enemies, sea mud, and shifting sands.

Out in the parks, seaweed suffuses the air with its briny smell. Oystermen clean the *poches* of clinging algae and seaweed so water can circulate freely. They also shake the sacks and even out the layer of oysters to equalize their chances of feeding on the phyto-plankton that floats by on the tide. All around you hear popping noises as the oysters open and close their shells.

When the growing oysters start to fill the sacks, they are hauled inland on tractors to be sorted. Oysters that have stuck together are pried apart. Now fewer of them are placed in new *poches* with larger mesh holes and then they are returned to the sea. One oystergrower calculated that each oyster is worked 36 times during its four year life.

This scene of oystermen on tractors plays not just at Pirou but on other beaches along both the west and east coasts of the Manche. When you dine in any of the fish restaurants in one of the oyster villages, you'll be served "*les huîtres d'ici*," as though there weren't any other oysters but these in the whole world. These oysters are the plump, oval Portuguese, known locally as *speciales*. The flat, round Belon oysters have virtually disappeared since 1982.

Though some restaurants cook with oysters, the preferred way to eat them is raw, on the half shell, with lemon juice or shallot and vinegar sauce, and plenty of white wine to drink.

Like oystermen, mussel farmers commute to work on tractors. As at Pirou, the mussel parks are always separated from the oyster area as mussels are faster growing and big eaters. They would quickly take over the food supply.

Mussels *de bouchots* also grow in the open sea in a fashion similar to oysters, but not on tables. Instead, they are in long mesh tubes twirled around *bouchots*, wooden stakes the size of telephone poles that are driven deep into the sand to withstand the stresses of tides and storms.

But mussels are harvested from boats as well as tractors. Off Barfleur, on the northeast tip of the Manche, wild mussels are fished with a dredge. Just as for scallop fishing elsewhere along the coast, regulations limit mussel dragging here to certain hours to prevent exhausting the *moulières*, or mussel beds.

OPEN-SEA OYSTERS

Around Blainville-sur-Mer, one of the major oyster-growing corners in Normandy, oystermen putter along, hauling loads of oyster sacks. "They are bringing them in from the oyster parks to work on them," says Jocelyne Ruault, member of CABANOR, the co-operative of independent oystergrowers in Blainville.

The beaches in the Manche slope so gently that when the sea recedes twice each day it uncovers a vast plain favorable for raising creuses, *the crinkly long oysters. Because oystergrowers here travel to the parks on tractors like farmers, they are called* paysans de la mer, *or fishermen-farmers. From the west coast of the Manche, as well as Saint-Vaast-la-Hougue and Isigny — the two other oyster regions — come 20,000 tons of oysters annually, nearly one-fifth the national total.*

Each "cru" of oysters has its own character. The oysters from the west coast are briny, tasting of Mont-Saint-Michel bay. Saint-Vaast is known for oysters with hazelnut overtones, Isigny for plump, meaty specimens.

Along with the mussels, *pétoncles* (tiny scallops), *palourdes* (a kind of clam), and cockles are all pulled up with metal nets. They are also cooked in the same ways – most simply just steamed open with a little white wine or dry cider. You can eat them scalding hot, as is, or plucked from their shells and folded into an omelet or tossed in an herbed vinaigrette. One popular recipe in the Manche grills the opened shellfish with garlic butter until bubbling (see page 136). Shellfish sautéed still in the shell with scallions and parsley is also wonderful.

But there are more unusual ways to fish than dredging, raking, digging in the warm sand with toes and even fishing by tractor. Traditional gray-mullet-fishing must be the most exotic custom.

Near the lambs that graze in the salt marshes around Mont-Saint-Michel bay, a few lone fishermen gently swing their cantilevered nets into the shallows. A spindly pole, stuck in the soft gray mud between the legs of each fisherman, supports the net, which hangs like an upside-down parachute.

The fishermen's feet slip in the silt as they dip their nets, hoping to catch the black-backed *mulets* as they swim by. Over and over they swivel the nets, moving them clockwise into the water. All too often the fishermen hoist heavy murky water but no fish.

Housewives in the Manche commonly poach the mullet – or salmon, skate, or other fish – in a court-bouillon, and serve it with boiled potatoes and a sauce of crème fraîche and mushrooms.

Although salt-marsh lambs come under the umbrella of farming and not fishing, they, too, are affected by the flux of the tides. The sea washes over their pastures and flavors their food. And if the grass is too salty, the lambs get sick. Every so often a sheep dawdles in the marshes and is caught in the rising tide. Some get stuck in quicksand-like potholes left behind by the receding tide.

The best-known *pré-salé* (salt-marsh) lambs feed in the salt meadows around Mont-Saint-Michel bay (see right). But authentic salt-marsh lambs also graze in the salty grasslands along the Cotentin coast in Régnéville-sur-Mer, Geffosses, Portbail, and Bricqueville-sur-Mer.

THE INLAND MANCHE

Normally it takes only a few minutes to motor between the fishing ports of Saint-Vaast-la-Hougue and Barfleur in northeastern Manche. But when cauliflower is at its peak in the Val de Saire, the jaunt can take twice as long. It is hard to make any progress behind all the tractors harvesting and bringing the crop to market on this coastal route. Better to relax and enjoy the view. "Vegetables and seafood," one resident of the area told me. "That is all there is here."

In the mild Saire Valley, fields of early vegetables stretch practically to the seashore. Still, for all the hungry farmers and fishermen, a few bakers provide the daily bread.

In addition to the *baguettes* and round country loaves found everywhere in France, *boulangers* in northern Manche continue to make strictly regional breads – *pains de Cherbourg* as they are called in this part of France. Even the modern bakeries in Bricquebec and Cherbourg list *pain plié, la gâche*, and *pain à soupe* (see page 126) on their pre-printed price sheets.

But few bakers still rise at five every morning to light the wood that will heat their oven. Jacques Leterrier, with his blue eyes and firm handshake, may do many things the old way in his *boulangerie* in Le Vast, but he prefers to fuel his 70-year-old wood-burning oven with the hardwood planks that lean against his bakery, not with faggots and gorse the way the old-timers did. And his bread is made

LEFT *Norman cows graze in sight of the sea and the
Goury lighthouse, Cap de la Hague.
With the sea never more than 30 miles
away anywhere in Manche,
the overlap between fishermen and farmers is
part of the distinctive culture of the area.*
BELOW *Mullet fishing at the mouth of the Séline
river near Mont-Saint-Michel. The scene could be a
subject for a traditional Chinese painting in ink
and pale brown and gray wash on paper.*

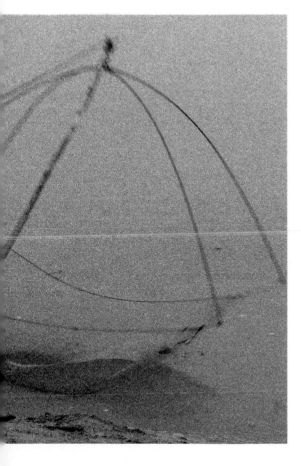

SALT-MARSH LAMBS

*It is a few days before Good Friday and, in salt-
meadow territory around Mont-Saint-Michel bay,
couturier-butchers dress their spring lambs with
colorful braids of camellias and paper frills.
Still, many butchers' windows are unornamented,
snubbing the age-old Easter custom.
"Traditions are disappearing, little by little," says
Jean-Robert Tiercelin, a butcher in Pontorson
near the Mont. "Twenty years ago all the lambs
were decorated."
Monsieur Tiercelin is one of only two local butchers
who still buy their lambs, on the hoof, from farmers
near Pontorson. His lambs are not the ordinary
variety, spending their lives in the sheep-pen. These
are* grévin *lambs, which graze in the* grèves, *or salt
marshes, around Mont Saint-Michel.
At Easter, Monsieur Tiercelin sells 60 to 70 of these
lambs, compared to the average 25 a week and
only 15 in winter. In addition to his shop, this
butcher supplies* grévins *to local restaurants,
including Mère Poulard, Au Vent des Grèves, Hôtel
Montgomery, and Terrasses Poulard.
Guy Lemouland is a typical pré-salé (salt-marsh)
lamb farmer. Monsieur Lemouland's flock
numbers 250* brebis *or mothers and as many*

*lambs. As these sheep are not good milkers, each
mother can feed only one lamb.
Like most lamb farmers here, Lemouland also does
other things to help pay the rent, like growing
carrots and taking in overnight guests. He tries to
arrange the lambing for when he and his wife
have time to care for the new-borns. Today, with
shepherds a luxury most farmers cannot afford,
they care for the flock themselves.
Each morning, they lead the black-faced* agneaux
de pré salé *out to the salt meadows, where the
lambs graze unchaperoned. During the day flocks
from different farmers mingle in the pastures.
These athletic animals cover nine to ten miles
each day in search of tasty local grasses that thrive
in this marshland covered by the sea during
the lunar tides. At nightfall, the flocks sort
themselves out and head home.
As a result of this far-ranging grazing from the
tender age of six weeks, there is little fat on the flesh
of the* grévin. *The meat is compact and fine-
textured, but still butter-like.
The flocks pasture in the* grèves *in all weather
unless the tide is exceptionally high or it is
unseasonably cold. "Last time it snowed," said
Monsieur Lemouland, "some sheep could not find
their way back to the* bergerie."

BREAD LIKE OLD TIMES

*On Sunday mornings there is a traffic jam in Le
Vast just past the cauliflower fields in front
of the bakery. In this village near
Saint-Vaast-la-Hougue, Jacques Leterrier is the
last baker to fire up his 1920s'
wood-burning oven for regional breads and
coarse-textured, buttery brioches
(above and above right).*

To make pain plié, *Monsieur Leterrier pats the
dough into a pancake, makes a crease
in the middle with his arm, and folds the dough
in half. Baked, it looks like a swollen turnover.*

La gâche *uses the same dough, but is flat
and looks like a frisbee. When baked for three
hours,* les gâches *become* pains à soupe,
which last practically forever.

What is the best way to keep pain plié *and* la gâche?
*Monsieur Leterrier is against bread boxes,
which he calls moisture traps. "The best thing is to
put them on the shelf above the kitchen table,"
he says. "That is what they still do
on the old farms I deliver to."*

ABOVE Apple tarts from the Courbaron bakery in Bricquebec; despite the dominance of the sea in this region, the culture of fruit-growing is almost as strong as elsewhere in the province. Baking traditions are alive and well in Manche, and even many of the modern bakeries here make top-quality pastries and regional breads. Sadly this is not so true of other regions of Normandy. LEFT The elegance of an old-fashioned pâtisserie, Cherbourg.

with some yeast, not pure sourdough starter. "People do not like that sourdough taste any more," he explains. "It is too acidic."

As soon as the oven reaches baking temperature, Monsieur Leterrier rakes the coals from the oven floor. With a bread paddle, he sends the loaves into the depths of the oven. First he fills the oven with *la gâche*, a puffy beret-shaped bread that bakes quickly before the other breads are added. *La gâche* is meant to be eaten the day it is baked.

Next the oven receives folded loaves of *pain plié*. Just folding the dough makes it a denser loaf than ordinary country bread. Monsieur Leterrier also makes flat-topped brioches, which he bakes once the heat diminishes after several *fournées* (or batches) of *pain plié, pain de campagne,* and *baguette.* His brioches are coarser and more buttery than the average.

Though their shapes may differ from other familiar breads, *pain plié, la gâche,* and brioche fall into the category of recognizable baked goods. The *pain à soupe,* however, is more curious. Deep brown and hard from long cooking, with mostly crust and little crumb, *pain à soupe* is twice-baked bread. It begins life as a *gâche,* baked at the highest temperature. Then it is removed and baked again for hours at a lower temperature. This bread does not go stale; it endures.

Pain à soupe, a bread hard enough to crack a tooth, was a staple in modest households in northern Manche until the 1950s. Every day, for breakfast as well as supper, ordinary people broke this bread into a *guichon* or unglazed pottery soup bowl and moistened it with *soupe à la graisse,* a nourishing vegetable and herb soup enriched with clarified suet (not butter).

When all the bread has been baked, the oven still holds a very hot temperature – about 475°F. It is now that Monsieur Leterrier pushes a roasting pan with a leg of lamb into the oven for Sunday lunch. "It will cook an hour and a quarter like that," he says. "This is the best way to cook it."

Numerous cheese factories in the Manche today produce Camembert, Pont-l'Evêque, and Coutances, a new raw-milk cheese. Yet there is no history of cheesemaking in the area. Farmers raised cows for milk, and once a week they churned butter from the cream. The closest farmers came to cheesemaking was with *fromage blanc* and *la piquette,* fresh curds that farmers still sell at market even today. *La piquette* is curdled milk that has not completely drained; *fromage blanc* is completely drained.

La piquette is served for dessert in the summer, with or without sugar. It is even better when blended with cream and fruits from the garden: raspberries or strawberries, for example. *La piquette* permits using milk that may have accidentally curdled during a summer storm.

The coastal plain that extends from the center of the Cotentin peninsula into eastern Calvados is low country, a place so localized that it is distinct even from the Val de Saire to the north and wooded Bocage to the south. The Vire, Taute, and Douve rivers, along with myriad tributaries and canals, form an intricate network of inland waterways that have provided a way of life here for centuries. Cargo boats used to ply these backwaters, ferrying people to church and goods to market. Fishermen caught eels in the rivers, and eel stew (see page 138) is still frequently included on auberge menus in the region.

Even today any family with a hearth has the right to graze one horse or two cows in the marshes, based on a system of common ownership. And a wickerware company in Remilly-sur-Lozon still weaves a variety of baskets with the rushes that grow in these wetlands, just the way country people have done for generations.

COPPERWARE COUNTRY

*Where do all those gleaming pots that hang
in restaurant kitchens come from? Most are
made in small foundries in the land of
copperware, Villedieu-les-Poêles. All the
untinned preserving kettles and sugar pans,
pommes Anna pans, tarte Tatin molds, and heavy
saucepans you have ever coveted crowd shop
windows in this medieval town.
Each shopkeeper claims to possess real copperware
from Villedieu and puts you on guard against
fakery. One way to sort through the offerings is to
visit the Atelier du Cuivre, an old copper workshop,
where metal is still worked on lathes by hand.
It is hard to understand the introductory film here,
for all the hammering in the background,
but still you glean the basic stages in making a
yellow-copper canne à lait, the traditional
pot-bellied milk flagon in the Manche. After the film
you can watch the copperworkers welding,
soldering, molding, and tinning just as artisans
have done for nine centuries in Villedieu.*

A THEATRICAL OMELET

*After a hike up Mont-Saint-Michel and a breath-
taking view of sea and sky, pause before the glass
doors at La Mère Poulard for the mealtime show.
The entrance to the restaurant acts as stage.
A towering wood pile is stacked next to the hearth,
ready for the week's omelets.
Baskets of brown eggs and mounds of butter
await the next order.
A buffet with recessed shelves and dairy armoire,
its doors of sheet-iron pierced for aeration,
stands against one wall.
A yellow-copper milk can and sumptuously carved
armoire complete the set.
Dressed in Norman smocks and black caps, men
with thick biceps whip up the famous omelet in
front of you. They beat the eggs rhythmically
in giant copper bowls with balloon whisks
until the volume quadruples.
The fluffy eggs are poured into a long-handled
frying pan and cooked in the flames
until the omelet puffs like a soufflé.*

SMOKEHOUSE HAMS

*Summer and winter, smoke rises from the
chimney of Les Jambons d'Antan in
La Chapelle-en-Juger. "Everyone used to
smoke his own ham on the farm," says Jacques
Lerouxel, owner of this smokehouse near
Saint-Lô. "But today fewer people keep a fire
burning in the hearth."*

*Since 1987, Monsieur Lerouxel has been stoking
slow-burning elm wood to smoke the meat he buys
locally. He has made a window along one side of
his smoker, which faces his no-frills shop, so clients
can see his hams are not artificially cured.*

*He first rubs the hams with seasoned salt and
leaves them to cure for three weeks. The hams are
then brushed and washed. A sock is slipped on
and the hams are smoked for four or five weeks.
He first hangs them on a low rung, then raises
them progressively during smoking.
Finally the hams are moved to a cold room for
four to six weeks, where they age to perfection.*

In the village of Mesnilbus, you can stay the night at the Auberge des Bonnes Gens. Here you can sample (if you call ahead) the virtually extinct daily fare of the area: *soupe à la graisse, fricassée de sarrasin*, made with buckwheat, and *jarret aux choux* or ham hocks with boiled cabbage.

In the Hague, the rugged northwest corner of the Manche, farmers still graze their cows next to the sea in small plots delimited by hedges and dry stone walls. The landscape has barely changed since Jean-François Millet painted "Norman Dairymaid in Gréville" here in 1874. In this oil, a milkmaid returns from the cow pasture balancing a milk flagon on one shoulder. Behind her in the twilight, a cow scratches its neck on a picket fence.

The rare *roussin de Vauville* lambs also pasture on these moors, covered with gorse in spring and heather in summer. They overlook the most dramatic seascape in Normandy: the craggy Ecalgrain bay and wild, windswept Nez de Jobourg promontory. Here the sea spray shapes the trees as it blows off the water, and the dark huddled villages resemble Brittany more than Normandy.

Besides lamb, other meat has always been plentiful in farm kitchens. The butcher provided less-expensive cuts not available at home. Poultry – chicken, guinea fowl, goose – and rabbit were common, and each often had its own day in the week. Friday was reserved for fish, and Sunday, invariably, for pot-au-feu.

The family pigs also provided a major source of food, and pork remains important today. Norman dampness makes preserving by drying absurd, so farmers traditionally smoke ham (on the bone), bacon, and sausage in the chimney. The fire does not burn hot enough to cook the meat; that would melt the fat. In Normandy, *jambon fumé* (see left) means raw but cured and smoked ham. Few people smoke their own hams nowadays, but if they raise pigs they may bring the hams to a smokehouse for *façonnage*, that is, for curing and smoking. In the Manche and western Calvados, where most of the smoking is done, ham is eaten either raw like prosciutto or cut into thick slices and then grilled or pan-fried and served with shallots and a cider sauce (see page 139).

While you see plenty of country terrines in *charcuteries* in the Manche today, they are recent imports. The meat that goes to make pâté or *rillettes* was traditionally forced into natural casing to make pork sausages. In the southern town of Saint-Hilaire-de-Harcouët, the Vikings du Bocage, a gastronomic brotherhood, organizes a sausage competition every year in June. *Saucisses* – fresh sausages as opposed to *saucissons*, the dried variety – are popular fried, grilled, and poached and are served with cabbage or Brussels sprouts.

Perhaps the best way to get an overview of the Manche, past and present, is to visit the country fair in Lessay, celebrated every year in September. Lessay sits halfway up the western side of the Cotentin, close by the mollusk farms of Pirou, the sandy fields of carrots and leeks in Créances (see opposite), and the salt-marsh grazing land of Geffosses.

The biggest fiesta in the Manche and one of the oldest in Normandy, this *foire de la Sainte-Croix* draws farmers, butchers, and livestock dealers as well as tourists. For four days fathers haggle over chains and tractor parts outside the livestock market (cows, horses, hunting dogs, and sheep – each has its day), while children enjoy the fairground rides. When they get hungry, the throngs move between wine and cider stands and tents where *rôtisseurs* tend sausages and legs of lamb on spits.

This is how people amuse themselves and get their business done in the Manche even today. Victor Letouzé, carrot farmer and president of the vegetable co-op in Créances near Lessay, agrees people in the Cotentin have not changed much: "We still keep our feet on the ground."

AN UNCOMMON CARROT

*The rain continues steadily as another tractor
backs up to the loading bay at Co-op Créances with
a wagonful of carrots. "The farmers bring them
in from mid-August to mid-May," says Victor
Letouzé, president of the vegetable co-operative and
a carrot and leek farmer here. "The co-op takes
care of washing and grading them."*
These are pedigree carrots, crowned with an AOC
since 1960. The appellation recognizes that,
like the best wines and cheeses, the carottes
de Créances *are unique.*
According to legend, their cultivation began as an
act of desperation by a local boy who
inherited no land. For his birthright, this spunky
farmer took the worthless mielles,
the reclaimed land by the sea. He nourished the sand
with the seaweed that washed up on the shore
and planted his seeds. Salty droplets watered
the developing shoots. The sandy carrots grew up
iodine-rich, deep orange, and with no woody core.

RESTAURANT LA MER

PIROU PLAGE, TEL 33 46 43 36

Do not come here expecting a black-tie maître d'hotel, polished silver, and baronial tables. At Restaurant La Mer, set on Pirou beach, locals feast on seafood platters at bargain prices. This is the place the marketing director of the vegetable co-operative in Créances takes his clients for glistening shellfish gathered a few feet from the restaurant's door.

The skyscraper plateau de fruits de mer *here comes posed on its pyramidal rack, leaving space below for such necessary accompaniments as lemons, shallot and vinegar sauce, chilled Muscadet, fresh, crusty bread, and butter. The* plateau *is loaded with delicious Pirou oysters, crabs,* langoustines, *whelks, shrimp, periwinkles, and clams.*

La Mer is not a fisherman's shack but a proper restaurant. However good the food, though, it is the panoramic view through the wrap-around windows that makes the dining room unique. As you plough through a mound of the very freshest shellfish, you can watch oystermen in yellow overalls heading out to the oyster parks on tractors, while other fishermen glide past, their wicker baskets laden with clams and whelks.

ABOVE Smoked Trout Salad with Avocados (recipe opposite).
RIGHT A heaping seafood platter as served at the Restaurant La Mer.

SALADE DE TRUITE FUMEE AUX AVOCATS

Smoked Trout Salad with Avocados

Here creamy avocado is blended with the smokiness of cured fish in an appealing salad from Restaurant La Mer. Chives and lemon juice add a fresh taste. The look of this dish is beautiful, too: pink and yellow-green slices alternate on a pile of greens. It is ideal for a summer lunch or to start an evening meal. (Illustrated far left)

SERVES 4

6oz mixed salad greens, such as romaine and red-leaf lettuce, lamb's lettuce (mâche), curly endive, Belgian endive, and watercress
1tbsp snipped fresh chives
2 avocados
½lb thinly sliced smoked sea trout, or salmon fillets

FOR THE DRESSING

1tbsp lemon juice
¼ cup vegetable oil
salt and freshly ground black pepper

Make the dressing: Whisk together the lemon juice and a little salt until the salt dissolves. Whisk in the oil and a little pepper until smooth.

Combine the salad greens and chives with the dressing in a bowl and toss until evenly coated. Taste for seasoning.

Peel, pit, and thinly slice the avocados. Cut the trout fillets in slices of about the same size as the avocado slices.

Arrange the dressed salad greens in small mounds on individual plates. Alternate the slices of trout and avocado on the greens in a pattern like the spokes of a wheel, and serve.

LA VERTE CAMPAGNE

LE HAMEAU CHEVALIER, TRELLY, TEL 33 47 65 33

Hidden in the countryside south of Coutances is La Verte Campagne, a dream of an inn covered in roses and ivy. Before you settle into a comfy dining room, you will be invited to sip an apéritif and choose your meal in the parlor. Here, a fire glows in the stone hearth, and darting flames reflect in your glass.

It is easy to warm to the cooking, too. Pascal Bernou, the chef-patron, apprenticed in some of the finest kitchens in France before falling in love with this manor of 1717 and starting out on his own. With his wife, Caroline, he is gradually sprucing up La Verte Campagne. And he is determined to bring the quality of the food up to the standard of the setting.

All the bread comes straight from his ovens, the herbs used in the dishes are picked in the garden at the back, and the menu is always stuck with bits of paper reflecting Monsieur Bernou's latest culinary inspiration.

A vintage Calvados follows dinner. Then you can float up to one of the inn's eight rooms for a sound sleep.

RAGOUT DE HOMARD DE CHAUSEY AU VIN MOELLEUX

Chausey Lobster in Ginger and Lime Sauce

The seafood Pascal Bernou serves at La Verte Campagne comes from nearby Granville, a minor commercial harbor compared to Cherbourg, but actually more important than Cherbourg as a fishing port.

Granville also offers passenger service to the Chausey Islands, a small archipelago of granite islands, where fishermen hunt for lobsters amid the islets and reefs.

In this recipe, Monsieur Bernou simmers these just-out-of-the-sea lobsters, briefly, in a court-bouillon, then quickly sautés the lobster meat in fruity olive oil. For a sauce, he infuses fresh gingerroot in sweet white wine, whisks in butter, and adds droplets of lime juice. Baby vegetables and herbs provide the garnish.

Though Monsieur Bernou changes his menu at whim, he insists this dish is a classic and will stick around. With the lobster, try a lightly chilled sweet white wine – Côteaux du Layon, Jurançon, Sauternes, Bonnezeaux.

SERVES 4

FOR THE LOBSTERS AND COURT-BOUILLON
1 onion, thinly sliced
1 carrot, thinly sliced
a bouquet garni
2¼qt water
1¼ cups dry white wine
4 live lobsters (each about 1lb)
15 black peppercorns, crushed
2tbsp extra-virgin olive oil

FOR THE GARNISH
8 baby leeks or scallions, trimmed to 2½in
8 baby carrots, peeled
1 cup shelled fresh fava beans or fresh or frozen, thawed green peas
1tbsp unsalted butter, cut into pieces
sprigs of mixed fresh herbs, such as chives, dill, and lemon grass

FOR THE SAUCE
1 cup sweet white wine
1½oz fresh gingerroot, peeled and cut into ¼-in pieces
10tbsp unsalted butter, cut into pieces
2tsp lime juice, or to taste
salt and freshly ground white pepper

For the court-bouillon, combine the onion, carrot, bouquet garni, water, and a little salt in a stockpot. Bring to a boil, then reduce the heat and simmer 15 minutes. Add the wine and continue simmering another 15 minutes.

Add the lobsters and peppercorns to the court-bouillon and bring back to a boil. Cover and simmer over moderate heat 3 minutes. Remove the lobsters to a platter and let them cool completely. Discard the court-bouillon.

To prepare the garnish, steam the vegetables, separately, until tender, 3–5 minutes. Rinse in cold water and drain thoroughly.

For the sauce, combine the wine and ginger with a little salt in a heavy saucepan. Bring to a boil, then reduce the heat and simmer until reduced by half. Gradually whisk in the butter over very low heat so the butter doesn't melt completely but softens to form a smooth sauce. Add the lime juice and season to taste. Strain the sauce and keep it warm in a water bath.

To finish, dry the lobsters well, then separate the tails and claws from the heads. Crack the claws gently and try to remove the meat in one piece. Remove the tail meat from the shells. If you like, save the lobster heads and the lower portion of the empty tail for the garnish.

Heat the olive oil in a large frying pan over moderately high heat. Add the pieces of lobster meat and sauté them quickly on both sides until heated through, about 2 minutes. Cut the tail meat of each lobster into ¼-inch slices.

Put the garnish vegetables in a frying pan with the butter and seasoning. Toss until heated through.

To serve, mound a quarter of the vegetables in the center of each warmed plate. Set the sliced tail meat on top, lifting each portion with a metal spatula to keep the slices together. Place a lobster head at the top of the plate and the tail shell at the bottom, if you like. Arrange the claw meat at the sides. Spoon the sauce over the lobster and garnish the plate with herbs. Serve immediately.

COROLLE D'ABRICOTS AU BEURRE D'ORANGES

Caramelized Apricots in Orange Butter Sauce

When I first visited La Verte Campagne in 1992, I wasn't expecting much on the food front. I had heard the farm manor was charming but the cooking was indifferent. However, Pascal Bernou and his lovely wife, Caroline, had taken over this secluded spot just the month before. And I knew from my first meal there that a talented chef was in the kitchen. This apricot dessert looks beautiful and tastes wonderful.

SERVES 4
½ cup sugar
16 apricots, halved and pitted
4 crêpes (see page 113), or 4 thin slices
gingerbread or toasted brioche, crusts
removed
4 scoops vanilla ice cream

TO DECORATE (OPTIONAL)
16 raspberries
fresh mint leaves

FOR THE SAUCE
½ cup sugar
2tbsp water
scant 1 cup orange juice
4tbsp unsalted butter, cut into pieces

For the sauce, combine the sugar and water in a small heavy saucepan. Heat gently until the sugar melts, stirring often. Continue cooking over moderately low heat, without stirring, until the sugar turns a deep amber color. Dip the base of the pan in cold water to stop the cooking. Pour the orange juice into the caramel. (It will sputter so take care.) Return the pan to moderate heat and stir the orange juice thoroughly into the caramel until melted and smooth. Cook the caramel sauce until it thickens, 3–5 minutes.

Allow the sauce to cool slightly, then gradually whisk in the butter so it softens but doesn't melt completely. Keep the sauce warm in a water bath.

Spread the sugar in a deep dish and coat the cut sides of the apricots with sugar. Set a large nonstick frying pan over moderately high heat. Arrange the apricot halves, sugar-side down, in the pan and cook on one side only until caramelized.

To serve, put a crêpe or a slice of gingerbread or brioche in the center of each plate. Arrange 8 apricot halves in a ring around the edge. Set a scoop of ice cream in the center. Spoon the sauce around the apricots. If you like, decorate each plate with raspberries and mint leaves. Serve at once. Pass any remaining sauce separately.

PETONCLES FARCIES

Scallops Broiled with Garlic and Herb Butter

Snail butter belongs in Burgundy, right? Yes, but not exclusively. Cooks in the Cotentin pair the garlicky herb butter not with snails but with the plentiful mollusks that are harvested along the shore. These sizzling pétoncles, *based on a recipe from the Château de Quinéville, fill your kitchen with the aromas of garlic and shallots.*

If you can't find pétoncles *in the shell, substitute mussels, clams, or cockles. If the shellfish are small, allow 12 per person and spoon ¼ teaspoon of the butter into each shell. (Illustrated left)*

SERVES 4 AS A FIRST COURSE
4tbsp unsalted butter, cut into pieces
3 cloves garlic
1tsp finely chopped shallot
1tbsp chopped fresh parsley
24 *pétoncles* or bay scallops in the shell
salt and freshly ground black pepper

Combine the butter, garlic, shallot, parsley, and a little salt and pepper in a food processor. Process the mixture until it is smooth. Chill the garlic butter until ready to use it.

Scrub the scallop shells. Put them in a heavy saucepan, cover with a lid, and set over high heat. Cook, stirring once or twice, just until the shells open, about 5 minutes. Remove from the heat and discard the flat top shells.

Preheat the broiler. Arrange the scallops, on their bottom shells, on flameproof plates. (Snail dishes with indentations for the shell work well.) Place ½ teaspoon of the garlic butter on each scallop. Put the plates on the broiler rack and cook about 3 inches from the heat until the scallops are lightly browned, 2–4 minutes. Serve at once, with plenty of fresh bread.

TERRINE DE POULET AU CAMEMBERT

Chicken and Mushroom Terrine with Camembert

I include this recipe as a curiosity. At La Pommer-aie in Macey not far from Mont-Saint-Michel, the chef, Monsieur Letertre, prepares a terrine stud-ded not with the usual morsels of foie gras or chicken livers, but – this being Normandy – with slices of Camembert.

Serve the terrine from its mold with a few leaves of lettuce and pass crusty bread, pickled onions, and cornichons or gherkins.

SERVES 10

1 chicken (about 3lb)
½ cup Calvados
2tbsp unsalted butter
1 large onion, finely chopped
¼lb mushrooms, finely chopped
¾lb pork sausage meat
¾ cup crème fraîche
½ cup dry hard cider
1tbsp salt, or to taste
1½tsp freshly ground pepper,
or to taste
1 egg white, lightly beaten
1 Camembert (8oz), rind removed
and cut into thin slices
2 bay leaves

Cut and scrape the chicken meat off the carcass, which you can save for stock. (Do not worry about doing this perfectly or about scraping the carcass perfectly clean.) Remove the skin from the chicken meat and save it.

Cut the breast meat lengthwise into thin strips and combine it in a glass bowl with the Calvados and reserved skin. Cover and chill this mixture 12 hours or overnight.

The next day, remove the chicken and skin and save the Calvados. Melt the butter in a frying pan over moderate heat. Add the onion and cook, stirring, until translucent, 3–5 minutes. Add the mushrooms and cook, stirring, until all the liquid evaporates, 3–5 minutes.

Cut the dark chicken meat into chunks and work it with the sausage meat in a food processor until coarsely chopped.

Beat together the onion mixture, chopped meat, crème fraîche, cider, salt, pepper, and reserved Calvados. Then beat in the egg white. Sauté a small piece of this forcemeat in a frying pan, taste it, and adjust the seasoning of the remaining mixture.

Preheat the oven to 350°F.

Line a 1½-quart terrine mold with the reserved chicken skin. (There will not be enough skin to line the mold completely.) Pack one-third of the forcemeat into the mold. Cover with half the Camembert slices and top with all the strips of chicken breast, laying them lengthwise. Spread one-third of the remaining forcemeat over the chicken. Make another layer of the remaining Camembert slices and cover with the rest of the forcemeat. Add the bay leaves.

Press a piece of buttered foil on top and cover with a lid. Set the terrine mold in a simmering water bath. Bake 1½ hours.

Take the terrine mold from the oven and the water bath and let it cool to tepid. Pour off the fats and juices. (If you like, save them for the next terrine.) Set weights on top (cans of food work nicely) to pack down the contents. Chill the terrine with the weights until cold.

Remove the weights and foil. Set the lid on the terrine mold and keep it chilled at least 3 days for the flavors to develop.

Slice the terrine for serving. Serve it at room temperature.

The famous Carottes de sable on sale at the market at Pirou.

CAROTTES A L'ETOUFFEE

Slow-Cooked Carrots with Onions and Herbs

A few carrots, onions, and a bundle of herbs – this is one of those dishes that adds up to far more than the sum of its parts. Monsieur Letouzé, president of the vegetable co-op in Créances, offered me this recipe. Even if you cannot find carrots grown in seaweed-nourished sand, like those in Créances, this vegetable side dish is impossible to bungle. Serve it with everything.

SERVES 4

3tbsp unsalted butter
1½lb carrots, cut into ¾-in pieces
on the diagonal
6oz onion, halved and thinly sliced
a large bouquet garni
¾tsp sugar
salt and freshly ground black pepper

Melt the butter in a heavy pan (cast iron works well) over low heat. Add all the remaining ingredients except the pepper and stir them until coated with the butter. Cover the pan and cook over the lowest possible heat until the carrots are tender, 20–30 minutes, stirring occasionally.

Discard the bouquet garni. Taste the carrots and add salt, pepper, or sugar to taste.

MATELOTE D'ANGUILLES

Eel Stew

The Auberge de l'Ouve sits along the Douve, one of the coastal rivers that cross the Marais du Cotentin, wetlands where horses and cows graze and country people still make a living by turf-cutting and selling their cows' milk to dairies. The Auberge is a favorite stopping place for bird watchers, equestrians, and hikers, who come for a crêpe and a glass of local cider.

Although not much more than a waterside café, the Auberge de l'Ouve sometimes prepares regional fare, including this humble matelote d'anguilles. *The eel is poached in a court-bouillon and served with thick farm cream. But the days remaining for such dishes are few. As one resident of the Marais remarked concerning eel stew: "I love it but bonjour le cholestérol!"*

SERVES 4
2 onions, thinly sliced
1lb carrots, thinly sliced
a bouquet garni
2 cups dry white wine or hard cider
2lb eel, without heads, skinned and cut into 2-in lengths
1tsp crushed black peppercorns
1tbsp unsalted butter
2–3 shallots, thinly sliced
½ cup crème fraîche
salt and freshly ground white pepper
1tbsp chopped fresh parsley

Combine the onions, carrots, bouquet garni, wine, and a little salt in a large sauté pan. Bring to a boil, then reduce the heat to low and simmer this court-bouillon 20 minutes.

Add the pieces of eel and peppercorns and bring the liquid back to a simmer. Reduce the heat to low, cover, and poach the eel until firm, about 5 minutes. Remove the eel and drain it on paper towels, then transfer it to a serving dish and keep it warm. Add the carrots from the court-bouillon to the eel. Discard the remaining court-bouillon.

Melt the butter in a saucepan over moderately high heat. Add the shallots and cook until golden, 2–3 minutes. Reduce the heat to low and stir in the crème fraîche with a little salt and pepper. Heat it through without boiling. Adjust the seasoning.

Pour the sauce over the eel, sprinkle with the parsley, and serve.

AILE DE RAIE GRATINEE AUX PATES FRAICHES

Skate in Golden Herb Sauce with Fresh Pasta

Here, fish is pan-fried and a quick sauce is made with shallots, white wine, cream, and herbs. To improve the color of the sauce and heighten the tarragon flavor, a little béarnaise is whisked in. Then the fish, napped with its sauce, is broiled until golden. At the Restaurant des Fuchsias, the chef likes to use skate in this dish, but any firm white fish such as sole or snapper will do. Allow 1⅓lb of fish fillets for four people.

SERVES 4
½lb fresh tagliatelle
3tbsp unsalted butter, clarified (see page 33)
2¼lb skate wing, filleted and skinned
2 shallots, finely chopped
2tbsp mixed chopped fresh herbs, such as tarragon, chives, and chervil
¾ cup dry white wine
1 cup crème fraîche
salt and freshly ground white pepper

FOR THE BEARNAISE SAUCE
2tbsp tarragon or white wine vinegar
3 black peppercorns, crushed
1 shallot, finely chopped
2 tsp chopped fresh tarragon
1 egg yolk
4tbsp unsalted butter, clarified (see page 33)
salt and freshly ground white pepper

For the béarnaise sauce, in a small heavy saucepan boil the vinegar with the peppercorns, shallot, and tarragon until reduced to 2 teaspoons. Remove from the heat and let cool. Add the egg yolk with a little salt and pepper and whisk 30 seconds until light. Return the pan to the lowest possible heat and continue whisking until the mixture is creamy and quite thick. Take the pan from the heat again and gradually whisk in the clarified butter. Taste and adjust the seasoning. Strain the sauce and keep it warm in a water bath.

Cook the pasta in boiling salted water until al dente; drain. Preheat the broiler.

Heat the butter over moderately high heat in a large frying pan. Sprinkle the fish fillets with salt and pepper. Add the fish to the butter and cook, turning once, until opaque throughout, 2–4 minutes in all. Drain the fish on paper towels.

Add the shallots to the same pan and cook them over moderate heat, stirring occasionally, until translucent, 2–3 minutes. Stir in the herbs until evenly coated with butter. Pour in the wine, scraping up the browned pan juices, and simmer until the wine reduces by half, 2–3 minutes. Add the crème fraîche and simmer until the sauce reduces by half again. Take the pan from the heat and whisk in the warm béarnaise sauce.

Spread the pasta in the center of a flameproof platter or plates. Arrange the fish on top and pour the sauce over all. Set on the broiler rack and cook about 3 inches from the heat until the top is lightly browned, 3–4 minutes. Serve at once.

JAMBON AU CIDRE

Ham in Cider Sauce

When you have a ham curing in the chimney and bottles of cider in the cellar, this dish is a natural. It crops up on farm tables and auberge menus throughout the Manche.

In this version, from the Auberge de l'Ouve in Les Moitiers-en-Bauptois, the ham is sliced and browned in butter, then simmered briefly in good farm cider. The most time-consuming thing about this recipe is peeling the shallots!

With the ham, serve Slow-Cooked Carrots with Onions and Herbs (see page 137) and baked potatoes or a big green salad. (Illustrated below)

SERVES 4
2tbsp unsalted butter
4 slices smoked ham (each about
¼in thick)
2–3 shallots, finely chopped
¾ cup dry hard cider
freshly ground black pepper
2tbsp snipped fresh chives

Melt the butter in a large frying pan over moderately high heat. Add the slices of ham, 1 or 2 at a time, without crowding the pan, and brown lightly on both sides, 2–3 minutes, then remove.

Add the shallots to the frying pan and cook over moderate heat, stirring occasionally, until golden, 2–3 minutes. Reduce the heat to low and replace the ham in the pan (the slices may overlap). Pour in the cider, scraping up the browned pan juices, and cook gently 5 minutes.

Add pepper to taste. (Salt is probably unnecessary as the ham is already highly seasoned.)

Arrange the slices of ham on a warmed platter or individual plates, moisten with the buttery cider and shallots, and serve immediately, sprinkled with the snipped chives.

PETIT RAGOUT D'AGNEAU DE PRE-SALE

Spring Lamb and Vegetable Stew

On the road to Mont-Saint-Michel, the Hôtel Montgomery in Pontorson evokes nostalgia and dignified charm. It is filled with polished silver, mementos of historic dinners, grandfather clocks, and beveled mirrors hung over the fireplace.

The food at this restaurant celebrates local ingredients, especially the athletic salt-meadow lamb, which covers a lot of ground during its daily grazing in the marshland at the foot of the Mont. This recipe calls for tender lamb (at the Hôtel Montgomery the choice is naturally pré-salé) and a brief cooking time, producing a spring-like stew in any season. (Illustrated left)

SERVES 4

1¾lb boneless lamb shoulder, cut into
1½-in cubes
3tbsp vegetable oil
¼lb shallots, finely chopped
4 tomatoes, peeled, seeded, and chopped
¼tsp tomato paste
2 cups dry white wine
½ cup water
¼lb carrots, halved lengthwise and
cut into 1½-in lengths
14oz potatoes, peeled, quartered
lengthwise, and cut into 1½-in lengths
1 cup fresh or frozen, thawed peas
salt and freshly ground black pepper

Season the cubes of lamb with salt. Heat the oil in a sauté pan or flameproof casserole just the size to hold the meat and vegetables in a single layer. Add the lamb to the oil and lightly brown the cubes all over, then remove them.

Add the shallots and cook over moderate heat until they are translucent, 2–3 minutes.

Pour off any fat from the sauté pan. Replace the lamb in the pan and stir in the tomatoes and tomato paste. Cook over low heat, stirring occasionally, 8–10 minutes.

Stir in the wine and water, scraping up the browned pan juices. Bring to a boil, then reduce the heat to low, cover, and simmer until the lamb is tender, 15–20 minutes.

Meanwhile, cook the carrots and potatoes, separately, in boiling salted water until barely tender, 3–5 minutes; drain.

Skim off any fat from the stew. Add the carrots, potatoes, and peas to the stew and cook gently 10 minutes. If the cooking liquid is still thin, remove the meat and vegetables and simmer the cooking liquid, skimming regularly, until it will lightly coat a spoon.

Reheat the meat and vegetables in the cooking liquid if needed, then taste and adjust the seasoning. Serve hot.

FILET DE CANARD AU POMMEAU ET AUX POMMES

Duck Breast in Pommeau Sauce with Apples

This recipe is a favorite with guests at the Restaurant des Fuchsias in Saint-Vaast-la-Hougue. It is even taught in a cooking class held in the restaurant's kitchen.

If you can find the beefy duck breasts known as magrets and a bottle of pommeau apple apéritif, preparing this dish is simple. The duck breasts and apple slices are pan-fried, and a fast sauce is made in the same pan with pommeau and cream. Frying the duck breasts slowly for a long time melts the fat and produces crisp, golden skin.

SERVES 4

2 duck magrets (each about ¾lb) or
4 ordinary duck breast halves
½ cup pommeau
1 cup crème fraîche
salt and freshly ground black pepper

FOR THE GARNISH

3tbsp unsalted butter
4 small, firm apples, cored and each
cut into 6 wedges
salt and freshly ground black pepper

Score the skin of the duck breast pieces. Put them in a dry frying pan, skin-side down, and set over low heat. Cook gently until most of the fat has been rendered and the skin is golden, 15–20 minutes (if using ordinary duck breasts, reduce the cooking time on the skin side to 10–15 minutes). Turn the breasts and cook on the other side until rare like steak, about 5 minutes more. Remove the duck breasts to a carving board with a juice catcher and set aside, covered loosely with foil.

Pour off the fat from the pan. Stir in the pommeau, scraping up the browned pan juices. Bring to a boil, then lower the heat and simmer until reduced by half. Add the crème fraîche and a little salt and simmer the sauce, stirring from time to time, until it thickens, 5–8 minutes.

Meanwhile, prepare the garnish. Melt the butter over moderately high heat in a frying pan. Add the apple wedges with a little salt and pepper and cook until they are tender and golden on both sides, 10–15 minutes.

Cut the duck breasts crosswise into thin slices. Stir any duck juices that have collected into the sauce and taste and adjust the seasoning. Coat warmed individual plates with the sauce. Arrange half a duck magret (or a duck breast half), with the slices overlapping, on each plate. Arrange the sautéed apple wedges in the same way on each plate. Serve immediately.

MOUSSE AU CIDRE

Sweet Cider Sabayon

This is a dessert for people who like to finish a meal with something sweet but not heavy. It must be prepared just before serving, but it literally whisks in minutes. Serve Sablés (see below) or other cookies with the sabayon. (Illustrated left)

SERVES 4
3 egg yolks
2tbsp sugar
⅓ cup sweet hard cider

In a large heatproof bowl, beat the egg yolks with a hand-held electric mixer or a whisk until creamy, about 30 seconds. Gradually beat in the sugar and then the cider. Set the bowl over a pan of simmering water, making sure the water does not touch the base of the bowl. Continue beating at high speed until the sabayon holds soft peaks, 6–8 minutes with an electric mixer, 8–10 minutes if beating by hand. Spoon the sabayon into champagne glasses or dessert bowls. Serve immediately.

SABLES AUX AMANDES

Buttery Almond Cookies

Around Mont-Saint-Michel bay, several cookie factories are open to the public. They display the giant metal rollers used for stamping the cookies and sell sablés, galettes, and other buttery cookies in tins decorated with scenes from the Mont.

But most pastry shops in Normandy also prepare their own recipe for sablés. Some have designs etched in the tops, some have scalloped edges. These differ slightly from the average as they contain ground almonds. (Illustrated left)

MAKES ABOUT 30

scant ½ cup blanched almonds

1 cup flour

6tbsp sugar

pinch of salt

1 stick unsalted butter, cut into pieces

2 egg yolks

Grind the almonds to a coarse powder in a food processor. Add the flour, sugar, and salt and work briefly until mixed. Add the butter and process until the mixture resembles coarse crumbs. Add the yolks and process just until the dough holds together when you pinch it with your fingers.

Transfer the dough to wax paper, flatten it into a disk, wrap, and chill until firm, at least 1 hour.

Preheat the oven to 375°F. Butter one or two baking sheets.

Roll out the dough on a floured work surface to a sheet ¼ inch thick. (If the dough is difficult to work with, roll it out between two sheets of wax paper.) Stamp out rounds with a 2-inch cookie cutter and transfer them to a prepared baking sheet. Trace decorations in the top of the sablés with a knife, if you like. Gather any remaining scraps, re-roll, chill, and cut more rounds.

Bake the sablés until pale golden, 8–10 minutes. Let them cool slightly on the baking sheet before putting them on wire racks to cool completely. Sablés will keep for months if they are stored in an airtight tin.

FEUILLANTINE DE POMMES AU CARAMEL DE CIDRE

Apple Napoleon in Cider Caramel Sauce

Chefs love to play with the classic napoleon, inventing new variations according to inspiration and the seasons. I have tasted chocolate ones, which are never chocolatey enough. Sometimes lacy wafers replace traditional puff pastry, and in summer juicy raspberries and whipped cream are often tucked between the layers.

At the Château de la Salle in Montpinchon, the version is pure Normandy. Sliced apples provide the filling, and apple compôte serves as edible glue. For the sauce, homemade caramel is flavored with cider, naturally.

SERVES 4

½ cup whipping cream

2tbsp confectioners' sugar

5oz best-quality puff pastry dough

4 small, firm apples

granulated sugar, for sprinkling

Calvados, for sprinkling

FOR THE APPLE COMPOTE

1 small apple, peeled and sliced

1 cup water

1½tbsp granulated sugar

FOR THE CIDER CARAMEL SAUCE

½ cup granulated sugar

scant ½ cup water

1¼ cups dry hard cider

For the apple compôte, put the sliced apple in a small heavy pan with the water and sugar. Cover and cook over low heat, stirring occasionally, until the apple is very soft and falling apart, 12–15 minutes. Work the mixture in a food processor until smooth. Set aside.

For the cider caramel sauce, combine the sugar and water in a small heavy saucepan. Heat gently until the sugar dissolves, stirring often, then continue cooking over moderately low heat, without stirring, until the sugar syrup turns a deep amber color. Dip the base of the pan in cold water to stop the cooking. Pour the cider into the caramel. (It will sputter so take care.) Return the pan to moderate heat and stir the cider thoroughly into the caramel until melted and evenly blended. Cook the caramel sauce until it reduces by half, 7–9 minutes. Cool to room temperature.

Whip the cream with the confectioners' sugar until it holds stiff peaks. Chill until ready to use.

Sprinkle a baking sheet with water. Roll out the dough on a floured surface to a sheet ⅛ inch thick. Cut into 8 rectangles, each about 3½ × 2 inches and transfer to the baking sheet. Prick the dough all over with a fork about every ½ inch, then chill until firm, at least 15 minutes. Preheat the oven to 425°F.

Core and peel one of the apples, then halve it lengthwise. Set an apple half, rounded side up, on a cutting board and cut it lengthwise into thin slices. Slip a metal spatula under the sliced apple half and, keeping the slices together, set it on a dough rectangle. Press the apple gently to flatten the slices a little. Sprinkle with granulated sugar and Calvados. Repeat with the remaining apples. Bake until the apples are tender and the pastry is risen around the edge and golden brown, about 15 minutes.

To assemble the napoleons, spread a tablespoon of the compôte over four of the apple rectangles. Cover each with a second rectangle. Scoop the whipped cream into a pastry bag and pipe rosettes of cream to cover the apple entirely; or spoon a dollop of cream on each. Spoon the caramel sauce onto plates and spread it out to cover evenly. Set a napoleon in the center of each plate and serve.

A VISITOR'S GUIDE

This guide draws from the vast assortment of restaurants, farms, museums, cheesemakers, stores, markets, distilleries, and festivals that I visited while researching *Normandy Gastronomique*. The entries roughly follow the regions as they are discussed in each chapter, grouped first by *département* and then by *pays* – Pays d'Auge, Bocage, Perche, and so on.

The eating establishments range from farmhouses and family restaurants to Michelin-starred restaurants (marked by one or two asterisks) and châteaux. They all serve regional food or make creative use of local ingredients. Cooks at *fermes-auberges* and *tables d'hôte* usually prepare meals only on request, and when you telephone, you may be asked what you would like to eat. It is worth remembering that even lavish restaurants offer bargain price-fixed menus during the week at lunchtime. Often the most interesting regional fare appears on these set menus.

Places of interest include traditional museums, gardens, and aquaria, as well as cheese factories, watercress farms, and mushroom caves. The local *offices de tourisme* and *syndicats d'initiative* can provide maps and the most current information and listings of events.

Under the specialties section, you will find addresses for the local products mentioned in the text, and also tea rooms, where you can stop for an afternoon pastry or a light lunch.

Calvados- and cidermakers are everywhere in Normandy, and many of them offer tours and tastings. Also, note the cider weekends where you can join the cidermaking.

As for opening times, bear in mind the way different people live. Farmers rarely leave their fields and pastures, but factory workers take off on the weekend. Family businesses often hang up the *fermé* (closed) sign at lunchtime.

Some storekeepers and restaurateurs like to spend Wednesdays, and school and public holidays *en famille*. Otherwise they often close Sunday after lunch and Monday. On the other hand, country museums, *fermes-auberges*, and out-of-the-way restaurants tend to open when families have free time: public holidays, weekends, and Easter to All Saints' Day (1 November). Many museums close on Tuesdays.

Every effort has been made to provide accurate information, but addresses, telephone numbers, festivals, and market days are liable to change.

SEINE-MARITIME

Restaurants

LA MARMITE DIEPPOISE
8 rue Saint-Jean
Dieppe
Tel 35 84 24 26

RESTAURANT AU TROU NORMAND
Pourville-sur-Mer
Tel 35 84 59 84

LES GALETS*
3 rue Victor-Hugo
Veules-les-Roses
Tel 35 97 61 33

AUBERGE DU DUN*
route de Dieppe, Bourg-Dun
Tel 35 83 05 84

FERME-AUBERGE DE BOUCOURT
Boucourt-Bénesville
Tel 35 96 55 99

LES HETRES
Ingouville
Tel 35 57 09 30

NICOLE AND HUBERT LOISEL
("*table d'hôte*")
Hamlet of Ecosse
Manneville-la-Goupil
Tel 35 27 77 21

FERME-AUBERGE DU PLESSIS
Goupillières
Tel 35 91 02 83

AUBERGE DU VAL AU CESNE
Yvetot-Duclair
Tel 35 56 63 06

AUBERGE DU BEAU LIEU
Le Fossé, Forges-les-Eaux
Tel 35 90 50 36
(see pages 30–2)

HOTEL DE LA POSTE
286 quai Libération, Duclair
Tel 35 37 50 04

MANOIR DE RETIVAL*
2 rue Saint-Clair
Caudebec-en-Caux
Tel 35 96 11 22

LE BEFFROY*
15 rue Beffroy
Rouen
Tel 35 71 55 27
(see pages 32–3)

RESTAURANT GILL**
9 quai de la Bourse
Rouen
Tel 35 71 16 14

RESTAURANT LE TOURVILLE
12 rue Danièle-Casanova
Tourville-la-Rivière
Tel 35 77 58 79

Places of interest

MUSEE DES TERRE NEUVAS
(cod-fishing museum)
27 boulevard Albert-1er
Fécamp
Tel 35 29 76 22

PALAIS BENEDICTINE
(Benedictine liqueur museum)
110 rue Alexandre-Legrand
Fécamp
Tel 35 10 26 00

CHATEAU DE MIROMESNIL
(ornamental kitchen garden)
Tourville-sur-Arques
Tel 35 04 40 30

CHATEAU DE BAILLEUL
(kitchen and utensils)
Bailleul
Tel 35 27 83 04

MUSEE DU PAYS DE CAUX
(cooking utensils museum)
18 rue Grand-Fay
Yvetot
Tel 35 95 03 69

CHATEAU DE MARTAINVILLE
(folk-arts museum and bread oven)
Martainville
Tel 35 23 44 70

ATELIER DU TONNELIER
(cooper's workshop)
Boissay
Tel 35 34 04 98

HOTEL DE VILLE
(faïence collection)
place Brevière
Forges-les-Eaux
Tel 35 90 50 39

LA FERME DE BRAY
(museum of rural life)
Hamlet of Bray, Sommery
Tel 35 90 57 27

MUSEE MUNICIPAL
(local history museum)
grande-rue Saint-Pierre
Neufchâtel-en-Bray
Tel 35 93 06 55

MUSEE DE LA MARINE DE SEINE
avenue Caumont
Caudebec-en-Caux
Tel 35 96 27 30

MUSEE DE LA CERAMIQUE
(ceramics museum)
rue Faucon, Rouen
Tel 35 07 31 74

Specialties of the region

**BOULANGERIE PATISSERIE
DIEPPOISE**
Demanneville
(regional pastries)
69 rue Saint-Jacques
Dieppe
Tel 35 84 22 54

DESCHAMPS
("galette au beurre")
18 place Théodule-Benoist
Saint-Romain-de-Colbosc
Tel 35 20 52 76

FRANCOIS CROCHET
(blood sausage)
25 place Théodule-Benoist
Saint-Romain-de-Colbosc
Tel 35 20 51 40

DANIEL AUVRE
(farmhouse Neufchâtel)
Mesnil-Mauger
Tel 35 90 41 22

LA FERME DU CANARDIER
Robert Maugard
(poultry farm)
Le Claquevel
Anneville Ambourville
Tel 35 37 56 41

CHRISTIAN ARTU
("pain brié")
11 place du Bateau
La Bouille
Tel 35 18 01 58

ROGER GRANGER
(pastry shop)
29 rue du Général-Leclerc
Rouen
Tel 35 70 10 64

PATISSERIE PAILLARD
(pastry shop)
35 rue du Gros Horloge
Rouen
Tel 35 71 10 15

Markets

Monday: *Bolbec, Bûchy, Cany-Barville, Havre (Le)*

Tuesday: *Dieppe, Duclair, Goderville, Gournay-en-Bray, Havre (Le), Rouen, Tréport (Le), Yerville*

Wednesday: *Baqueville-en-Caux, Criel-sur-Mer, Havre (Le), Lillebonne, Mont-Saint-Aignan, Rouen, Saint-Etienne-du-Rouvray, Saint-Nicolas-d'Alièremont, Valmont, Yport, Yvetot, and Veules-les-Roses during July and August*

Thursday: *Dieppe, Etretat, Fontaine-le-Dun, Forges-les-Eaux, Havre (Le), Londinières (p.m.), Pavilly, Rouen, Saint-Etienne-du-Rouvray*

Friday: *Auffay, Clères (p.m.), Eu, Fauville, Havre (Le), Mont-Saint-Aignan, Nôtre-Dame-de-Cravenchon, Rouen, Saint-Valéry-en-Caux, Sainte-Adresse*

Saturday: *Aumale (p.m.), Barentin (p.m.), Bolbec, Caudebec-en-Caux, Dieppe, Doudeville, Envermeu, Fécamp, Havre (Le), Monville, Neufchâtel-en-Bray, Rouen, Ry, Saint-Laurent-en-Caux, Saint-Romain-de-Colbosc, Trait (Le) (pm), Tréport (Le), Veules-les-Roses (July and August only), Yvetot*

Sunday: *Blangy-sur-Bresle, Harfleur, Longueville-sur-Scie, Rouen, Saint-Etienne-du-Rouvray, Saint-Nicolas-d'Alièrement*

Cidermakers

CIDRERIES MIGNARD
Auffay
Tel 35 32 81 01

DUCHE DE LONGUEVILLE
Anneville-sur-Scie
Tel 35 83 32 64

LE VERGER D'AUGUSTIN
La Folletière
Tel 35 91 19 20

Fairs and festivals

Late March: Longueville-sur-Scie,
Concours de cidre (*cider contest*)
Late May: Le Tréport, Foire aux
moules (*mussel fair*)
June: Auffay, Fête du cidre (*cider
festival*)
July: Le Mesnil-sous-Jumièges (*base de
plein air*), Marché aux cerises
(*cherry market*)
August: Le Mesnil-sous-Jumièges (*base
de plein air*), Marché aux prunes
(*plum market*)
Mid-August: Callengeville, Fête du
battage à l'ancienne (*threshing
festival*)
Late August: Béaubec-la-Rosière,
Grande foire aux melons (*melon
fair*)
Mid-September: Gournay-en-Bray,
Foire aux herengs, fromage, cidre
(*herring, cheese and cider fair*)
Third Sunday in September:
Caudebec-en-Caux, Concours de
pâtisseries normandes (*Norman
pastry contest*)

Last weekend in September of even
years: Caudebec-en-Caux, Fête du
cidre (*cider festival*)
First weekend in October: Saint-
Pierre-les-Elbeuf, Fête
gastronomique (*gastronomic
festival*)
October: Sommery, Weekend
champignons (*mushroom
weekend*)
October: Le Mesnil-sous-Jumièges
(*Base de plein air et de loisirs*),
Marché aux pommes (*apple
market*)
Mid-October/early November: Yvetot,
Pilaison à la ferme cauchoise du Fay
(*cidermaking*)
Early November: Dieppe, Foire aux
harengs (*herring fair*)
Early November: Sommery, Grande
fête de la pomme et du cidre (*apple
and cider festival*)
Mid-November: Neufchâtel-en-Bray,
Foire Saint-Martin (*local fair*)
Late November: Londinières, Foire aux
fromages et aux plaisirs de la table
(*cheese fair*)
Late November: Saint-Valéry-en-Caux,
Fête du hareng et du cidre (*herring
and cider festival*)

EURE

Restaurants

HOTEL DE LA CHAINE D'OR
place Saint-Sauveur
Les Andelys
Tel 32 54 00 31

LES JARDINS DE GIVERNY
1 rue Milieu
Giverny
Tel 32 21 60 80

CHATEAU DE LA RAPEE
La Rapée
Bazincourt
Tel 32 55 11 61

LUCIEN NUTTENS
(*table d'hôte*)
20 rue de l'Eglise
Reuilly
Tel 32 34 70 65

AUBERGE DE PARVILLE*
route de Lisieux
Parville
Tel 32 39 36 63

LA FERME DE COCHEREL
rue Aristide-Briand
Cocherel
Tel 32 36 68 27

FERME-AUBERGE DE L'EGLISE
Coulonges-Sylvains-les-Moulins
Tel 32 34 52 46

AUBERGE DU VIEUX LOGIS*
Conteville
Tel 32 57 60 16

LE CLOS POTIER
(*table d'hôte*)
Conteville
Tel 32 57 60 79

AUBERGE DU VIEUX PUITS
6 rue Notre-Dame-du-Pré
Pont-Audemer
Tel 32 41 01 48
(see pages 60–1)

ODETTE AND JACQUES
BOUTEILLER
(*table d'hôte*)
route Epaignes
Martainville
Tel 32 57 82 23

AUBERGE DE L'ABBAYE
place de l'Eglise
Le Bec-Hellouin
Tel 32 44 86 02

FERME-AUBERGE DE GIVERVILLE
Hamlet of Dommenesque
Giverville
Tel 32 45 96 69

RESTAURANT LA TOQUE BLANCHE
18 place Carnot
Conches-en-Ouche
Tel 32 30 01 54

L'ETAPE LOUIS XIII*
Beaumesnil
Tel 32 44 44 72

HOSTELLERIE DU CLOS
98 rue Ferté-Vidame
Verneuil-sur-Avre
Tel 32 32 21 81

Places of interest

MUSEE CLAUDE MONET
(house and garden)
84 rue Claude-Monet
Giverny
Tel 32 51 28 21

CHATEAU DE BOURY-EN-VEXIN
(kitchen and utensils)
Boury-en-Vexin
Tel 32 55 15 10

LE PAYS DE LYONS CENTRE
D'EXPOSITION TEMPORAIRE
(local history exhibits)
Lyons-la-Forêt
Tel 32 49 31 65

MUSEE DE LA FERME ET DES VIEUX
METIERS
(museum of rural life)
Bosquentin
Tel 32 48 07 22

LA FERME DE ROME
(museum of rural life)
Bézu-la-Forêt
Tel 32 49 66 22

MOULIN DE PIERRE
(working windmill)
Hauville
Tel 32 56 86 11

MAISON DES METIERS DU PARC DE
BROTONNE
(trades museum)
Bourneville
Tel 32 57 40 41

MAISON DE LA POMME
(apple museum)
Sainte-Opportune-la-Mare
Tel 32 57 16 48

MONSIEUR ROBERT VASSEUR
(house of broken dishes)
80 rue Bal-Champêtre
Louviers
Tel 32 40 22 71

MUSEE DU CIDRE
(cider museum)
Montaure
Tel 32 50 64 99

MUSEE DU BRAS ET DE LA BIELLE
(local crafts exhibits)
Thevray
Tel 32 54 00 19

MUSEE DES OUTILS DU TERROIR
NORMAND
(farm machinery)
Caugé
Tel 32 37 13 00

MUSEE DE L'ANCIEN EVECHE
(folk arts exhibits)
rue Charles-Corbeau, Evreux
Tel 32 31 52 29

JOEL COULON
(mushroom caves)
route de la Noë-Poulain
Epaignes
Tel 32 57 87 99

GERARD HAMON
(watercress farm)
route de Beuzeville, Epaignes
Tel 32 57 40 76

MUSEE MUNICIPAL DE BERNAY
(folk-art exhibits)
2 place Guillaume-de-Volpiano
Bernay
Tel 32 46 63 23

LA CHARRETTE
(folk-arts museum)
15–17 rue Gaston-Folloppe
Bernay
Tel 32 43 05 47

Specialties of the region

AU PATE DE LYONS
("pâté de Lyons")
place Isaac-Benserade
Lyons-la-Forêt
Tel 32 49 60 68

LA HAYE-DE-ROUTOT BREAD OVEN
(regional breads and pastries)
La Haye-de-Routot
Tel 32 57 30 41 (town hall)

LE BRETON
(regional pastries)
41 rue du Maréchal-Foch
Louviers
Tel 32 40 01 05

BOULANGERIE-PATISSERIE MICHEL
LANGLOIS
("pain brié")
10 rue de la Libération
Beuzeville
Tel 32 57 71 88

CLAUDE TREHET
(cheese shop)
7 rue Gambetta, Pont-Audemer
Tel 32 41 04 98

FROMAGERIE QUESNEY
(cheesemaker)
route Epaignes
Beuzeville
Tel 32 42 14 83

MICHEL CAUVET
(farmhouse Cormeillais)
Saint-Pierre-de-Cormeilles
Tel 32 57 83 55

MICHEL COUTURIER
("pomme Calvados" pastry)
61 rue Thiers
Bernay
Tel 32 43 00 74

AU COCHON D'OR
(trout pâté)
50 rue Thiers
Bernay
Tel 32 43 14 59

Markets

Monday: *Bourg-Achard, Gisors,
Pont-Audemer*

Tuesday: *Beaumont-le-Roger,
Beuzeville, Damville, Fleury-sur-
Andelle, Gaillon, Montreuil-l'Argillé*

Wednesday: *Barre-en-Ouche,
Breteuil-sur-Iton, Etrepagny,
Evreux (center), Le Neubourg,
Nonancourt, Routot, Saint-Georges-
du-Vièvre, Vernon*

Thursday: *Brionne, Conches, Ezy-sur-
Eure, Lieurey, Lyons-la-Forêt, Pacy-
sur-Eure, Quillebeuf-sur-Seine*

Friday: *Beaumont-le-Roger, La
Bonneville-sur-Iton, Broglie,
Cormeilles, Gisors, Pont-Audemer,
Val-de-Reuil (p.m.)*

Saturday: *Les Andelys, Bernay,
Bourgtheroulde, Charleval, Evreux,
Fleury-sur-Andelle, Ivry-la-Bataille,
Louviers, Lyons-la-Forêt, Pont-
Saint-Pierre, Rugles, Verneuil-sur-
Avre, Vernon, Lieurey*

Sunday: *Brionne, Epaignes, Evreux,
Ezy-sur-Eure, La Ferrière-sur-Risle,
Pont-de-L'Arche, Saint-Pierre-du-
Vauvray, Le Vaudreuil,
Lyons-la-Forêt*

Calvados- and cidermakers

MAISON DE LA POMME
*(apple museum, cider, Calvados,
"pommeau")*
Sainte-Opportune-la-Mare
Tel 32 57 16 48

RENE LESUR
(cider only)
La Godinière
Noyer-en-Ouche
Tel 32 44 46 71

JULIEN GRIEU
(cider only)
Pallière
Le Bois-Hellain
Tel 32 57 15 17

Fairs and festivals

First Sunday of the month November–
April: Sainte-Opportune-la-Mare,
Marché aux pommes (*apple
market*)
First Sunday of the month March–
November: La Haye-de-Routot
(*bread oven*), Cuisson du pain
(*bread-making*)
First Sunday in March: Bourneville
(Maison des Métiers),
Démonstration de charcuterie
("*charcuterie*" *demonstration*);
Hauville (Moulin de Hauville),
Dégustation de beignets (*fritter
tasting*)
Palm Sunday: Le Neubourg, Comice
agricole (*agricultural fair*)
Mid-March: Bernay, Concours du pâté
de truite (*trout pâté contest*)
First weekend in April: La Haye-de-
Routot (Bread oven/Musée du
sabotier), Fêté du pain et des
sabots (*bread and clog festival*)
First of May: Marais-Vernier, Fête de
l'estampage (*cattle branding*)
Second Sunday in May: Bourneville
(Maison des métiers),
Démonstration de boulangerie
(*baking demonstration*)
Late May/early June: Vernon, Foire
aux cerises (*cherry fair*)
Late October/late November/late
December: Le Neubourg, Marché au
foie gras ("*foie gras*" *market*)
11 November: Lieurey, Foire aux
harengs (*herring fair*)
6 December: Evreux, Foire Saint-
Nicolas (*Saint-Nicolas fair*)

CALVADOS

Restaurants

L'ASSIETTE GOURMANDE*
2 quai Passagers
Honfleur
Tel 31 88 24 88

LES VAPEURS
160 boulevard Fernand-Moureaux
Trouville
Tel 31 88 15 24

LE SPINAKER*
52 rue Mirabeau
Deauville
Tel 31 88 24 40

LES DEUX TONNEAUX
Pierrefitte-en-Auge
Tel 31 64 09 31

AUBERGE DU DAUPHIN*
Le Breuil-en-Auge
Tel 31 65 08 11

RESTAURANT LA HAIE TONDUE
La Haie Tondue, Drubec
Tel 31 64 85 00

AUBERGE DE L'ABBAYE
Beaumont-en-Auge
Tel 31 64 82 31

LE PAVE D'AUGE*
Beuvron-en-Auge
Tel 31 79 26 71

FERME-AUBERGE LE DOUX MARAIS
Sainte-Marie-aux-Anglais
Tel 31 63 82 81

FERME-AUBERGE DES POMMIERS
DE LIVAYE
Notre-Dame-de-Livaye
Tel 31 63 01 28

LA BOURRIDE**
15 rue Vaugueux
Caen
Tel 31 93 50 76
(see pages 82–3)

DANIEL TUBOEUF*
8 rue Buquet
Caen
Tel 31 43 64 48

HOTELLERIE DU MOULIN DU VEY
Clécy
Tel 31 69 71 08

LE LION D'OR*
71 rue Saint-Jean
Bayeux
Tel 31 92 06 90

CHATEAU D'AUDRIEU*
Audrieu
Tel 31 80 21 52

LA RANCONNIERE
route Arromanches
Crépon
Creully
Tel 31 22 21 73

FERME-AUBERGE DU LOUCEL
Colleville-sur-Mer
Tel 31 22 40 95

FERME-AUBERGE DE LA RIVIERE
Saint-Germain-du-Pert
Tel 31 22 72 92

Places of interest

MUSEE DU VIEUX HONFLEUR
(local history museum)
quai Saint-Etienne
Honfleur
Tel 31 89 14 12

MUSEE EUGENE BOUDIN
(folk-art exhibits)
place Erik-Satie
Honfleur
Tel 31 89 54 00

AQUARIUM ECOLOGIQUE
Promenade Planches
Trouville
Tel 31 88 46 04

MUSEE DU CALVADOS ET
DES METIERS
(Calvados and trades museum)
Pont-l'Evêque
Tel 31 64 12 87

MUSEE DU VIEUX LISIEUX
(local history museum)
boulevard Pasteur
Lisieux
Tel 31 62 07 70

MUSEE DU FROMAGE DE LIVAROT
(cheese museum)
Manoir de l'Isle
68 rue Marcel-Gambier
Livarot
Tel 31 63 43 13

MUSEE MUNICIPAL D'ORBEC
(local history museum)
rue Grande, Orbec
Tel 31 32 82 02

CHATEAU DU
CREVECOEUR-EN-AUGE
(local history exhibits)
Crèvecoeur-en-Auge
Tel 31 63 02 45

MUSEE DES TECHNIQUES
FROMAGERES
(cheese museum)
rue Saint-Benoit
Saint-Pierre-sur-Dives
Tel 31 20 97 90

MUSEE DE NORMANDIE
(local history museum)
Caen
Tel 31 86 06 24

CENTRE GUILLAUME LE
CONQUERANT
(Bayeux tapestry)
13 bis rue de Nesmond
Bayeux
Tel 31 92 05 48

MUSEE BARON GERARD
(folk-art exhibits)
1 rue la Chaine
Bayeux
Tel 31 92 14 21

MUSEE DE LA MEUNERIE
(flour-milling museum)
Le Moulin de Marcy
Molay-Littry
Tel 31 21 42 13

MUSEE DE LA FERME
(farm museum)
Parfouru-sur-Odon
Villers-Bocage
Tel 31 77 01 13

FERME DE SAINT-QUENTIN
(working cider press)
Soumont-Saint-Quentin
Tel 31 90 88 18

MUSEE DE VIRE
(local history museum)
4 place Sainte-Anne
Vire
Tel 31 68 10 49

Specialties of the region

LA PETITE CHINE
(tea room)
14 rue Dauphin
Honfleur
Tel 31 89 36 52

CHARLOTTE CORDAY
(pastry shop/tea room)
172 boulevard Fernand-Moureaux
Trouville
Tel 31 88 11 76

HUG
(pastry shop/tea room)
20 place Morny
Deauville
Tel 31 88 20 79

LE GLOBE
("teurgoule")
44 rue des Bains
Houlgate
Tel 31 91 22 51

PENNEC
(cheesemaker)
Saint-Benoit-d'Hebertot
Tel 31 64 25 38

MICHEL THOMAS
("brioche")
61 rue Saint-Michel
Pont-l'Evêque
Tel 31 64 04 08

LA REINE AIMEE
(pastry shop/tea room)
6 rue Pont-Mortain
Lisieux
Tel 31 62 04 51

EUGENE GRAINDORGE
(Livarot factory)
42 rue du Général-Leclerc
Livarot
Tel 31 63 50 02

ALBERT LALLIER
(farm Pont-l'Evêque)
La Moissonnière
Fervaques
Tel 31 32 31 23

PLESSIS
(farm Pont-l'Evêque)
Putot-en-Auge
Tel 31 79 69 05

DOMAINE DE SAINT-LOUP
(Camembert factory)
Saint-Loup-de-Fribois
Cambremer
Tel 31 63 04 04

JEAN-MARIE AND ODILE GASSON
("confiture de lait")
Les Patis
Mery-Corbon
Tel 31 23 66 21

MICHEL TOUZE
(farm cheeses)
Le Bôquet
Vieux-Pont-en-Auge
Tel 31 20 78 67

LES FROMAGERS DE TRADITION
(small cheese factory)
Boissey
Tel 31 20 64 00

STIFFLER
(pastry shop/tea room)
72 rue Saint-Jean
Caen
Tel 31 86 08 94

COLLETTE
("tripe à la mode de Caen")
31 rue de la Mer
Courseulles-sur-Mer
Tel 31 37 45 02

PATISSERIE PAUL DUPONT
(regional pastries)
7 rue Saint-Martin
Bayeux
Tel 31 92 09 45

LA REINE MATHILDE
(regional pastries)
47 rue Saint-Martin
Bayeux
Tel 31 92 00 59

ANDRE TAILLEPIED
(oyster, mussel farms)
Grandchamp-Maisy
Tel 31 22 76 82

JEAN-PIERRE LASNON
(oysters)
55 rue du Docteur-Bautrois
Isigny-sur-Mer
Tel 31 22 19 13

DUPONT D'ISIGNY
(caramel factory)
La Cambe, Isigny-sur-Mer
Tel 31 22 70 12

BOULANGERIE VIGOT
("pain brié")
27 rue Demagny
Isigny-sur-Mer
Tel 31 22 02 64

EMILE ROUSSEL
("brasillé")
Clinchamps-sur-Orne
Tel 31 79 82 22

PANIER
("teurgoule")
Trois-Monts
Tel 31 79 76 10

MONSIEUR AND MADAME
MICHALKE
(snail farm)
La Goutière, Donnay
Tel 31 79 77 67

GILBERT BERTRAND ET FILS
(farmhouse Camembert)
La Graverie
Tel 31 67 74 89

DANJOU
("andouille de Vire")
5 rue aux Fèvres, Vire
Tel 31 68 04 00

TRIPES VIROISES
("tripe à la mode de Caen")
Michael Ruault
1 rue des Usines
Vire
Tel 31 68 05 78

CHARLES AMAND
("andouille de Vire")
rue du Calvados
Vire
Tel 31 67 01 79

LEVEILLE
(smoked ham)
route de Granville
Saint-Martin-de-Tallevende
Tel 31 68 29 55

Markets

Monday: *Langrune (in season), Pont-d'Ouilly, Pont-l'Evêque, Saint-Pierre-sur-Dives, Vierville-sur-Mer*

Tuesday: *Balleroy, Blonville (in season), Caen (rue de Bayeux), Courseulles, Deauville, Dozulé, Grandcamp-Maisy, Ouistreham (bourg), Thury-Harcourt, Vassy, Villers-sur-Mer, Villerville*

Wednesday: *Bayeux, Bernières, Bonnebosq, Cabourg, Caen (boulevard Leroy), Creully, Evrecy, Ifs, Isigny, Landelles-et-Coupigny, Lisieux (haute ville), Luc-sur-Mer (in season), Mery-Corbon, Orbec, Potigny, Thaon, Trouville, Villers-Bocage*

Thursday: *Argences, Asnelles (in season), Le Bény-Bocage, Blangy-le-Château, Bretteville-sur-Laize, Caen (La Guérinière), Caumont-l'Eventé, Condé-sur-Noireau, Douvres, Houlgate, Lion-sur-Mer (in season), Livarot, Le Molay-Littry, Mondeville, Saint-Aubin*

Friday: *Blainville-sur-Orne, Blonville (in season), Caen (place Saint-Sauveur), Cahagnes, Cambremer, Colombelles (p.m.), Courseulles, Deauville, Falaise, Langrune, May-sur-Orne, Ouistreham (Riva-Bella), Saint-Julien-le-Faucon, Trévières, Villers-sur-Mer, Villerville, Vire*

Saturday: *Amfreville, Aunay-sur-Odon, Bayeux, Beaumont-en-Auge, Beauvron (a.m.), Bretteville-l'Orgueilleuse, Caen (boulevard Leroy), Dives-sur-Mer, Epron, Fleury-sur-Orne, Grandcamp-Maisy, Honfleur, Isigny, Lisieux, Louvigny, Luc-sur-Mer, Mouen, Ouistreham (bourg), Saint-Martin-des-Besaces, Saint-Sever, Touques, Troarn, Verson*

Sunday: *Cabourg, Caen (Saint-Pierre), Clécy (Easter–end of October), Le Home-Varaville, Mézidon-Canon, Noyers-Bocage, Port-en-Bessin, Tilly-sur-Seulles, Trouville, Villerville (in season)*

In season there are daily markets in the following seaside resorts: *Cabourg, Deauville, Dives, Houlgate, Luc-sur-Mer, Ouistreham, Trouville, Villers-sur-Mer*

Old-time markets

Cambremer: Sunday (a.m.) during Easter, Pentecost, July, and August

Le Molay-Littry: Sunday (a.m.) during July and August

Pont-l'Evêque: Sunday (a.m.) during July and August

Calvados- and cidermakers

DOMAINE DE LA POMMERAIE
(cider only)
Gonneville-sur-Honfleur
Tel 31 89 20 11

DISTILLERIE DES FIEFS DE SAINT-ANNE
Coudray-Rabut
Tel 31 64 30 05/31 98 80 16

CHAIS DU PERE MAGLOIRE
(Calvados only)
Etablissements Debrise-Dulac
Le Lieu-du-Champs
Pont-l'Evêque
Tel 31 64 12 87

DISTILLERIE MOULIN DE LA FOULONNERIE
(Calvados only)
Coquainvilliers
Tel 31 62 29 26

LE PERE JULES
Léon Desfrièches
route de Dives
Saint-Désir-de-Lisieux
Tel 31 61 14 57

LA FRICHE MENUET
(cider only)
Saint-Germain-de-Livet
Tel 31 31 18 24

ROGER GIARD
(Calvados only)
Manoir de Montreuil
Grandouet
Tel 31 63 02 40

CIDER WEEKENDS
Office du tourisme
Cambremer
Tel: 31 63 08 87

LE PRESSOIR DAJON
(also Calvados, "pommeau")
Dampierre
Tel 31 68 72 30

Fairs and festivals

March. Noyers-Bocage, Concours de la meilleure terrine de campagne (country terrine contest)

Early May: Le Molay-Littry, Fête au Moulin de Marcy (festival at the Marcy windmill); Pont-l'Evêque, Concours du fromage de Pont-l'Evêque (Pont-l'Evêque cheese contest)

Mid-May: Crèvecoeur-en-Auge, Foire aux produits locaux (local food fair)

Late May: Falaise, Weekend gourmand (gastronomic weekend)

Late June: Avenay, Concours interrégional du pain (bread contest)

First weekend in August: Livarot, Foire aux fromages et produits régionaux (local food and cheese fair)

Early August: Lisieux, Foire aux picots (turkey fair)

Late August: Pont-l'Evêque, Concours d'animaux gras et dégustation d'entrecôtes grillées (livestock contest and grill)

Mid-September: Dives-sur-Mer, Foire aux melons (melon fair)

Mid-September: Clinchamps-sur-Orne, Fête du brasillé (local pastry festival)

Mid-October: Caen, Concours de la tripe à la mode de Caen (tripe contest)

Mid-October: Soumont-Saint-Quentin, Fête du cidre (cider festival)

Late October/early November: Beuvron-en-Auge, Fête du cidre (cider festival)

Last weekend in October: Pont-d'Ouilly, Foire de la pomme (apple fair)

Early October: Houlgate, Concours de teurgoule ("teurgoule" contest)

Late October/early November: Beny-Bocage, Concours de rillettes d'oie et de foie gras (goose "rillettes" and "foie gras" contest)

All Saints' Day (1 November): Vire, Foire à l'andouille ("andouille" fair)

Late November: Livarot, Foire Saint-André et dégustation de tripes (Saint André fair and tripe tasting)

Late December: Bayeux, Marché au foie gras ("foie gras" market)

ORNE

Restaurants

FERME-AUBERGE DU HAUT DE CROUTTES
Crouttes
Tel 33 35 25 27

LA RENAISSANCE
20 avenue de la 2eme-Division
Argentan
Tel 33 36 14 20

CHEZ OCTAVE
23 rue Saint-Denis
La Ferté-Macé
Tel 33 37 01 19

GERARD CHATEL
31 rue Saint-Denis
La Ferté-Macé
Tel 33 37 11 85

MANOIR DU LYS
route de Juvigny-Croix-Gauthier
Bagnoles-de-l'Orne
Tel 33 37 80 69
(see pages 108–9)

FERME-AUBERGE LA CHEVAIRIE
Juvigny-sous-Andaine
Tel 33 38 27 74

HOTEL DE LA POSTE
70 rue Maréchal-Foch, Domfront
Tel 33 38 51 00

FERME-AUBERGE LA FERARDIERE
La Gonfrière
Tel 33 34 81 05

HOTEL DU DAUPHIN*
place Halle
L'Aigle
Tel 33 24 43 12

MOULIN DE VILLERAY
Villeray
Tel 33 73 30 22
(see pages 106–8)

AUBERGE DES 3 JEUDI
1 place Docteur-Gireaux
Nocé
Tel 33 73 41 03

AUBERGE DE LA VALLEE
Saint-Cénéri-le-Gérei
Tel 33 26 57 98

HOTELLERIE DE LA FAIENCERIE
Saint-Denis-sur-Sarthon
Tel 33 27 30 16

Places of interest

MUSEE DES ARTS ET TRADITIONS
POPULAIRES DU PERCHE
(*museum of rural life*)
Sainte-Gauburge
Tel 33 73 48 06

L'EPICERIE
(*grocery museum*)
Lignerolles
Tel 33 25 91 07

CHATEAU DE CARROUGES
(*folk-art exhibits*)
Carrouges
Tel 33 27 20 32

BISCUITERIE DE L'ABBAYE
(*cookie factory*)
route Val
Lonlay-l'Abbaye
Tel 33 38 68 32

MUSEE MATERIEL AGRICOLE
(*farm-machinery museum*)
16 rue Durmeyer
Flers
Tel 33 65 42 22

DOMAINE DE LA BONNERIE
(*venison farm*)
Sevigny
Tel 33 36 50 11

MUSEE DU CAMEMBERT
(*Camembert museum*)
10 avenue du Général-de-Gaulle
Vimoutiers
Tel 33 39 30 29

Specialties of the region

FERME DE LA HERONNIERE
(*farmhouse Camembert*)
Camembert
Tel 33 39 08 08

MICHEL DELORME
(*farmhouse Camembert*)
Le Tordouet
Tel 33 39 12 56

C. LINTE CHARCUTIER-TRAITEUR
(*"cervelas d'aiglon"*)
6 rue Romain-d'Archy
L'Aigle
Tel 33 24 18 89

AU ROI DU BOUDIN
(*blood sausage*)
Claude Guillochon
50 place du Général-de-Gaulle
Mortagne-au-Perche
Tel 33 25 16 43

CHARCUTERIE CHARTIER
(*white sausage*)
2 place du Général-de-Gaulle
Le Mêle-sur-Sarthe
Tel 33 27 63 07

JACQUES GLATIGNY
(*regional candies*)
44 Grande-Rue
Alençon
Tel 33 26 18 23

JACKY PEDRO
(*regional candies*)
39 Grande-Rue, Alençon
Tel 33 26 00 47

PATRICK RUEL
(*"andouillette d'Alençon"*)
21 Grande-Rue
Alençon
Tel 33 26 20 24

AU PAIN D'AUTREFOIS
(*bakery*)
Maurice Hélaine
3 place à l'Avoine
Alençon
Tel 33 32 22 43

GERARD CHATEL
(*"tripes en brochettes"*)
31 rue Saint-Denis
La Ferté-Macé
Tel 33 37 11 85

BOULANGERIE MARIE
(*"bourdelots"*)
70 rue 6-Juin
Flers
Tel 33 65 23 37

JEAN-CLAUDE DESVAUX
(*"bourdelots"*)
7 place Saint-Vigor
Athis-de-l'Orne
Tel 33 66 42 42

Markets

Monday: *Briouze, Rémalard,
    Tinchebray, Vimoutiers (p.m.)*

Tuesday: *Argentan, Athis, Nocé,
    Passais-la-Conception, L'Aigle*

Wednesday: *Carrouges, Flers, Longny-
    au-Perche, Le Mêle-sur-Sarthe, Le
    Theil-sur-Huisne*

Thursday: *Alençon, Bellême, La Ferté-
    Macé, La Ferté-Fresnel, Moulins-la-
    Marche, Putanges-Pont-Ecrepin,
    Trun*

Friday: *Argentan, Courtomer,
    Ecouché, Tourouvre, Vimoutiers*

Saturday: *Alençon, Domfront, Flers,
    Mortagne-au-Perche, Gacé (p.m.)*

Sunday: *Alençon, Mortrée*

Calvados- and Cidermakers

CAVE CIDRICOLE DE L'HERMITIERE
(cider only)
Lieu-dit La Cour
l'Hermitière
Tel 37 49 67 30

YVES SALLARD
Champs de la Vallée
La Ferté-Macé
Tel 33 37 45 92

CHAIS VERGER NORMAND
rue du Mont-Saint-Michel
Domfront
Tel 33 38 53 96

ROGER LEMORTON
Le Pont-Barrabé, Mantilly
Tel 33 38 76 60

Fairs and festivals

February: Moulins-la-Marche,
Concours de la meilleure brioche
("brioche" contest)
Early April: La Ferté-Macé, Concours
de tripes en brochettes (tripe contest)
Third weekend in March: Mortagne-
au-Perche, Foire internationale du
boudin (international blood sausage
fair)
Eastertime: Vimoutiers, Concours de
cidre et de tarte aux pommes (cider
and apple tart contest)
First of May: Longny-au-Perche,
Concours national du meilleur plat de
tripes (national tripe contest)
Ascension: L'Aigle, 4 jours de L'Aigle –
spécialité cervelas aiglon – (food fair
with local sausage)

Second weekend in July, alternate
years: Mantilly, Fête du poiré
(sparkling pear wine festival)
Last Sunday in July: Camembert, Fête
du Camembert (Camembert festival)
Last Sunday in September: Bellême,
Journées mycologiques (mushroom
days)
Last weekend in November: Essay,
Foire au boudin blanc (white sausage
fair)
October: Flers, Concours de tourte au
canard (savory duck pastry contest)
Late September: Argentan, Concours
de daguet cuisiné (venison recipe
contest)
First weekend in October: Longny-au-
Perche, concours de terrine forestière
(mushroom terrine contest)
Early October: Carrouges, Exposition
pomologique (apple exhibition)
Third Friday in October: Athis,
Concours de bourdelots et charlottes
("bourdelot" and "charlotte" contest)
Late October: Vimoutiers, Foire de la
pomme (apple fair)
Last weekend in October: Pont-
d'Ouilly, Foire de la pomme (apple
fair)
Early November: Gacé, Marché au foie
gras (foie gras market)
Last weekend in November: Essay,
Concours de boudin blanc (white
sausage contest)
Mid-December: L'Aigle, Marché au foie
gras cru (raw foie gras market); Sées,
Foire à la dinde (turkey fair)

MANCHE

Restaurants

LE DRAKKAR
rue Havre
Quinéville
Tel 33 21 24 90

LA CHAUMIERE
place du Général-de-Gaulle
Le Quettehou
Tel 33 54 14 94

RESTAURANT DES FUCHSIAS
18 rue Maréchal-Foch
Saint-Vaast-la-Hougue
Tel 33 54 42 26

AUBERGE LES GROTTES
Nez de Jobourg
Tel 33 52 71 44

LA MARINE*
2 rue Paris
Carteret
Tel 33 53 83 31

AUBERGE DE L'OUVE
Village Longuerac
Les Moitiers-en-Bauptois
Tel 33 21 16 26

RESTAURANT LA MER
avenue Ferdinand-Desplanques
Pirou-Plage
Tel 33 46 43 36
(see pages 132–3)

AUBERGE DES BONNES GENS
Le Mesnilbus
Tel 33 07 66 85

CHATEAU DE LA SALLE*
Montpinchon
Tel 33 46 95 19

LA VERTE CAMPAGNE
Le Hameau Chevalier
Trelly
Tel 33 47 65 33
(see pages 133–5)

LE JARDIN DE L'ABBAYE
La Croix de Saint-Pierre
Saint-Pierre-Langers
Tel 33 48 49 08

MONSIEUR AND MADAME CLOUET
(table d'hôte)
Manoir de Vaucelles
Saint Léger
Tel 33 51 66 97

LA MERE POULARD
Grande-Rue
Le Mont-Saint-Michel
Tel 33 60 14 01

AU VENT DES GREVES
route du Mont-Saint-Michel
Moidrey
Tel 33 60 01 63

HOTEL MONTGOMERY
13 rue Couesnon, Pontorson
Tel 33 60 00 09

Places of interest

MUSEE DE LA FERME DU COTENTIN
(farm museum)
chemin Beauvais
Sainte-Mère-Eglise
Tel 33 41 30 25

MUSEE DU LAIT
(milk museum)
rue des Perruquettes
Montebourg
Tel 33 41 13 48

MUSEE REGIONAL DU CIDRE
(cider museum)
Maison du Grand-Quartier
rue Petit-Versailles
Valognes
Tel 33 40 22 73

MUSEE DES VIEUX METIERS ET DE
L'EAU DE VIE DE CIDRE
(trades and Calvados museum)
Hôtel de Thieuville
rue Pelouze
Valognes
Tel 33 40 26 25

EXPOSITION PERMANENTE DE
POTERIES ANCIENNES
(pottery exhibits)
Mairie
Vindefontaine
Tel 33 71 14 21

BISCUITERIE DU COTENTIN
(cookie factory)
5 Les Hauts Vents
La Haye-du-Puits
Tel 33 46 03 54

ETABLISSMENTS REAUX
(Camembert factory)
avenue Gare
Lessay
Tel 33 46 41 33

LA MAISON DES MARAIS
(restored farmhouse)
Marchésieux
Tel 33 07 15 20

VANNERIE LEHODEY
(basket museum)
Remilly-sur-Lozon
Tel 33 56 21 01

MUSEE DU BOIS-JUGAN
(farm museum)
Saint-Lô
Tel 33 56 26 98

MUSEE QUESNEL-MORINIERE
(pottery exhibits)
2 rue Quesnel-Morinière
Coutances
Tel 33 45 11 92

BISCUITERIE L'ANNOVILLAISE
(cookie factory)
Annoville
Tel 33 47 50 00

MUSEE DE LA POESLERIE ET DE LA
DENTELLE
(copper and lace museum)
rue Général-Huard
Villedieu-les-Poêles
Tel 33 90 20 92

ATELIER DU CUIVRE
(copper workshop)
54 rue Général-Huard
Villedieu-les-Poêles
Tel 33 51 31 85

MUSEE DU MEUBLE NORMAND
(rural furniture museum)
9 rue du Reculé
Villedieu-les-Poêles
Tel 33 61 11 78

MAISON DE L'ETAIN
(pewter museum)
54 rue Général-Huard
Villedieu-les-Poêles
Tel 33 51 05 08

MUSEE DU VIEUX GRANVILLE
(folk-arts museum)
2 rue Lecarpentier
Granville
Tel 33 50 44 10

MAISON DE LA PECHE A PIED ET
DES ANCIENNES SALINES DE LA
BAIE DU MONT-SAINT-MICHEL
(fishing museum)
Vains
Tel 33 70 81 42

MAISON DE LA POMME ET DE LA
POIRE
(apple and pear museum)
La Logeraie
Barenton
Tel 33 59 56 22

Specialties of the region

ABBAYE NOTRE-DAME DE LA
PROTECTION
("pâtes de fruits")
8 rue de Capucins
Valognes
Tel 33 95 01 41

GUILBERT-CHAMBON
(charcutier)
18 rue Armand-Levéel
Bricquebec
Tel 33 52 20 65

COURBARON
(regional breads/pastry shop)
16 rue Armand-Levéel
Bricquebec
Tel 33 52 50 20

JACQUES LETERRIER
(regional breads and "brioches")
Hameau Boisnel
Le Vast
Tel 33 54 13 56

HELIE ET FILS
(oyster grower)
31 rue d'Isamberville
Saint-Vaast-la-Hougue
Tel 33 54 42 70

LES JAMBONS DU COTENTIN
(smoked ham)
route de Périers
Lessay
Tel 33 46 47 67

LES JAMBONS D'ANTAN
(smoked ham)
La Chapelle-en-Juger
Tel 33 57 68 47

JAMBON NORMAND JOURDAN
(smoked ham)
3 l'Hotel-Rihouet
Carantilly
Tel 33 56 62 41

MEISS
(*regional pastries*)
7 rue Saint-Nicolas
Coutances
Tel 33 45 00 75

ANDOUILLERIE DE LA
VALLEE-DE-LA-SIENNE
(*"andouille"*)
Pont-La-Baleine
Saint-Denis-le-Gast
Tel 33 61 44 20

CHARCUTERIE CHALENDE
A La Bonne Fumée
19 rue Général-Huard
Villedieu-les-Poêles
Tel 33 61 02 65

FRANCOIS AND HERVE
CHAMPOISEAU
(*foie gras*)
Le Cacquevel
Villedieu-les-Poêles
Tel 33 61 06 23

FERME DE LA MAURICIERE
(*farm Pont-l'Evêque*)
Sartilly
Tel 33 48 93 40

JEAN-ROBERT TIERCELIN
(*salt-marsh lamb*)
36 rue Couesnon
Pontorson
Tel 33 60 10 90

MICHEL HUET
(*"saucisse à l'oignon"*)
20 avenue du Maréchal-Leclerc
Saint-Hilaire-du-Harcouët
Tel 33 49 11 39

Markets

Monday: *Bricquebec, Carentan, Juvigny-le-Tertre, Saint-James, Torigni-sur-Vire*

Tuesday: *Barfleur, Brehal, Cherbourg, Coutainville, Ducey, Hambye, Lessay, Notre-Dame-de-Cenelly, Portbail, Le Quettehou, Saint-Clair, Sourdeval, Villedieu*

Wednesday: *Cerisy-la-Forêt, Condé-sur-Vire, Granville, La Haye-du-Puits, La Haye-Pesnel, Marigny, Montmartin-sur-Mer, Pontorson, Saint-Hilaire-du-Harcouët, Saint-Pierre-Eglise, Tessy-sur-Vire*

Thursday: *Bacilly, Belval, Cerences, Cherbourg, Coutances, Ger, Montbray, Le Passou, Remilly, Sainte-Mère-Eglise, Saint-Pois, Saint-Sauveur, Le Teilleul*

Friday: *Brecey, Canisy, Les Pieux, Montsurvent, Picauville, Roncey, Saint-Denis-le-Vetu, Saint-Jean-de-Daye, Saint-Laurent-de-Terregatte, Sartilly, Valognes*

Saturday: *Avranches, Barfleur, Barneville-Carteret, Beaumont, Cerisy-la-Salle, Coulouvray, Coutainville, Gavray, Granville, Montebourg, Mortain, Notre-Dame-du-Touchet, Percy, Periers, Quettreville-sur-Sienne, Saint-Lô, Saint-Sauveur-le-Vicomte, Saint-Vaast-La-Hougue, Agon*

Sunday: *Barenton, Barfleur, Créances, Lingreville, Octeville, Saint-Martin-de-Brehal*

Calvados- and cidermakers

PIERRE HAMEL
Les Petits Bois
Saint Joseph
Tel 33 40 17 12
Tours during summer

FERME DE L'HERMITIERE
Saint-Jean-des-Champs
Tel 33 61 31 51

GILBERT CALVADOS
(*Calvados only*)
Manoir du Coquerel
Milly
Saint-Hilaire-du-Harcouët
Tel 33 49 00 63

MAISON DE LA POMME ET DE LA
POIRE
La Logeraie
Barenton
Tel 33 59 56 22

Fairs and festivals

early May: Cherbourg, Concours et foire gastronomique (*gastronomic fair and contest*)
June: Saint-Hilaire-du-Harcouët, Concours de saucisses (*sausage contest*)
July: Bas-Courtils, Fête du pré-salé (*salt-marsh lamb festival*)
Second Sunday in August: Créances, Fête de la carotte (*carrot fair*)
Late September: Lessay, Foire de la Sainte-Croix (*county fair*)
October: Valognes, Fête de la pomme (*apple fair*)
Early October: Barenton, Exposition pomologique (*apple exhibition*)
First of December: Valognes, Marché au foie gras (*foie gras market*)
Early December: Avranches, Foire du boudin blanc (white sausage fair)

LIST OF RECIPES

INDEX

AUTHOR'S ACKNOWLEDGMENTS

Help came from all the cheese-makers, farmers, bakers, chefs, cider-makers, and museum curators mentioned in these pages. Pascal and Caroline Bernou, Michel Bruneau, Janine Chatel, Jacques Leterrier, Christian and Muriel Eelson, Odile Engel, Hélène Foltz, Roger Lemorton, Victor Letouzé, Franck Quinton, Patrick and Marie-France Ramelet, Jean-Robert Tiercelin, and Michel Touzé went out of their way to assist.

More than anyone else, Michael Saklad was in on the day-to-day work of this book. He crisscrossed Seine-Maritime and Manche with me and, back in Paris, he hunted down ingredients and tasted my recipes, often again and again until I got them right. My parents, Barbara and Ronald Sigal, took time from their very busy retirement schedule to help with driving, shopping, and recipe testing. I also want to thank Juliette Birnbaum, Jackie Bobrow, Katia Boissevain, Janet and Marjorie Fradin, Michael Seiler, and Joshua Sigal for their help and companionship, whether on the road, in the kitchen or office, or at the dining room table. Thanks to Debbie Patterson for her beautiful photographs and an endlessly cheerful disposition as we raced from appointment to appointment. Help has also come from Sarah Pearce and Jane Chapman at Conran Octopus. Norma MacMillan edited carefully. I am grateful to my agents, Maureen and Eric Lasher, for letting me have my way on this book. For hand-holding, I would particularly like to thank Jessica Bond, Paul Chutkow, and Claudie Massaloux.

Index by Karin Woodruff

PHOTOGRAPHIC ACKNOWLEDGMENTS

All pictures have been specially taken by Debbie Patterson except the following:
6–7 Explorer/J.L. Bohin; 8 centre left Agence Top/Tripelon-Jarry; 14 above left Girts Gailans/ Robert Harding Picture Library; 25 Robert Tixador/Agence Top; 57 below left Explorer/Jalain. F; 72–73 Explorer/Thouvenin. G; 77 below Explorer/Girard. L; 80 above left Philippe Perdereau; 97 above right Philippe Perdereau; 120–21 Explorer/Jalain F.